Archibald R. Adamson

Rambles round Kilmarnock

With an Introductory Sketch of the Town

Archibald R. Adamson

Rambles round Kilmarnock
With an Introductory Sketch of the Town

ISBN/EAN: 9783337013516

Printed in Europe, USA, Canada, Australia, Japan

Cover: Foto ©Andreas Hilbeck / pixelio.de

More available books at **www.hansebooks.com**

RAMBLES

ROUND KILMARNOCK,

WITH AN INTRODUCTORY

SKETCH OF THE TOWN.

BY

ARCHIBALD R. ADAMSON.

"*Still o'er these scenes my memory wakes,*
And fondly broods with miser care;
Time but the impression stronger makes,
As streams their channels deeper wear."

KILMARNOCK:
PRINTED AND PUBLISHED BY T. STEVENSON, "STANDARD" OFFICE.
MDCCCLXXV.

PREFACE.

THE following pages are a record of some pleasing Rambles in and around the town of Kilmarnock. A considerable portion appeared in the *Kilmarnock Standard*, and met with such a favourable reception, both at home and abroad, that I have yielded to the solicitation of numerous friends, and now present them to the public in their present form. In doing so, I have carefully revised them and added much new matter suggested by further inquiry, and have endeavoured to make the work as useful, entertaining, instructive, concise, and accurate as possible. In nearly every instance, although one visit is only mentioned, I have repeatedly gone to the places described; but, nevertheless, it must be borne in mind that the "Rambler" does not rise to the dignity of the historian, therefore he is not to be censured if he omits some things which fall within the province of one who aims at giving a minutely detailed history of a locality or place. The district is one of singularly romantic interest, and replete with memories of patriot and bard; so much so, that the Scotchman must be soulless indeed who can tread its classic ground and pass by the haunts of heroes and the graves of martyrs, and look upon scenes that once inspired the tongue of Coila's bard, without being susceptible to a feeling of pride that the land of Wallace and Bruce is that of his nativity.

The time-shattered ruins, auld kirkyards, and quaint villages which nestle in many a picturesque nook in the vicinity of the town are dear to every Kilmarnockonian, but more so to those whom fate or circumstances have removed from the scenes of youthful days; therefore I trust that this work will not only serve to awaken fond memories of each loved spot, but act as a handy guide to the numerous places of interest in and around the town, for a want of a knowledge of the topography, historic, and traditionary lore of a district often robs a ramble of an amount of pleasure which otherwise would be derived from it.

With the idea of making the Rambles more complete, an introductory description of the town has been given. In doing this I frankly acknowledge my indebtedness to the *History of Kilmarnock*, for no historical notice of the town can be written without reference to its pages, the author having carefully collected almost everything regarding the subject. Nevertheless, there will be found in the following sketch not a little that is new and entertaining.

In conclusion, the writing of this work has been

"My leisure's best resource."

I now respectfully dedicate it to the Natives of Kilmarnock and surrounding district at home and abroad, and trust that they will experience as much pleasure in its perusal as I have had in my walks and wanderings.

THE AUTHOR.

KILMARNOCK.

CHAPTER I.

Rise and Progress of the Town—The Cross—Flesh Market Bridge—Corn Exchange—Clerk's Lane—Fore Street—High Church and Burying Ground — King Street — Wellington Street — Fever Hospital—Portland Street, ... 1

CHAPTER II.

Green Bridge and its environs—London Road—Milldykes—The Irvine and Struthers' Steps—Saint Andrew's Burying Ground and Church—Glencairn Square and its associations—High Glencairn Street—King Street—King Street U.P. Church—The Council House, ... 18

CHAPTER III.

Cheapside Street—The Old Tolbooth—The Low Church of former days and its associations—The Churchyard—Dickie Street—Dunlop Street—The Astronomical Observatory—Langlands Street—The New Theatre—St. Marnock Street—The Court-House—Kilmarnock House—Dundonald Road—The Public Park—Waterside—Sandbed Street, ... 27

RAMBLES ROUND KILMARNOCK.

CONTENTS.

CHAPTER I.
Page

The Bridges connecting Kilmarnock with Riccarton, and the objects of interest in their vicinity—Caprington Castle—Riccarton Castle: its site and traditions—Traditions of Sir William Wallace—Riccarton—The Parish Church—Sandy M'Crone—The Churchyard—Old Stones—The East Shaw Street Miser—The Old Church—Village Worthies—The Village past and present—The Manse, ... 47

CHAPTER II.

Craigie Road—Knowehead and its surroundings—The Buchanan Bequest—Treesbank Manor House—Scargie—John Burtt—Knockmarloch—Craigie Hill—Craigie Church—The Village—The Witch Stane—Craigie Castle—A Strange Story—A Curious Stone, ... 56

CHAPTER III.

From Craigie to Barnweill—Barnweill Kirk and Graveyard—The Wallace Monument—Fail Castle—The Warlock Laird—Tarbolton—Willie's Mill—Peden's Pulpit and Cave—Through the Fields to Ayr Road—The Halfway House—The Estate of Coodham—Peace-and-Plenty—Back to Kilmarnock, ... 66

CHAPTER IV.

Wild Flowers—The Macwheelan Murder—The Cairn—Symington—The Church and Graveyard—Witherington—Old Sandy Neil—"Laird" M'Pherson—"Jock o' the Whalps"—The Glen, ... 76

CHAPTER V.

The House of Auchans—Dundonald Castle—The Village and Parish Church—Extracts from the Parochial Registers—Smuggling—Tam Fullarton—Newfield—"Fairlie o' the Five Lums"—Old Rome—Home again, ... 85

CHAPTER VI.

Beansburn—Dean Castle: its situation and appearance—The Castle besieged—Destroyed by fire—A Tradition of the Persecution—The Boyd Family—From the Dean to Craufurdland—Craufurdland Castle and Grounds—Craufurdland Bridge—Up the Stream to Fenwick, ... 95

CHAPTER VII.

Low Fenwick—Old John Kirkland—"The Kirk-town"—The erection of the Parish and origin of the name—The Parish Church and Burying Ground—The Rev. William Guthrie—The Burial Place of the Howies—Captain Paton, ... 106

CHAPTER VIII.

The Churchyard continued—John Fulton—King's Well—Lochgoin: its Traditions and Relics—Duntan Cove—Back to Kilmarnock, 115

CHAPTER IX.

The influence of sunshine—Glasgow Road and its scenery—An Adventure—Specimens of Kilmaurs cutlery—The Reservoir—From it to Rowallan Castle—The situation and appearance of the Castle described—The interior of the building—The garden—A fox story—Traditions, ... 134

CHAPTER X.

The origin and descent of the Mures of Rowallan—A letter from Queen Mary to Sir John Mure—Sir William Mure: his writings and version of Psalm xxiii.: events in his life—The last of the Mures—The late Countess of Loudoun's attachment to the Castle—The grounds the resort of pleasure parties—An Address to Rowallan—A ride into the town, ... 144

CHAPTER XI.

From Kilmarnock to Stewarton—The Parish and its Boundaries—The Town: its Buildings, Trades, and Eminent Characters—Corsehill Castle and its Traditions—The Parish Church—The late William Cunninghame of Lainshaw—The Churchyard—The Viaduct—Lainshaw Castle—The Murder of Hugh, fourth Earl of Eglinton, 152

CHAPTER XII.

From Stewarton to Kilmaurs—The appearance of the Village—The Council House and Juggs—Kilmaurs of the olden time: its Government and Churches—The Monk's Well—My Lord's Place—Jock's Thorn—Kilmaurs Castle—The Glencairn Family—An Incident, ... 163

CHAPTER XIII.

Kilmaurs continued—The old Church: its appearance and history—An Anecdote of the Rev. Hugh Thomson—The Glencairn Aisle and Monument—The appearance of the Vault when opened—A Ghastly Keepsake—The Rev. George Paxton—"Wee Miller"—"The Double Suicide"—The Old Manse—Covenanting Relics—A Stroll along Crosshouse Road—The Estate of Plann—Busbie Castle—The Tumulii at Greenhill Farm—Home again, ... 171

CHAPTER XIV.

From Kilmarnock to Grougar—The Ruins of Tammie Raeburn's Cottage—His self-imposed vow, personal appearance, courtship, witticisms, &c.—Grougar Row—Loudoun Kirk—The Queir—Lady Flora Hastings: her melancholy death: the character of her poems—Janet Little, the poetical correspondent of Robert Burns—George Palmer—An obscure Covenanter—A relic of Loudoun Kirk, ... 181

CHAPTER XV.

The Policies of Loudoun Castle—The external and internal appearance of the building—The Family Portraits—The Library—The old Yew Tree—The Loudoun Family, and salient points in the history of some of its members—The old Castle of Loudoun: its destruction by the Kennedys, &c., ... 190

CHAPTER XVI.

Loudoun Braes—Newmilns: its appearance, history, and trade—The Radical proclivities of the inhabitants—The old Tower, and incidents associated with it—The Parish Church—Norman Macleod—The Churchyard—Interesting Tombstones commemorative of Nisbet of Hardhill and other Covenanting natives of the Parish who suffered during the Persecution—The Workmen's Institute —"The Lass o' Patie's Mill," 196

CHAPTER XVII.

The Village of Darvel: its appearance and trade—Loudoun Hill and its Historic Associations—Wallace's Attack on the English Convoy—A Scottish Victory—Drumclog—The Laird of Torfoot's account of the Battle—His fight with Captain Arrol and his encounter with Claverhouse—The appearance of the field after the engagement—The Covenanters and their achievements, ... 204

CHAPTER XVIII.

From Newmilns to Galston—The Institute—Barr Castle—The Boss Tree—Cessnock Castle—The appearance of the buildings—The Campbells of Cessnock—Sir Hew, and the charges brought against him—The Alienation of the Castle and Lands—The Main Street of Galston—The Parish Church and Graveyard—Stones commemorative of local Covenanters—John Wright, the Galston Poet—Titchfield Street—A Mining Settlement—From Galston to Hurlford—The Village: its buildings and inhabitants—Crookedholm—Back to Kilmarnock—Conclusion, ... 212

RAMBLES THROUGH KILMARNOCK.

CHAPTER I.

Rise and Progress of Kilmarnock—The Cross—Flesh Market Bridge—Corn Exchange—Clerk's Lane—Fore St.—High Church and Burying Ground—King Street—Wellington Street—Fever Hospital—Portland Street.

BEFORE starting on a ramble *through* Kilmarnock, I deem it necessary to give a sketch of the town in former times, seeing that it owes much of its present prosperity to the enterprise of days gone by. The knowledge that "Auld Killie" may be justly considered the metropolis of Ayrshire may suggest comparisons highly satisfactory to our sense of vanity, and the glories of progress, but let it not be forgotten that all things of which we may be inclined to boast will have their day, and that nothing is immutable below,

"The glories of our birth and state
Being shadows, not substantial things."

With this simple introduction, then, I open my subject by stating that the origin of the town is shrouded in obscurity. It is generally supposed that an early promoter of Christianity named Saint Marnock built a church and therein expounded the tenets of his creed. Houses in time sprang up in its vicinity and formed a village, which gradually increased into the proportions of a town.

As far back as authentic history goes, Kilmarnock seems to have been under the feudal jurisdiction of the Lords Boyd, who were barons of the district, and dwelt in Dean Castle, the ruins of which still stand in a vale on the bank of the Kilmarnock Water, about a mile and a-half north-east of the town. In 1591 it was created a burgh of barony, and in 1672 a second charter was conferred upon it, that endowed it with further privileges. In 1609 Timothy Pont visited it when surveying Cunninghame, and makes mention of it thus:— "Kilmernock—tounc and kirk—is a large village, and of great repaire. It hath in it a veekly market; it hath a faire stone bridge over the river Mernock, vich glyds hard by the said toune till it falles in the river Irving. It hath a pretty church, from vich the village, castllo, and lordschipe takes its name," &c. At that early date Kilmarnock seems to have been a place of considerable importance, manufactures being carried on to some extent in it. In 1695 the first magistrates were appointed; these were chosen by the Superior from a list presented to him by the Council annually. This system continued until 1745, afterwards the Council appointed the bailies.

Kilmarnock did not make much progress as a town until the middle of the eighteenth century, or until after it was freed from baronial jurisdiction; then it began to prosper civically and commercially. About this time, the author of "The History of Kilmarnock" says, "the town presented a mean and inelegant appearance. The streets were crooked and narrow; the houses were low and poorly lighted; and to many of them that were two storeys high were attached outside stairs that not only confined the already limited thoroughfares, but gave to the houses themselves a rude and clumsy aspect. The principal streets at that time were those now called High Street, Soulis Street, Fore Street, Back Street, Croft Street, Strand Street, and Sandbed Street, which, with some buildings at the Cross, Nethertonholm, and a few back tenements and lanes, formed the whole of the town." In 1777, or nearly fifty years after the introduction of the manufacture of woollen fabrics, Loch in his "Essays" makes mention of it as a place of considerable manufacturing importance, and states that it was possessed of two hundred and forty looms for the weaving of silk, sixty for the weaving of carpets, forty for the weaving of linen, thirty for the weaving of blankets, thirty for the weaving of serges and shalloons, twenty for the weaving of duffles, and six stocking frames; also of being possessed of two tanyards and a good trade in shoes. As business increased so grew the population, and from an obscure village Kilmarnock came to be the most important town in Ayrshire. Dr. Webster states that the town " in 1763 contained nearly 5000 inhabitants ; in 1792, 6776 ; in 1801, 8079 ; in 1811, 10,148 ; in 1821, 12,769 ; in 1831, 18,093 ; in 1841, 19,398." In 1871 it numbered 23,709. In the *Edinburgh Magazine* for July, 1831, there is an article which gives some curious statistical information. I make the following extract :—" In Kilmarnock about 1200 weavers and 200 printers are engaged in the manufacture of harness and worsted printed shawls. From 31st May, 1830, to June 1, 1831, there were no less than 1,128,814 of these shawls manufactured, the value of which would be about £200,000. In the manufacture of Brussels, Venetian, and Scottish carpets and rugs, the quality and patterns of which are not surpassed by any in the country, there are upwards of 1000 weavers employed. The annual amount of this important branch of manufacture cannot be less than £100,000. About 2400 pairs of boots and shoes are made every week, of which three-fourths are for exportation ; annual value about £32,000. The manufacture of bonnets is also extensive, there being upwards of 224,640 yearly made by the corporation, the annual value of which is £12,000. The number of sheep and lamb skins dressed annually exceeds 140,000."

Since that time the advancement of mechanical science and the appliance of machinery has in a manner revolutionised the trades of the country, and weaving and block-printing have received an irreparable shock in Kilmarnock, as elsewhere. The sound of the shuttle has now a faint echo in her streets, and block-printing is all but extinct ; but for the manufacture of carpets Kilmarnock is still a rival to Brussels and other more pretentious seats of this industry. Within the last thirty years prodigious advances in business and manufactures have been made. Engineering, and also brass and iron founding, have been added to the trades of the town to such an extent that it is better known now-a-days by such products than for carpets and bonnets. Within the same period the old portion of the town has in a great measure been swept away or remodelled. New streets and new localities have been formed, and the Kilmarnock of to-day may be said to be a minor city ; but I will now conclude this imperfect sketch and start on a ramble

"Through a' the streets and neuks o' Killie,"

and thereby convey to the reader some idea of the present appearance of the town.

The Cross being the great local centre, I will make it the starting-point; but as it is possessed of considerable historic interest, perhaps a few words regarding it may not be inappropriate. Kilmarnock Cross is most spacious, although of a most peculiar form, having no less than seven streets branching off it. In the centre stands a marble statue of Sir James Shaw, who rose from a humble position to that of Lord Mayor of London. He was born in the parish of Riccarton in 1764, and died in 1843. The statue was erected in 1848. The form of the Cross has been compared to the turned-up root of an old tree, but a nearer comparison, I think, is the right hand palm downwards, with the fingers extended and spread out, the index finger being held in a line with the wrist. The wrist represents King Street; the thumb, Cheapside Street; the index finger, Portland Street; the mid finger, Fore Street; the one next to it, Regent Street; and the little finger, Duke Street. To account for Waterloo Street you must add an imaginary finger, or get some one with six, and the illustration will be complete. The appearance of the Cross is not inelegant; it contains some fine shops, and the principal streets leading off it are wide and spacious. Looking up Portland Street, which is a handsome thoroughfare, the George Hotel stands prominently out. Looking down King Street, which is similar in appearance, the eye rests on the Council Buildings, the Relief Church, and the hills of Craigie in the distance. In Cheapside Street the old tower and clock of the Laigh Kirk present themselves, and in looking along Duke Street the principal object that arrests attention is the Corn Exchange. At an early period a corn mill stood in the Cross, the wheel of which was driven by a lade connected with the river. In the southern corner of the Cross John Nisbet was executed in 1683. The spot where the gallows stood is marked with white stones, which are best seen in wet weather. Nisbet was a Covenanter, and was accused of being concerned in the rising at Bothwell, and refusing to give information regarding the whereabouts of certain of his friends. Every step of the ladder he considered to be a step nearer Heaven. Tradition has it that the crowd at the execution was so great that the roofs of the houses were covered with people who were anxious to get a glimpse of the martyr. There is a stone in the Low Church burying ground to his memory which will be noticed hereafter. In 1740 "the roaring game" was practised in the Cross by some ingenious curlers, who obtained water from a pump and retained it by daming. Previous to 1802 the Cross was confined and inconvenient, but power from Parliament being obtained to improve the town, many of the houses were torn down and the area widened. In 1804 King Street was opened up, and shortly afterwards Portland Street was formed. Duke Street was formed in 1859 and opened with civic honours, a procession headed by the Provost and Town Council walking along it. In April, 1820, the town was invaded by a regiment of Edinburgh Yeomanry Cavalry, who placed a loaded cannon at the Cross ready for execution while a search for Radicals was going on. The scene at the Cross that day was one to be remembered, and many still living recollect it.

In the summer of 1830 Green the æronaut ascended in a balloon from the Cross amidst the acclamations of assembled thousands. The Magistrates and Council, who superintended the affair, had barricades erected at all the entrances, intending to make a charge for admission; but the people, upon the example being set, broke them down and thronged the reserved ground. In December, 1808, in a passage called Nailers' Close, that led from the Cross to Green Street, but which has been removed by the formation of Duke Street, a soldier was mortally stabbed by a deserter. The ruffian escaped and was never more heard of, although a reward of twenty pounds was offered for his apprehension. A knife that was supposed to belong to the assassin was afterwards found sticking in a tree in the neighbourhood. By the overflowing of the Kilmarnock Water the Cross was flooded to the depth of about four feet on the morning of the 14th July, 1852. I will close this brief notice with an account of the ludicrous battle, known as "the Sour Milk Rebellion," that took place in the Cross in 1829. At that period the farmers who drove their milk into the town vended it at the Cross,* and from a dozen to eighteen carts thronged the area

---

* The Cross was the market place of the town. Stalls stood in it for the sale of vegetables, fish, "blackman," &c., and on market days boots, shoes, and other articles of domestic use were sold.

every morning. The farmers agreeing amongst themselves to raise the price of sour milk by reducing the measure intimated their intention to the guidwives of "Auld Killie," who strenuously denounced and oppposed what they considered "an extortion." Combining, they refused to purchase sour milk until the old measure was restored, and threatened to smash both the jug and head of any one who should pay the increased price. Their threats were in some instances carried into effect, and the uproar occasioned brought business to a standstill, for amazons flocked from all quarters to the scene of the disturbance. An officious Bailie, accompanied by a town officer (there were no police then) made his appearance with the intention of restoring order. Matters now became worse, a general row commenced, in which the sour milk taps were set running, and wherever the Bailie and his man went they were hustled by the dames and well soused with canfuls of the liquid until they were half-blinded and drenched to the skin. Crestfallen and whitewashed with the milk they made a hasty retreat amid jeers and laughter, and left the Cross in the hands of the rioters. It is needless to say that the old measure was restored. A similar rebellion took place in the town about thirty years ago. I might mention several meal mobs that gathered in the Cross, but space forbids.

Turning Mr. M'Kie's corner I enter Waterloo Street, which is narrow, but widens as it reaches Fleshmarket Bridge. The houses are dingy and old-fashioned in appearance. It was in Waterloo Street the first edition of the poems of Robert Burns was printed. The house in which the printing office was is said to be that on the left hand side of the Star Inn Close. This circumstance has entwined Kilmarnock inseparably with the memory of Burns.

In November, 1807, two women were found murdered in the back apartment of the shop in Waterloo Street, at the corner of the bridge. Two men were tried for the crime but acquitted. Here the Flesh Market Bridge spans the Kilmarnock Water, and connects Waterloo Street with Market Place. On the bridge there is a row of shops, and here, as the name implies, the Flesh Market was held. Space is so valuable that a great portion of the stream as it passes through the town is arched over and built on. The principal erections are the Council House and Police Offices. The bridge bears the following inscription :—" Flood, 14th July, 1852," which refers to one of the greatest calamities that ever visited Kilmarnock. In consequence of a waterspout or extraordinary rainfall at an early hour on the morning of the above date the usually placid Kilmarnock Water rose far above its banks, and rolled in a torrent along the course of its channels, sweeping before it almost everything that obstructed its progress. Large boulders were rolled by the current as if they had been pebbles, and trees, rock-rooted, that had withstood many a storm, were torn from their beds and whirled along by the eddy, like twigs. Machinery was washed out of workshops, furniture out of houses, and goods out of stores. Walls, houses, and bridges were swept away, and the lives of many of the townspeople were jeopardised. The water in the street at Flesh Market Bridge was five and a half feet deep. It poured up Waterloo Street, Guard Lane, and Market Lane, flooded the Cross, and rushed in a torrent down King Street, bearing on its bosom tables and chairs, and many articles out of shops, the doors of which had been burst open by the force of the flood. The value of the property destroyed within the Parliamentary bounds was estimated at £15,000. Passing along Waterloo Street the view on the opposite side of the stream embraces Tankardha' Brae and two or three tall factories that raise themselves against the steep bank that rises conically from the channel. It is said that stage coaches to and from London used to pass up and down Tankardha' Brae, but the path is so steep and narrow that it is difficult to conceive how the feat was accomplished.

Turning into Green Street I pass the Butter Market, where maids and matrons from the country dispose of their butter, eggs, and poultry on market days, and arrive in Duke Street, pausing before the entrance to the Corn Exchange Hall.

The Corn Exchange is the finest structure in the town, if not in the whole county. It is situated at the corner of Green Street and London Road, and extends one hundred and thirty-six feet along the first-mentioned thoroughfare, and ninety-two along the latter. It is two storied, and the style of the architecture is Italian. Above the hall entrance there is a tower one hundred and ten feet high, surmounted with three clock dials. The tower is called the Albert Tower, and was erected by public subscription to the memory of the late Prince Consort. The building was opened in September, 1863. The under storey consists of shops, and in the upper storey are the Kilmarnock Library, Athenæum, Reading-room, and two small offices which are allotted to the Registrar and Sanitary Inspector. Attached is the Butter Market. The hall is spacious, and seated for twelve hundred. It has a commodious gallery, and behind the platform there is a large finely-toned organ that cost £800, and which is held by trustees for behoof of the public.

I now pass along Duke Street, which, as already stated, was opened for traffic in 1859. It forms a direct communication from the Cross to London Road, instead of the tortuous approach by Waterloo Street. The street is wide. One side is occupied by a row of handsome buildings, the other as yet is only partly built on. The corner block which faces the Cross is, in an architectural point of view, very chaste in design. Passing Regent Street, I pass through the Cross and enter Fore Street, or, as it is generally termed, the Foregate; but before proceeding on my way I will say a word about Clerk's Lane Church, which is situated in Regent Street, and seen from the corner of Duke Street. Clerk's Lane Church is at present an Evangelical Union place of worship, and the pastor is the Rev. Robert Hislop. The building originally belonged to a sect called "Antiburghers." It is a plain block, with something resembling a flower-plot in front of it, close to which stands a house that was at one time the manse. Several eminent divines have laboured in Clerk's Lane Church, not the least of whom was the Rev. James Robertson: he was ordained in 1777 and died in 1811. Although of scholastic attainments, he was most eccentric in his habits, and often pointed and personal in his discourse. Many anecdotes are preserved regarding him, only one of which space permits me to relate:—When preaching one day on the Atonement, he observed two individuals in his audience who had failed in business, and met the demands of their creditors—one with five shillings in the pound, and the other with two and sixpence. " Christ paid it all," said he; then with a fixed look at the one bankrupt and then at the other, he added, "it wasna five shillings in the pound

Christ paid, O no; nor was it two and sixpence in the pound, but the whole pound; and that's what every man who wishes to be considered honest should do."

It was in Clerk's Lane Church that the celebrated Dr Morison was tried by the Presbytery in 1841. He was plain Mr then, and in the morning of manhood. He had published a pamphlet which many considered contained doctrines that were at variance with the *Confession of Faith*. He also took a more liberal view of the Atonement of Christ than divines were wont to do, and did not hesitate to preach his opinions from the pulpit. Of course he was a reformer, and like all who interfere with use and wont, he suffered. The Presbytery got wind of his heresy; he was tried, and suspended; he appealed to the Synod; it sustained the decision, and ultimately expelled him from the Secession Church. The trial began in the morning, and lasted until midnight. Mr Morison spoke for five hours in his own defence. His address was earnest and eloquent, so much so that he carried the sympathies of the majority of the audience with him. During the trial the excitement throughout the town was intense. Prayer meetings were held in various quarters to beseech the Almighty to sustain and uphold him, and the church was so packed that several of the pews were broken down, while hundreds who were unable to gain admission blocked up the lane. I need not state how Mr Morison rose Phœnix-like, how he laboured in fitting students for the ministry, and founded the denomination known as the Evangelical Union.

I elbow my way along the Foregate—which, by-the-bye, is a narrow, confined thoroughfare, lined on both sides with low-roofed, old-fashioned houses. Their ground floors are mostly occupied with brokers' shops, at the doors of which furniture, old boots, and clothing of every description are exposed for sale. Strange smells greet the nostrils, and stranger sights the vision. Here unwashed children gambol in the gutter, and poverty-stricken men and women jostle each other as they pass up and down. Notwithstanding all this, the Foregate was at one time a most respectable street, and the first families lived in it. A short distance along it, on the left, there is a roofless ruin of a house, and behind it a store. On the site of this store there stood a two-storied thatched cottage, with a court in front of it. It was taken down in June,

1863, and while workmen were engaged in its demolition, one of them discovered a leathern bag in a hole beneath the thatch. On being lifted out it burst, and a quantity of silver coins showered from it, which created a general scramble, in which every one engaged who was conveniently near. The coins were about the size of our present five shilling pieces, and were supposed to amount to several hundreds. Why they came to be there is an insoluble mystery. The house was at one time an inn, but this fact does not account for the hidden treasure. The coins, however, were possessed of a language. They were principally of the reign of Charles the First and Charles the Second, which intimates the era of the Persecution, when bloodshed and robbery were perpetrated to drive terror into the hearts of inoffensive people, and compel them to square their creed to Act of Parliament. Any one at all acquainted with the history of Kilmarnock must be aware of the atrocities committed in the town about this time; therefore it is not at all improbable that the concealer of the bag left the house—which probably was his or her home—and never returned; that banishment or death for ever separated the individual from the town, and that the secret of the concealment was swallowed up in the oblivion of the grave.

Opposite the old building referred to is Caprington Close, so called from the circumstance of a cadet of the Caprington family having resided in it in those days when

"Lairds sae spruce, an' leddies braw,
Proudly thronged the Foregate."

Next to it is a public house, styled Kay's Tavern. The building is modern, and stands on the site of a low-roofed, thatched cottage, wherein Mr Kay, the testator of a large sum of money for schools and a public park, is alleged to have been born.

Picking my steps along this ancient street for some distance, and squeezing through a crowd of slatternly women and lazy, lounging men gathered round a ballad-singer, I pass Bond Lane, a vile-looking passage, then New Street—which, by-the-bye, has every appearance of being a very old street—and step into Soulis Street, which is just a continuation of the Foregate. Passing Paddy's Close, a cluster of houses that still retain a look of faded grandeur, I pass under an arch of the railway viaduct that spans the street, and emerge into a more respectable-looking locality.

A little up the street, on the left, stands the High Church. It is surrounded by a burying-ground. In the wall that separates it from the street there is a niche in which stands a fluted pillar, surmounted by an urn. Over the whole there is a kind of pediment, on which the following inscription is graven :—

> "To the memory of Lord Soulis, A.D. 1444.
> Erected by subscription, A.D. 1825.
> 'The days of old to mind I call.'"

Prior to this monument, a rude stone pillar, surmounted by a cross which was much decayed and time-worn, stood in the middle of the street. The circumstance that the monument commemorates is merely traditionary, and to the effect that Lord Soulis was an English nobleman who was shot by an arrow from the bow of one of the Boyds of Dean Castle. It is said that Boyd fired the fatal shot from the opposite bank of the Kilmarnock Water, which flows in the vicinity. In the centre of the street there is a diamond figure in the causeway, which marks the spot where the ill-fated Soulis fell. The grave-yard contains many handsome tomb-stones. One of polished granite bears the following inscription :— "Sacred to the memory of Thomas Kennedy, water meter manufacturer, who died 6th Sept., 1874, aged 77 years———." Thomas Kennedy was not, *strictly speaking*, the inventor of the water meter, yet it was owing to his persistent perseverance that the wonderful piece of mechanism was brought to its present state of perfection. In the infancy of the invention, difficulties were encountered and obstacles met with that would have disheartened any ordinary man, and had it not been for him a water meter manufactory would never have been in Kilmarnock. He added much to the trade and importance of the town, and the extensive works in Low Glencairn Street are his best monument. Meters of his patent are in use in all quarters of the civilised world.

The eccentric Rev. James Robertson that I mentioned in connection with Clerk's Lane Church is interred here. There is a handsome stone to his memory. Here also lie the remains of John Wilson, the printer of the first edition of the poems of Burns. He was, as every reader of Burns is aware, unmercifully lampooned by the bard in the following epitaphical stanza:—

HIC JACET WEE JOHNNIE.

"Whoe'er thou art, oh reader know,
That death has murder'd Johnnie!
And here his body lies fu' low—
For saul he ne'er had ony."

There is another stone that I may mention. It is "to the memory of Robert Laurie, Waterlooman, late of the Scots Greys." It is stated by William Scott Douglas, in his little work on the County of Ayr, that this individual acquired a small property adjoining the churchyard, and felt a great desire that his bones should repose at the back of his house. But a trifling obstacle lay in the way of accomplishing his purpose. His father, John Laurie, was buried in the Laigh Kirkyard, and Robert disliked the idea of being separated from him in death. The method he adopted to reconcile matters was very singular. After procuring a lair on the desired spot, he erected a fine stone, with inscription to his father's memory and his own, and proceeded under cloud of a winter evening to the Laigh Kirkyard, where he dug up his father's bones and carried them away in a bag. Being thirsty by the way after his resurrection feat, he stepped into a public house and refreshed himself with liquor, placing the bag of bones by his side. How long he sat we have not been told; but eventually he got his father fairly buried in the other churchyard close to his own house, and he used to boast in his cups that he once sat and got drunk in a public house, in the company of his father, many years after his father's death.

The High Church stands in the centre of the burying ground, and bears the date 1732. It is a large, plain, square building, with a spire in which there are clock dials. When viewing Kilmarnock from the vicinity of the Townhead it is a prominent object. In 1731 the population had so increased that the Parish Church was found insufficient, and the Town Council resolved to erect an additional church in consequence. The scheme met with the approval of the Earl of Kilmarnock and Mr. Orr of Grougar, who between them contributed 1000 merks towards the fund. The Town Council gave £30 sterling, and the rest was raised by subscription. The building, exclusive of the spire, cost £850.

The Earl, besides his subscription, gave the ground at the nominal feu-duty of one penny Scots, which was to be paid at a certain spot "if asked."

Upon the erection of the new kirk the ministers of the old preached by turns in it, but in 1764 a clergyman was appointed to the charge, and in 1811 the union between the old and new churches was severed by the latter being created a parish church. The diocese was termed "The High Kirk Parish." Such is a brief outline of the origin and history of the High Church. Amongst the early ministers of the High Church may be mentioned the Rev. John Russell, who is said to have established the first Sabbath School in Kilmarnock. He was robust and very dark complexioned, was a strict disciplinarian, and used to go through the streets "between the preachings" with a stout stick in his hand in quest of Sabbath-breakers. His sermons were always replete with references to the torments in store for the ungodly. He seems to have thought that terror of future punishment was more conducive to make men virtuous than appealing to the finer feelings of the breast by showing that the pleasure of doing good brings its own reward. Burns refers to him as follows in "The Holy Fair," and no doubt his description is a correct one:—

> "But now the Lord's ain trumpet touts
> Till a' the hills are rairin',
> And echoes back return the shouts :
> Black Russell is na' spairin';
> His piercing words, like Highland swords,
> Divide the joints and marrow ;
> His talk o' hell, where devils dwell,
> Our vera sauls does harrow
> Wi' fricht that day."

The present minister of the High Church is the Rev. James Aitken. He takes a deep interest in the homeless, destitute children of the town, and other matters connected with it. In the graveyard, a gate opens into Soulis Street, and another into Back Street. It was in Back Street that Sandy Patrick's bit "public" was situated. It is said to have been a favourite "ca' house" of the poet Burns, and that he drank many a social glass of the *cap ale* that the landlord brewed on the premises. Recent town improvements have swept the house away, and left its site an uncertainty.

Leaving the churchyard, I pass along High Street, and stop before an odd-like building with an inscription on it stating that it was built in 1705, and rebuilt, 1840. This is the meal market, a place at which that ingredient which composes

"The halesome parritch, chief o' Scotia's food,"

was at one time vended ; in fact, it was the only place in the town where it could be procured, for the Council enacted in 1711 "that all persons sell or retail their meal in the meal market, and not elsewhere."

Passing Menford Lane, Townhead Bridge and "Willie Mair's Brae" come in view. From the brae a beautiful view can be obtained of the ruin of Dean Castle and the valley stretching before it. Turning into Dean Lane, a steep, narrow thoroughfare, I come to Boyd Street. It is a very ancient street, and is lined on either side with old-fashioned houses that speak of "the days o' auld lang syne." Like Fore Street, it was at one time inhabited by people who were well-to-do in the world, but it is changed days with it now. In this street the notorious "Timmer Land" is situated. In one of its rooms a man named Wallace lately dashed the brains of a little child out against the hearthstone. He was tried for it, and received twenty years' penal servitude! Twenty years for dashing out a child's brains? Yes, human life is at a discount, and hanging has become unfashionable. Across the lane from Boyd Street, on the right, stands a solitary, strange-looking thatch cottage. It was at one time a toll-house, and stood on the old line of road to Glasgow in the days of stage-coaches. The road originally passed in front of it, and the coaches rattled down Dean Lane, along High Street, Soulis Street, Fore Street, and into the Cross ; and when going to Ayr, down Sandbed Street and on through Riccarton. Opposite the toll-house is Gallows-knowe, a place that derives its name from the circumstance that a gibbet was erected here in the days of feudalism whereon to hang individuals who were convicted of theft and lesser crimes than the fellow Wallace received twenty years for. In these days there were nice distinctions observed. For instance, if a man was convicted of theft he was hanged, but if a woman was convicted of the same offence they drowned her in a hole that was kept for female malefactors. This was called "pit and gallows," the power of which was conferred upon the Lords Boyd. The first Dissenting church in Kilmarnock was built on Gallows-knowe in 1772. It was taken down in 1861 upon the congregation removing to a more commodious place of worship in Portland Road.

I now enter Dean Street, opposite Witch Road. Witch Road is a handsome street of recent construction. It is said to derive its name from a weird-like path that at one time existed in its locality, and along which (tradition states) those convicted of witchcraft were led to execution. Turning into Wellington Street, I enter what may be appropriately termed the main artery of the town, and pass on my right the High Church Manse, a quaint building, surrounded by a garden; and farther down, on my left, Kay School, a pretty little Gothic structure, with a playground attached. The cost of erecting this and another school similar to it in Bentinck Street was defrayed from a legacy of £5000 bequeathed to the town for educational purposes by the late Mr Kay. the location of whose birthplace I pointed out when entering the Foregate. Besides these buildings, Wellington Street contains some fine villas and substantial houses of a superior order. At its termination I pause to view Henderson Church (the Rev. David Landsborough's) and the Fever Hospital. The first is a plain but neat edifice. It was erected in 1818, and its congregation then formed a splinter off that of Gallows-knowe. It is at present under the wing of the Free Church. The second is a beautiful building, in the Grecian order of architecture, and consists of a centre and two wings. The right wing is recently added; the other portions were built in 1869. This noble Institution stands on a piece of rising ground called Mount Pleasant, and from its elevated position has a handsome appearance. It is wholly supported by subscriptions and donations bestowed by the benevolent. Since it has been opened three gifts of £500 each have been given to it by natives of Kilmarnock who have realised competencies. As yet it has never lacked support, and I trust it never shall, for to many a poor mortal it is a haven in the day of affliction, and not a few are nurtured and cared for within it when stricken down by disease who otherwise would pine from want and inattention.

In the vicinity of the Fever Hospital, but at a higher

elevation, stands Saint Joseph's Roman Catholic Chapel. It was erected in 1847, and occupies a site that overlooks the town, and commands an extensive view of the surrounding district. It is attended by a large congregation. The pastor is the Rev. Peter Forbes.

Wellington Street merges into Portland Street. Passing along it, the next object that attracts attention is the Free High Church, a very handsome building of a mixed kind of architecture. It was erected in 1844 at a cost of £3,000, but since then it has undergone many alterations and improvements. The Rev. Thomas Main may be said to be its founder. He was some time minister of the High Church, but seceded from the Establishment in 1843. The present pastor is the Rev. Ivie M. Maclachlan, B.A.

Passing under the railway bridge, a short walk brings me to East and West George Streets. At the corner of the first named is situated the George Hotel, the largest place of the kind in town.

Portland Street now assumes a thorough business aspect. Down to the Cross, where it terminates, both sides are lined with tall buildings, in which there is a continuous row of well-stocked shops. On the left, a little below East George Street, are situated the premises of the Kilmarnock Equitable Co-operative Society. On the ground floor there is a large retail provision store named "the Central," and two doors from it a shop devoted to cloth and drapery goods. The flat above "the Central" contains the library, reading-room, and offices of the Society. The library possesses over one thousand volumes, and the reading-room is well supplied with newspapers, magazines, and periodicals. Beside "the Central," the Society have seven branch stores scattered through the town, five of these retail provisions and groceries, one boots and shoes, and one butcher meat. Their united drawings average £643 per week. The share capital amounts to £5,424. The turnover for last year amounted to £30,357, and the divisible profit to £2,286. These figures will convey to the reader a slight idea of what Co-operation is accomplishing in Kilmarnock. The business is conducted wholly by working men—men who have thought out the problem, "What can be done to better the condition of the working classes?" Co-operation, when conducted on sound principles, proves that the working classes can better their own condition morally, physically, and intellectually. The science is but in its infancy, Co-operators are but feeling their way, but most assuredly as it gathers strength and expands it will become the germ of that great Millenium that men are so anxiously looking forward to. Jostling along Portland Street, there is nothing remarkable beyond what is to be met with in business thoroughfares in all populous districts, and arrive once more in the Cross.

CHAPTER II.

Green Bridge and its environs—London Road—Milldykes—The Irvine, and Struthers' Steps—Saint Andrew's Burying-Ground and Church—Glencairn Square and its Associations—High Glencairn Street—King Street—King Street U.P. Church—The Council House.

TAKING the Cross again as my starting-point, and traversing Duke Street, I pass the Corn Exchange and arrive at Green Bridge. Tradition states that there was a ford in early times at this spot, and a popular anecdote has it that a certain farmer and a female servant crossed it every Sabbath on their way to church—the farmer most ungallantly, for he did so on the back of the maid, it being part of her duty to carry her master across. In course of time the worthy farmer resolved to take Jenny to wife, and finding her acquiescent they repaired to Kilmarnock on foot to get the knot tied. At the ford Jenny bore her wonted burden across in safety, after which they proceeded to the minister and had their wish consummated. Reaching the ford on their way home, Jenny kilted her coats and paddled across, leaving her now husband behind. "Jenny, lass," cried he, "ye maun carry me owre."—"Na, na," she replied, "when we cam to the toun I was yer servant; noo I'm yer wife an' yer equal, sae ye can strip yer shoon an' come awa'."

Looking up the river—if the Kilmarnock Water can be designated such—the scene is murkily romantic. The view is terminated by the railway viaduct, and almost beneath the arch that spans the stream the water falls over the weir of the Bark Brae dam and purls along its polluted channel, tainted with extraneous matter. To the right a steep bank clothed with wood rises abruptly from the water edge. On its brow an old-fashioned mansion called Brachead House, the residence of Mr T. B. Andrews, peers from its sylvan retreat, and near to the bridge, some distance below the level of the road, there is a small nursery and a neat bowling green. On the left are the works of Gregory, Thomsons, & Co., and between them and the road is the Town Green, a small piece of ground the townspeople have the right of bleaching their clothes on. It was at one time of much greater extent, but the erection of the Academy and other buildings, and the construction of the road over the bridge, have greatly narrowed its limits. Above the house-tops in the distance the Roman Catholic Chapel and the Fever Hospital stand prominently out, and more near the gilded, dome-like spire of the High Church is a conspicuous object.

Down the stream the scene still retains a degree of picturesqueness. On the right, surrounded by a playground, stands the Kilmarnock Academy, a plain, unassuming edifice. It was erected in 1807. Many eminent teachers have laboured within it, and not a few natives who were educated in it have distinguished themselves and attained honourable positions. The opposite bank is an almost perpendicular steep. It is studded with trees, and over its summit passes the old line of road to the town. The houses which line it are primitive in construction and quaint-like in appearance. From Green Bridge I push along London Road, and pass a cluster of old houses at the entrance to Tankard Ha' Brae. Beyond these, a short walk along this truly pleasing highway brings me to Burnside. Opposite is Elmbank, the beautiful residence of Mr John Gilmour, coalmaster; and a little further on I pass the handsome villa of our worthy Provost, Mr Peter Sturrock; then that of Orchardhill, the residence of Mr Gross, procurator-fiscal. From Orchardhill to the Newmill burn there is a long row of elegant villas, with flower-plots in front and gardens behind. In style of architecture they are very dissimilar, but they are all graceful and neat, and are on the whole very handsome residences. The last two buildings of the range are beautiful specimens of domestic architecture, and are equal to any of the merchant princes' houses in the West End of Glasgow. One is the property of Mr Gavin Anderson, coalmaster, and the other of Mr Alexander Walker, wine merchant. Others equally palatial are in course of erection. London Road undoubtedly contains the finest houses of any thoroughfare in Kilmarnock.

Crossing Newmill burn, I turn to the right and enter a rural avenue which skirts the trickling streamlet. Strolling by the side of its hedgerows admiring the wide expanse of country before me, I soon arrive at the Irvine and at a small bridge that crosses the burnie a little above where it falls into the river. The road over the bridge was and still is a favourite walk of the lads and lasses of the town, and also of older people whose daffin' days have long since passed away. It is called the Milldykes. It leads to Struthers' Steps, a romantic spot, where there is a ford and where stepping-stones connect the banks of the river. The scene is well described by Mr David Smith, of Aberdeen, in a poem entitled "Youthful Days." Musing on the haunts of his boyhood he says—

> "And now appears another scene:
> The Struthers' Steps, with banks so green,
> Stand out before me bright and clear,
> And bring a flood of memories dear.
> Low, nestling close beside the hill
> Stands Riccarton's old famous mill;
> The railway bridge lifts high its head
> Above the Irvine's lowly bed;
> By Kameshill's dark and gloomy wood
> The river pours its silent flood."

Near to the bridge that crosses Newmill burn the Irvine takes one of its fantastically abrupt turns, after which it pursues a tolerably straight course until it passes the village of Riccarton. Here also the Newmill lade enters the river, and the mill itself is seen in the distance looking picturesque beneath the shade of some tall trees. Straying along the river bank, I pass the Small-Pox Hospital, and after a short walk arrive at the foot of Welbeck Street. Here stands a large print-work named the Defiance; it was at one time a busy place, but it has long stood inactive, and it is only occasionally of late that the quiet which pervades its interior is broken by the busy clatter of blocks. Near to the Defiance stands the recently-erected bonnet yarn mills of Messrs Douglas, Reyburn, & Co. They are somewhat extensive, and contain wonder-working machinery of the most approved description. There are also adjacent the skin-works of Messrs Adam Crooks & Son, and the tweed weaving factory of Messrs Hannah & Company. Passing up Welbeck Street, I arrive at Robertson Place, or, as it is more commonly called, "the Newton;" but as it contains nothing of interest I turn to the left and enter what is termed Richardland Road.

Richardland Road is the new name of what formed part of the Milldykes. Beyond its entrance there are as yet no buildings. It still retains its hedges and much of its original rusticity. When about half-way through this quiet thoroughfare, I arrive at Saint Andrew's Burying-Ground. It is a small place, and has long been inadequate to the wants of the population; but at present a fine new Cemetery is in course of formation on the farm of Holehouse, in the vicinity of London Road. Saint Andrew's Burying-Ground was opened in 1837, and from that date until now (1875) over nineteen thousand interments have taken place in it. I might state how the sextons have managed to crowd a number nearly equal to the entire present population of the town into such a small area, but the subject is a disagreeable one, and therefore I decline. In this burying-ground there are several neat monuments and many handsome head-stones, but none commemorating any very remarkable individual. There is a stone to the memory of Thomas Hendrie, who was sexton in Saint Andrew's for thirty-five years. He died in April, 1874, at the ripe age of seventy-five. A relative of his kindly allowed me to examine the graveyard books, and I find that during the time he held office he buried no less than 17,605 bodies. I knew the man. His heart and soul were in his occupation. He delighted to speak of his "yard," and nothing gave him greater pleasure than to recount incidents of his life as a gravedigger. Often have I listened to him with a kind of shudder, but although somewhat eccentric on this point he was nevertheless a decent, honest old man. He used to boast of the quality of the earth in Saint Andrew's, and declare that it was so dry that it was fit for Queen Victoria to lie in. I have heard it said that he carried a sample of it in his vest pocket, but I rather think he was too sensible a man for that.

Adjoining Saint Andrew's Burying-Ground is Saint Andrew's Established Church (the Rev. Thomas Martin's). It was built in 1841, and is a plain square block, with a belfry. Near to it Milldykes merges into Bentinck Street, opposite East Netherton. The houses in East Netherton are mostly thatched cottages. It is a very old street, and was at one time almost entirely occupied by weavers. Carpets were woven in it, and in reference to this Burns in his "Ordination," when speaking of the Rev. Mr Robertson, says—

> "Or, nae reflection on your hair,
> You may commence a shaver;
> Or to the Netherton repair,
> And turn a carpet weaver."

Turning down Bentinck Street, I pass Kay School, a Gothic building similar to the one already noticed in Wellington Street. It is surrounded by a spacious playground. In 1872 Bentinck Street was extended to East Shaw Street. This was a much-needed improvement, for it cleared away an unsightly old printwork, and opened up what yet will become a handsome thoroughfare.

Arriving in East Shaw Street, I turn down to Glencairn Square. East Shaw Street has not an elegant appearance; the houses are, with few exceptions, one-storeyed and covered with thatch. Environed with pleasant grounds, in this neighbourhood is Shawbank, the handsome villa of Mr James Wilson, banker. At the foot of East Shaw Street flows the river Irvine, and beyond it there is a fine view of an extensive track of open country. There also stands the hydraulic engineering works of the Glenfield Iron Company; they employ about one hundred and fifty hands, and carry on a large export trade.

Entering Glencairn Square, I pause to look about me before turning my face towards the Cross. The square is spacious, but the buildings in it, with two or three exceptions, are thatched, low-roofed, dingy dwellings. Four streets branch off it, viz., High Glencairn Street, Low Glencairn Street, and East and West Shaw Streets. These streets are parallel to each other. High and Low Glencairn streets form part of the main artery of the town. Intersecting Glencairn Square, the thoroughfare passes through the adjacent village of Riccarton and on to Ayr. In Low Glencairn Street are situated the works of the Water Meter Company; they employ about one hundred and thirty hands, and carry on an extensive business in the manufacture of meters alone. At the foot of the same street are the Holm Foundry and the engineering works of Messrs Barclays & Co. At the foot of West Shaw Street is the carpet and rug factory of Mr John Wilson. The works, which are pretty extensive, are situated near the Kilmarnock Water, and close to the residence of the proprietor.

Glencairn Square, and also the handsome line of street— nearly three-quarters of a mile in length—that passes through it, were opened up in 1765 by William, thirteenth Earl of Glencairn, who acquired the lands and superiority of Kilmarnock in 1749. Upon his acquisition this nobleman did much to improve the town, and none of the many schemes he entered into for the purpose have been more beneficial to the community than his doing away with the tortuous narrow path which connected Kilmarnock with Riccarton, and opening a highway that has been compared by an eminent topographist to Leith Walk.

In April, 1800, many of the houses in Glencairn Square were destroyed by fire. At that date a malt-house stood next door to the old school-house in East Shaw Street, and by the overheating of one of its kilns the place took fire. Tongues of flame shot through the roof, which like those in its vicinity was covered with thatch, and rendered combustible by continuous dry weather seized upon the school, lapped up every thing flammable, gathered into a huge mass of fire, voraciously leaped from roof to roof, rounded the corner of the square, and passed down Low Glencairn Street on its course of devastation; nor was it stayed until it had left thirty-five dwellings a smoking mass of ruins, and rendered nearly eighty families homeless and destitute who two hours previous had not dreamt of danger or misfortune.*

An appeal that was made to the public for subscriptions to aid the sufferers from the calamitous catastrophe was liberally responded to, and they were aided to tide over what would have been to many of them absolute ruin.

Many of the weavers and shoemakers of the Holm were zealous Radicals, and in the year 1819 they were so persuaded that nothing but physical force would ever compel the Government to listen to the cry of the people, that they collected all the swords, guns, pistols, and pikes they could

---

* A landlord of one of the burned houses in Low Glencairn Street wished to get rid of an obnoxious tenant, but failing to give him notice to quit at the proper time the individual refused to give up the house. This, of course, caused a dispute between the parties; but the landlord had his revenge, for when the flames laid hold of the building he thrust his head into the door of the house, and in the most sarcastic manner cried, "Sit still noo, John; sit still and be d——d to ye."

lay hands on, in the expectation that a general rising would take place. The men of the Holm quarter, however, were not the only individuals engaged in those warlike preparations, for nearly the whole of Kilmarnock, and a great portion of the people of the West of Scotland, were affected with the same mania. An assimilation of opinions naturally draw men together, and the Radicals of the Holm met during mealtimes and spare hours in the evenings in Glencairn Square to take into consideration and discuss the affairs of the nation. These meetings were the origin of what was known in after years as "the Holm Parliament;" and no man was more respected in them than the late worthy James, or, as he was generally called, "Colonel" Osborne. He was looked to as a kind of authority in matters of politics, and was generally the principal speaker. The reason he was daubed "Colonel" was that he was appointed commander of a party of Radicals who attended a county meeting at Ayr in November, 1819. They met in Glencairn Square, and having been put in marching order by the "Colonel," he cast his eye along the line, and with a flourish of his staff and in a voice of thunder gave the word "March." The procession, which was preceded by two females bearing a cap of Liberty on a pole, moved forward to the strains of music, and passed through Riccarton with banners flying.

On the morning of the 14th April, 1820, when the Edinburgh Yeomanry Cavalry invaded the town, Glencairn Square presented an unusual appearance. Members of the corps rode up and down it and the adjoining streets with drawn sabres, and would allow no one to leave their houses until a search for suspected persons had been completed. The enthusiasm of the Radicals was on the wane that morning, for there was a general scramble amongst them to gain Caprington Woods or any other place of concealment.

"The Holm Parliament" continued its *standings* in Glencairn Square for fifty-two years, but time cooled the enthusiasm and silvered the hair of many of its members, and death and removals to other districts so thinned its numbers that it gradually dissolved. The "Colonel" continued a prominent speaker of the "Parliament," and lived to see many political changes; and when age and infirmities began to tell on him he was considerately accommodated with a chair, and the knights of the shuttle and the awl crowded round him and fought with voice and gesture the battles of the House of Commons over again. The "Colonel" remained a Radical to the end of the chapter, and died in March, 1859, aged seventy-eight.

From the Square I pass up High Glencairn Street and arrive at East and West Netherton Streets. In West Netherton stands the extensive power-loom factory of Messrs T. & J. Ferguson. At the Nethertons Titchfield Street begins, but like Glencairn Street, it possesses few modern buildings. Behind is the village of Riccarton, and beyond it the romantic hills of Craigie. In front, and looking as if it blocked up the thoroughfare, stands the Relief, or—beg its pardon—King Street United Presbyterian Church, with its tapering spire. On my right is the Galleon Brae, a row of old thatched cottages that stand above the level of the road. Opposite is the neat mansion of Ex-Provost Dickie, with a lamp in front of it, on the top of which is the "loupin' hand." Mr. Dickie filled the civic chair for thirteen years, and for a long period has taken a deep interest in the welfare of the town. Upon his retirement from the Provostship he was presented with a handsome testimonial by the members of the Council and other friends. Passing onward, a sharp walk brings me to the entrance of King Street. Branching off to the right is Fowlds and Saint Andrew Streets. In the first-named is Free Saint Andrew's Church, a large, gloomy-like building. Beyond it is the Meeting-House of the Original Seceders, and farther on, on the same side, is the Baptist Chapel. It is of recent erection, and is a neat little place of worship. The second-named street is undergoing a transformation. Buildings are springing up rapidly, and new streets are being formed off it in the direction of the Newton. A short distance up King Street I pause before the Presbyterian Church referred to above. It stands at the corner of Saint Marnock Street, and is a beautiful building of a mixed kind of architecture. From the centre of its front towers a graceful spire, one hundred and twenty-six feet in height, which gives to the whole structure an imposing appearance. This church is well attended, and internally it is commodious and neatly fitted up. It was erected in 1832. The present minister is the Rev. Alexander Brown. There is little of importance connected with the history of its congregation. Its founders were a few individuals who left the Parish Church of Riccarton, in 1798, because the patron denied them the choice of a minister. Erecting a meetinghouse in the village, at the top of New Street, they worshipped in it until the year 1814, when they removed to Kilmarnock, having built a church on the spot that the present building occupies. The reason of the change was that their numbers had greatly increased, and the augmentation coming principally from Kilmarnock they considered it prudent to have their place of worship more central. The congregation after its removal rapidly increased, and the new church becoming too small it was pulled down, hence the erection of this commodious building.

I now pass up King Street, which is the principal business thoroughfare of the town. It is broad, well paved, and regularly built, and is lined on either side with large and roomy shops. On my right I pass the Post-Office, a miserable-looking place of the kind, and anything but a credit to a town of the size and importance of Kilmarnock. Higher up on the same side, and near to the entrance of the Cross, stands the Council House. It is built on the top of the arch through which the Kilmarnock Water flows on its way through the town. It was erected in 1805, and is a plain, graceful building of two storeys. The ground floor is occupied by shops; the upper floor contains the Town Hall, Town Clerks' Office, and a waiting room. The hall is small, and only capable of seating little over two hundred individuals. In it are held the Police and Justice of Peace Courts. The walls are decorated with beautiful portraits in oil. One is that of Sir James Shaw in his Lord Mayor's robes; another that of Sir John Dunlop of Dunlop, the first M.P. for the Kilmarnock District of Burghs; a full length of the late Earl of Eglinton, and a well-executed likeness of the poet Burns by William Tannock, after Nasmyth's celebrated picture. Leisurely strolling along the street, I once more enter the Cross, and again make it my starting-point.

CHAPTER III.

Cheapside Street—The Old Tolbooth—The Low Church of former days and its Associations—The Churchyard—John Dickie Street—Dunlop Street—The Astronomical Observatory—Langlands Street—John Finnie Street—The New Theatre—St. Marnock Street—The Courthouse—Kilmarnock House—Dundonald Road—The Public Park—Waterside—Sandbed Street.

OBSERVING that the beautiful statue of Sir James Shaw, which adorns the centre of the Cross, appeared to be intently gazing down Cheapside Street, I took it as a hint and passed into that short thoroughfare. In front is the massive square tower of the Low Church. It bears the date 1410, and now stands prominently out since the old buildings that clustered about its base have been removed. At the Crown Hotel I pause and muse on other days, for, according to M'Kay, it was nearly opposite it where the Old Tolbooth stood. He says—" It was a gloomy-looking structure two storeys high, with a small 'bell-house,' and shops on the ground floor facing the street. The bell that belonged to it is still used in the present Council-house, and bears this inscription:— 'This bell was gifted by the Earl of Kilmarnock to the town of Kilmarnock for their Council-house. A.M., Edin., 1711.' Down a lane at the west end of the building was the Thieves' Hole, and above were two dungeon-like apartments called the Tolbooth, at the stairhead of which hung the *Juggs*, or iron collar, in which petty delinquents were doomed to stand for a given time exposed to the gaze of the multitude. The part of the upper flat nearest the Cross formed the Hall, or Courthouse, the entrance to which was by a broad outside stair faced with a parapet. From the head of this stair the whole of the market-place was seen; and here, on public occasions, such as Kings' birthdays, the Bailies and Councillors, accompanied sometimes by the lord of the manor, would assemble to drink His Majesty's health and give other loyal and patriotic toasts. The Old Tolbooth was taken down about the beginning of the present century."

From the above quotation we learn that Cheapside, as it is now called, has been a street of considerable importance. It still remains so, but contains nothing nowadays worthy of notice, therefore "swith to the Laigh Kirk" I now take my way. It stands at the end of Cheapside, and about a stone-throw from the Cross; but, oh, what a change has taken place in its vicinity since last year! Low Church Lane has all but disappeared, and only a portion of the Strand is now left, the hand of improvement having swept away the old buildings that lined these thoroughfares, and their sites form a handsome new street which is named after our late provost. It runs from Bank Street to John Finnie Street, and doubtless in future years it will be the main way between the western portion of the town and the Cross. The present Low Church is a massive, plain building. It was erected in 1802 on the site of a less commodious edifice that has been rendered classical by the poet Burns as the scene of *The Ordination*—a poem brimful of that biting sarcasm that he so unerringly hurled at the hypocritical shams of his day. All that now remains of the former building—and very probably of one anterior to it—is the square tower already referred to, which has withstood the blast for centuries.

The Low Church of Burns's day was the scene of a disgraceful riot at the induction of a distasteful minister, and of a melancholy catastrophe that sent a wail of grief and lamentation through the streets of Kilmarnock. The first-mentioned event took place in 1764, and the facts may be briefly related as follows:—Upon the death of the Rev. Robert Hall the second charge became vacant, and the Earl of Glencairn—the then patron—appointed the Rev. Mr. Lindsay of Cumbray to the office. This appointment the people of Kilmarnock did not approve of, and they determined to oppose it, for the following reasons:—In the first place, they did not consider Mr. Lindsay qualified to be their minister; and, secondly, it was through the influence of his wife, Margaret Lauder, who had been a governess in the Earl's family, that he had obtained the appointment, and not through any merit he possessed as a preacher. In spite of the opposition to the nomination of Mr. Lindsay, the Earl took his own way in the matter, and fixed the 12th of July as the day on which his ordination was to take place. "Time brought the day, the hour, the man," but it also brought the town's-people from workshop and dwelling, who, armed with every obnoxious missile they could lay hands on, thronged the approaches to the Low Church. The excitement was intense, and when the patron, the presentee, and other clergymen and gentlemen made their appearance, they were hooted, jostled, and pelted with mud and filth to such an extent that it was with the utmost difficulty they gained the interior of the church; but they were not safe even there, for, to quote from a metrical account of the tumult that was written at the period by a poet of some local fame :—*

* * * * * *

> While Brown was praying, I suppose,
> A stane cam whirring near his nose;
> Says he, 'Our wark we now maun close.'
>   Good people hear my ditty.
>
> Puir Taylor Steen, precentor there,
> They rave his wig aff ilka hair,
> And left the body's noddle bare.
>   Good people hear my ditty.
>
> And Bailie Baps he gat a shog,
> Outowce the head, wi' Lambert's dog,
> That laid him senseless as a log.
>   Good people hear my ditty.
>
> Though meek and gentle Lindsay was,
> And had at heart the guid auld cause,
> Yet nocht could mak' the rabble pause.
>   Good people hear my ditty.
>
> Their fury raise to sic a height,
> That here he durst not pass the night,
> But aff to Irvine took his flight.
>   Good people hear my ditty.
>
> Pursued with hisses, yells, and groans,
> And mony a shower o' dirt and stones,
> Their wicked rage he sair bemoans.
>   Good people hear my ditty.

* * * * * *

> At e'en Lang Tam, that howkes the stanes,
> Gaed to the inn to pike the banes,
> And to gie in the leaders' names.
>   Good people hear my ditty."

Ten ringleaders of the riot were apprehended, as the poet

---

* Burns refers to it as "a scoffing ballad." It is preserved by M'Kay in his "History of Kilmarnock," and by James Paterson in "Songs and Ballads of Ayrshire."

states, upon the information of Lang Tam. They were tried at Ayr. Three were found guilty and sentenced "to be imprisoned for one month, and whipt through the streets, and to find caution for keeping the peace and a good behaviour for a twelvemonth." The other seven were liberated. The Rev. Mr. Lindsay entered on his duties in the Low Church, but died ten years after, and was succeeded by the Rev. Mr. Mutrie, who was succeeded by the Rev. James Mackinlay. All three are mentioned by Burns in the "Ordination."

From the riot and its ludicrous incidents I will now turn to a more grave subject, and briefly refer to the melancholy catastrophe that occurred in the Low Church of former days. The building, which was incommodious and badly constructed, had long been considered unsafe—so much so that a popular prophecy stated that it would one day fall and bury the congregation in its ruins. This foolish prediction seems to have had some little weight in the public mind, for upon Sabbath, the 18th of October, 1801, when the church was unusually crowded a panic was occasioned, some say by a piece of plaster falling from the ceiling, others by the cracking of a seat in the gallery. Imagining that the prophecy was about to be fulfilled, and that the walls of the building were about to collapse, the bulk of the congregation rushed to the doors, and in their anxiety to escape crushed and trampled each other in their wild haste. Agonizing screams issued from the struggling mass of human beings in the corridors that rang through the building, and heightened the terror and dread that prevailed in the minds of the deluded throng. Unmindful of the fostering care of the Almighty Being whom they had assembled to worship, many for the moment discarded all their vaunted trust in Him, and allowed the brutal instinct of self-preservation to predominate, and sought to gratify it by throwing down and treading upon the weak and the helpless.

"Then shrieked the timid and stood still the brave."

Many sought refuge by jumping through the windows into the graveyard, and others in their despair threw themselves from the gallery into the body of the church, and heightened the pandemonium by their cries and maniacal actions. Tidings of the occurrence spread. People flocked to the scene, and the greatest excitement prevailed among the excited, horror-stricken mob who thronged every approach to the church. Ladders were procured and the building was entered by the windows, for the doors, which opened inwardly, had become shut by the pressure of those who blindly struggled to escape from the interior. The scene presented was indescribable. Behind the doors and along the passages the dead, the dying, the maimed, and the mangled, lay piled together in a trodden mass, and it was with much difficulty they were extricated and borne to the churchyard, where they were laid for recognition. This in some instances was most difficult, for many of the bodies were so disfigured that they were unrecognisable, and it was only by dress and other marks they were identified. I need not dwell upon the scenes of anguish in the churchyard, or tell of the agonizing wails of grief that rent many a bosom that afternoon. Suffice it to say that when all were got out of the building it was found there were twenty-nine killed and upwards of eighty injured, many severely. Homes in Kilmarnock and its vicinity that had resounded in the morning with family glee were by the going down of the sun abodes of mourning. Parents bewailed children, children parents, sisters brothers, and brothers sisters, while relatives and friends wept and lamented those who in the full vigour of life had been cut down and gathered into the garner of death. After the melancholy occurrence the church was taken down and the present one built. It is possessed of the opposite qualities of its predecessor, being spacious, comfortable, and well provided with means of egress.

The Low Churchyard contains several tombstones of peculiar interest, not the least of which are those to the memory of Tam Samson of elegaic fame, the Rev. John Robertson, and John Mackinlay, D.D., who, as the handsome new tombstone states, was " minister of this parish for fifty-four years." The tablet on Mr. Robertson's grave is not in the best order, but that to the memory of the famous Tam, which is railed in, is in excellent condition. On it is inscribed the following epitaph from the pen of Robert Burns which is appended to the worthy sportsman's elegy—

"Tam Samson's weel-worn clay here lies,
  Ye canting zealots spare him!
If honest worth in heaven rise,
  Ye'll mend ere ye win near him."

These three stones are situated at the north-west corner of the church. The two clergymen lie side by side, and the "weel-worn clay" of Mr Samson rests at the head of their graves, all three being buried in close proximity, which is a remarkable coincidence, seeing that they are all mentioned in the first verse of Tam's elegy in the following order—

> " Has auld Kilmarnock seen the Deil ?
> Or great Mackinlay thrawn his heel ?
> Or Robertson again grown weel,
>   To preach and read ?
> ' Na, waur than a' !' cries ilka chiel,
>   ' Tam Samson's dead.' "

Want of space compels me to omit noticing this old churchyard at any great length, therefore I will briefly refer to stones commemorating local heroes who suffered for "Christ and the Covenanted Work of Reformation," and pass on my way. The first of these stands at the back of the church, near the gravel walk, and bears the following inscription:— " Here lie the heads of John Ross and John Shields, who suffered at Edinburgh, Dec. 27th, 1666, and had their heads set up in Kilmarnock.

> " Our persecutors mad with wrath and ire,
> In Edinburgh members some do be, some here;
> Yet instantly united they shall be,
> And witness 'gainst this nation's perjury."
>   (See " Cloud of Witnesses. ")

These men were spies from the ranks of the Covenanters, and when apprehended they were found in the possession of arms, and to be in the town for the purpose of conveying intelligence of the movements of the King's troops to their confederates. Either crime at the period was a capital offence. Ross was a native of Mauchline, and Shields was a cottar on the estate of Nether Pollock. The next stone stands about the centre of the churchyard and is elaborately carved. On the top is a pistol, cross swords, and flags, the stems of which pass behind a scroll on which is graven "Solemn League and Covenant." One flag bears the inscription "God and our Country," and the other the device of a crown. The inscription is as follows :—" Here lies John Nisbet, who was taken by Major Balfour's party, and suffered at Kilmarnock, 14th April, 1683, for adhering to the word of God and our Covenants.—Rev. xii. and 11. Renewed by public contribution A.D., 1823.

> "Come, reader, see, here pleasant Nisbet lies,
> His blood doth pierce the *high* and lofty skies;
> Kilmarnock did his latter hour perceive,
> And Christ his soul to heaven did receive.
> Yet bloody Torrence did his body raise
> And buried it into another place;
> Saying, 'Shall rebels lye in graves with me!—
> We'll bury him where evil doers be.'"

For the account of Nisbet's accusation and execution I refer the reader back to the notice of the Cross.

The next and last stone to the memory of the martyrs is indented into the churchyard wall nearly opposite the old manse. On the top is an open book with the inscription, "Psalm XLIV., 17. Rev. ii., 10." Beneath is the following:—"Erected 1823. Repaired 1846. Sacred to the memory of Thomas Findlay, John Cuthbertson, William Brown, Robert and James Anderson (natives of this parish), who were taken prisoners at Bothwell, June 22nd, 1679, sentenced to transportation for life, and drowned on their passage near the Orkney Isles. Also, John Findlay, who suffered martyrdom 15th Dec., 1682, in the Grassmarket, Edinburgh."

> "Peace to the church! when foes her peace invade,
> Peace to each noble martyr's honoured shade!
> They, with undaunted courage, truth, and zeal,
> Contended for the church and country's weal;
> We share the fruits, we drop the grateful tear,
> And peaceful altars o'er their ashes rear."

The first-named five were, as the stone states, transported for life for their share in the battle of Bothwell Bridge. America was the country assigned them, and they, with 245 others who had been found guilty of the same offence, were—after undergoing much hardship and ill-usage—put on board of a vessel at Leith and confined under hatches. They received brutal usage at the hands of the captain and crew, but this had a sudden termination, for a storm arose and dashed the vessel against the rocks of Darness, near Orkney, and laid her a total wreck. Fifty escaped and 200 were drowned. The last named (John Findlay) who suffered martyrdom seems to have been the tenant of Muirside and to have been a man of sterling worth, and, according to the light he had, of great piety.

The charges brought against him were, 1st. Keeping company with the persecuted people of God. 2nd. For refusing to call Bishop Sharp's death murder, and the battle of Bothwell Bridge rebellion. 3rd. For giving food and shelter to the Covenanters. His last speech and testimony is given at length in "The Cloud of Witnesses." He considered himself greatly honoured by the laying down of his life for the cause he loved so well. The Laigh Kirkyard, as it is called, was at one time of much greater extent. Tradition states that it extended down to the brink of the river, and excavations that have from time to time been made in its neighbourhood prove that where streets are now formed and buildings erected has at one time been part of God's Acre, but at what period history saith not. I was much interested in some excavations that were made during the formation of John Dickie Street. Human skulls and bones, and, in many instances, entire skeletons were exhumed. These remains—which were carefully collected and buried in the graveyard—were no sheep shanks, but many bones were of surprising size and thickness. One thighbone that I lifted and examined would have served me for a walking stick, and a skull I had in my hand appeared to have belonged to some one *with a head*. It was unusually large, finely formed, and the region of the intelligent organs well developed. One sight I will not readily forget was that of a skeleton over six feet long imbedded in clay beneath the surface of what had been Low Church Lane. A labourer carefully removed the clay with his spade from about it, collected the bones, and had them removed to the graveyard. The sight impressed me very much, and even as I write I think I see the grinning skull—grinning as if the remnant of all that was mortal resented being disturbed. At one time these bones had formed the framework of some one's idol, which possibly had been laid there by loving friends who long ago

"Have been ordained the same cold bed,
   The same dark night, the same long sleep."

But a truce to this moralizing. To judge by the bones that I saw exhumed, men are degenerating—yes, degenerating in natural worth—and if they continue, doubtless they will arrive back at what some people would have us believe was the starting-point, viz., Darwin's ape; for the brawny brose and porridge fed Scotchmen of yore, who seemingly were possessed of greater physical qualifications and greater power of endurance than is generally met with in the men of to-day, have passed away, and a generation who have fallen off in stature and bodily strength now occupy their places. But I am beginning to moralize again.

Leaving the churchyard, I pass up John Dickie Street, and stop to view the remnant of Low Church Lane. It is meagre indeed, and consists of a few old biggins facing the wall at the back of the churchyard. The first of these is a two-storeyed venerable building, with a mansion-like appearance, that has had a narrow escape of being pulled down, for the new street passes alongside its gable. This is called "the Manse." It is now occupied by tenants, but in the olden time it was a clerical residence of some note. The last clergyman who lived in it was the Rev. Robert Jaffray, first minister of Gallows-knowe Church. He died in 1814. At the north-west corner of the churchyard, facing College Wynd, stands a tumble-down-like old house that is said to have been at one time a college; if so, it must have been of small dimensions, but from the name of the wynd it is reasonable to infer that it is only a remnant of some educational establishment whose history is swallowed up in the oblivious past.

Reaching the top of John Dickie Street, I cross John Finnie Street and enter Dunlop Street. It is a short, narrow street. On my left is the office of the Parochial Board, and set on a hill on my right, with sloping gardens in front, are three handsome mansions that overlook the town. The centre one with the niche—which is doubtless waiting for a statue of Burns—is the residence of Mr. James M'Kie, the well-known publisher. Passing Grange Street, at the corner of which is the extensive carpet factory of Hugh Wilson & Son, I begin to climb Park Street—or "the Wee Gas Brae" as it is more commonly called—and arrive at Morton Place. Situated in a back court, and towering over the house-tops, is a square block of masonry seventy feet high. It is the Astronomical Observatory. It was built in 1818 by the late Thomas Morton, who was born at Mauchline in 1783, and died at Kilmarnock in 1862. Mr. Morton was a famed constructor of telescopes and other optical instruments, and was also an ingenious machinist. He conferred a great boon on carpet manufacturers by inventing the "barrel" machine for carpet manufacture, and by improving other pieces of mechanism in connection with the trade. The Observatory is now the property of Mr. Thomas Lee, F.R.A.S. Passing along Langlands Street, which is lined on either side with working men's houses, I pass the Academy of Mr. Rose, and enter West Langlands Street. In it are situated the principal workshops of the town, viz., the extensive engineering establishment of Messrs. Barclay & Son, also that of Messrs. M'Culloch, and Allan Andrews & Co. Beyond these are the workshops of the South-Western Railway Co., in whose service over 600 men are employed. Near to the railway workshops is Bonnyton Square, which consists of a series of blocks of substantial dwelling-houses erected by the Company for the accommodation of their workmen. The buildings are finely situated, and command a view of a wide range of country. Besides a large saw mill, the gas work is situated in this street. It belonged to a joint-stock company that was formed in 1822, but it is now the property of the town, being lately purchased by the Corporation.

Turning down Langlands Brae, I have on my left the Railway Station. Vast improvements are going on at it; old buildings have been pulled down, and new premises erected. When the alterations are complete, a station worthy of the town will be the result.

At the top of West George Street I turn to the right and enter John Finnie Street. This street was opened up about ten years ago by the liberality of a native whose name it bears. It is fast assuming importance, and bids fair in an architectural point of view to be the finest thoroughfare in town. It runs from the foot of Langlands Brae to Saint Marnock Street, is broad and straight, and fully a quarter of a mile in length. A short distance along it on the left stands the New Theatre, a building that far surpasses anything of the kind in the West of Scotland. It is just completed, licensed, and opened under the management of Mr. William Glover, of the Theatre-Royal, Glasgow. The interior is commodious, beautifully fitted up, and seated for twelve hundred. Externally it is of large proportions. The front—which is Corinthian and elaborately ornamental—is gracefully chaste. It may not be inappropriate to refer to former theatres in Kilmarnock, for the drama has had several unsuccessful struggles to gain a footing in the town, not the least of which was the attempt in "Back Causeway" somewhere about thirty years ago. This theatre—or at least the stabling that was converted into such—was a rude affair of the kind; yet nevertheless the proprietors did their best to awaken a theatrical taste in the townspeople by engaging such actors as Edmund Kean, G. V. Brookes, Charles Vernon, and others; but they did not meet with the encouragement that their efforts merited, and after struggling for some years they had to give up for want of support. Shortly after its close a Mr. Scott erected a wooden theatre near to where the railway arch now crosses Portland Street. He also secured good talent, but his exertions proved futile, and like his predecessors he had to relinquish the attempt. Its successor—a wooden one also—was opened by a Mr. Bostock at the top of Langlands Brae. For a time large audiences were attracted, but gradually, in spite of stars and puffs, the interest waned and it collapsed. Shortly it was followed by another of a higher class, which was conducted by Mr. Edmund Glover. It was a neat wooden erection, and occupied nearly the same spot as the last-mentioned. Success attended it for some considerable time, but gradually the audience thinned, and after struggling for two or three winters it was taken down. The next effort worthy of notice was made by the late John Simpson and Mr. Bostock in the theatre under the railway arch in Back Street, but the expense of the erection was so great that Mr. Bostock grew terrified, disappeared, and left Simpson to wrestle with the concern as best he might. For several years Simpson struggled with adverse circumstances, tried many attractions, not the least of which was his engagements of Sir William Don, Mr. Parry, Mr. Mortimer Murdoch, G. V. Brookes, Mr. Christdale, and others, but all would not do; the Puritan spirit was too strong in Kilmarnock, support was denied, and as a last effort, after a chequered career, he dropped the price to "the low charge of one penny," but even at that figure it would not do, and John gave up in despair, having reached a state beyond bankruptcy. Since then —between six and seven years ago—various theatrical companies have visited the town, but now that it is possessed of a theatre more worthy of support, it remains to be seen whether the Puritan spirit of "Auld Killie" be sufficiently relaxed to give it the encouragement it deserves. Old John Simpson, the leading spirit in the theatre under the railway arch, was a well known character, and is still spoken of with respect. He was a shoemaker to trade, but discarded the last to tread the boards, "the profession" being more congenial to his nature. He was a fair actor, and as such was a favourite with the people of Kilmarnock, and nothing gave the juveniles more pleasure than to see him killed in a piece, he having a way of his own of dying that gave universal satisfaction. Once when playing "Burke and Hare," and when simulating death on the gallows, he would have done so in earnest had it not been noticed that the prop under his feet had given way, and that he was black in the face. He was of a congenial nature, and whether in prosperity or adversity had always a kind word for everybody. When the playgoing inhabitants denied him their support he travelled the country with a booth, and in it "played many parts;" but having met with an accident whereby he lost the sight of an eye, and age and infirmity beginning to tell on him, he came to Kilmarnock, and by the kindness of a few friends was admitted into the Infirmary, where after a short illness the curtain of death fell and closed the last scene of his eventful life on 21st December, 1873.

Passing along John Finnie Street, the next building worthy of notice is that destined for the office of Archibald Finnie & Son, coalmasters. It is in the ornate Corinthian style of architecture, and for beauty of design and sculptured embellishment there is nothing, with the exception of the Corn Exchange, to equal it in town. It stands opposite the opening in front of the Union Bank, and attracts universal attention. The Union Bank, although situated in Bank Street, faces John Finnie Street. It is of recent erection, large, and very ornamental, and forms a fine background to the short street that connects both thoroughfares.

Arriving at the termination of John Finnie Street I pause and look round me. In front is Dundonald Road; to the right, Portland Road; and to the left Saint Marnock Street. The two last-named are parallel and form a splendid line of street that merges into Irvine Road. At the corner of Dundonald and Portland Roads is Trinity Episcopal Church and Parsonage. The present minister is the Rev. A. G. Creighton. The church was enlarged last year, and a square tower yet in an unfinished state was then added. Its style of architecture is early English, and altogether it is a very neat place of worship. It was erected in 1857. Opposite it in Portland Road stands what is termed Portland Road U.P. Church (the Rev. George F. James's). It is an elegant structure, and is what may be termed Byzantine in style. It was erected in 1859 by the congregation of Gallows Knowe Church, who desired to have their place of worship more central. Besides these churches, Portland Road contains very many handsome villas and substantial houses of the first order. At its extremity is Springhill, the beautiful residence of Mr. Archibald Finnie. It stands on a slight eminence and presents an imposing appearance, with its green lawns and finely planted grounds. Behind Springhill, salubriously situated near Irvine Road, stands Grange Terrace. It also overlooks the town and consists of a row of substantial houses. Kilmarnock is stretching to the east and the west, and before many years pass away it will assume a degree of compactness that will remove the reproach so long cast upon it of being straggling and irregular.

But to return. At the corner of John Finnie and Saint Marnock Streets stand the Court House and Prison. The former is a massive building in the Grecian order of architecture. It was erected in 1852, and consists of a centre and two wings. The facade fronts Saint Marnock Street and is very imposing. By its side there is a neat flower plot inside an iron railing, in which stands a piece of ordnance in all the indolence of peace. In the hall of the Court House Sheriff Courts are held, and the offices of the Procurator Fiscal and Sheriff Clerk are situated within the building. The prison is behind, and connected with the Court House, and to it is attached the dwelling-house of Mr. Geddes, the governor, and an exercise court for the prisoners. Crime is not heavy in the burgh, but nevertheless this institution never lacks inmates, and never shall so long as the sale of intoxicating liquors is sanctioned by the Government. On the opposite side of Saint Marnock Street, and a little farther down than the Court House, stands Saint Marnock's Church (the Rev. John Thomson's). It was erected in 1836, and like the other churches in its neighbourhood is a very handsome building. From its front rises a massive square wing Gothically ornamented, symmetrical, and chaste in design. It became a Parish Church in 1862, and is well attended.

Opposite Saint Marnock's Church, and next to the Court House, stands an old-fashioned manor house, with a small garden before it. Its doors, windows, and general construction speak of former times. It is called Kilmarnock House. After the destruction of Dean Castle by fire in 1735, it was the residence of William, fourth Earl of Kilmarnock. It is supposed to have been built towards the close of the seventeenth century. Its policies were extensive and well wooded, and a portion of a shady avenue still remains a sad memento of the fallen house of Boyd. The unfortunate Earl—as the fourth Earl of Kilmarnock is generally called—left the threshold of this mansion in 1745 to join the standard of Prince Charlie, never more to enter its baronial shade. What induced him to allow himself to be drawn into the vortex of a hopeless civil war I know not, nor does any writer I have consulted throw any light upon the subject, although several have formed conjectures. The Kilmarnock people were opposed to the house of Stuart, and the Earl was never suspected of entertaining revolutionary principles, for he had been always friendly to the house of Hanover, and took a deep interest in the affairs and prosperity of the town, and up to the very hour of his departure retained his seat in the Council. The quiet, unostentatious life that he led in Kilmarnock formed a strange prelude to his brief career of adventure while following Prince Charlie and to his tragic and melancholy end. Space forbids me going at any great length into the Earl's history after he left Kilmarnock, but perhaps a brief account of what he passed through may not be uninteresting to the reader. Upon his arrival at the Prince's quarters he met with a cordial reception from the young adventurer, and was at once " made Colonel of the Guards and promoted to the degree of a General." At the battle of Falkirk, which was fought on the 17th of January, 1746, he distinguished himself, and by his bravery materially assisted the arms of the Prince in winning that victory, and in every other engagement evinced great courage. But the end came—the melancholy end. It was on the 16th April; the scene Culloden Moor, a few miles eastward of Inverness. There the Duke of Cumberland, accompanied by twelve thousand men, encountered the Prince's army, which amounted to half that number, and was principally composed of starving, dispirited Highlanders. The battle commenced; the Prince's little army fought bravely; but, to quote from *Chambers's History of the Rebellion,* "Notwithstanding that the three files of the front line of the English poured forth their incessant fire of musketry—notwithstanding that the cannon, now loaded with grape-shot, swept the field as with a hailstorm—notwithstanding the flank fire of Wolfe's regiment—onward, onward went the headlong Highlanders, flinging themselves into, rather than rushing upon, the lines of the enemy, which, indeed, they did not see for smoke till involved among the weapons. . . . Almost every man in their front rank, chief and gentleman, fell before the deadly weapons which they had braved; and, although the enemy gave way, it was not till every bayonet was bent and bloody with the strife." At the close of the battle, when the army of the Prince had been defeated and the remnant were seeking safety in flight, the account states that "the Earl of Kilmarnock, being half-blinded with smoke and snow, mistook a party of Dragoons for the Pretender's horse, and was accordingly taken. He was soon after led along the lines of the British Infantry, in which his son, then a young man, held the commission of ensign. The Earl had lost his hat in the strife, and his long hair was flying in disorder around his head and over his face. The soldiers stood mute in their lines, beholding the unfortunate nobleman. Among the rest stood Lord Kilmarnock, compelled by his situation to witness, without the power of alleviating, the humiliation of his father. When the Earl came past the place where his son stood, the youth, unable to bear any longer that his father's head should be exposed to the storm, stepped out of the ranks, without regard to discipline, and taking off his hat, placed it over his father's disordered and wind-beaten locks. He then returned to his place, without having uttered a word, while scarcely an eye that saw his filial affection but confessed its merits by a tear." With the Earl the scene had now changed—the Stuarts' star had set—the Prince was now a fugitive and he a prisoner. He was consigned to the tower of London, in due time was tried and convicted of high treason, and sentenced to be beheaded. He met his doom with resignation, and suffered on Tower Hill, London, on the 18th of August, 1746. Kilmarnock House is now converted into an Industrial Ragged School, and in it many poor children who have lost their parents, and others who would otherwise become waifs of society, find a home.

No portion of Kilmarnock has undergone a greater transformation of late years than that in the vicinity of Kilmarnock House. Forty years ago the old building was surrounded by venerable trees, and stood in all its baronial dignity as if waiting for those who would nevermore return. Then the Kilmarnock Water flowed along its unconfined channel in greater pelucidity, and where Saint Marnock Street now crosses it, a rickety old wooden bridge connected both its banks. The place was strictly rural, trees waved their verdant boughs, and birds sported among the foliage in all the consciousness of security. But a change has taken place. The town has grown into proportions that has swallowed up the Baron's pleasure grounds. The axe has been laid to the trees, and where Nature's carpet was spread, handsome streets have been formed and buildings reared; and where once the melody of birds was heard comes the rattling sound of wheels, and the busy hum of domestic life.

I now enter Dundonald Road; but before proceeding farther, I may state that the portion of the highway from Saint Marnock Street to Pointhouse Toll is of recent construction. The old road to the spot indicated was tortuously crooked, but by doing away with it and continuing the highway in a straight line through what was known as Ward's Park*, the present handsome thoroughfare was the result. A long range of graceful residences and beautiful villas are now erected on it, and altogether it has a handsome appearance.

Passing on my way, I pause before Winton Place Evangelical Union Church (the Rev. William Bathgate's). It is a neat building in the early English Gothic style, and has a fine appearance from the road. It was erected in 1860 by the members of Clerk's Lane Church, the majority of whom removed to it, and left those who adhered to the old

---

* It was in Ward's Park where Fastern's E'en Races were held. These races were "discontinued by the Magistrates and Council about 1831, after having been observed annually for five centuries."

building to form a new congregation. From Winton Place to the entrance of the Public Park every building is so chastely neat in design that the eye rests with delight upon the whole; and to avoid giving prominence to any one in particular, I add no more to what has been already stated regarding them.

Entering what is at present dignified with the name of a Public Park, I find it thronged with youths engaged in sports and pastimes. Here, a little band with bats and wickets are busy at cricket; there, another deeply engrossed in the game of rounders, and not a few are engaged in the more laborious game of football; while groups, not otherwise employed,

" Scour awa' in lang excursion,
And worrie ither in diversion."

Stretching along the top of a bank, and overlooking the park, is a belt of tall trees. They consist of two rows, and seem at some period to have lined the sides of a drive. A solemnity pervades the spot; and no wonder, for there is a sorrowful tale connected with it. The place is called "The Lady's Walk." It at one time extended down to Kilmarnock House, and in it the Lady of the unfortunate Earl of Kilmarnock, who is said to have died of a broken heart, wandered and mourned the sad fate of her lord. A little poem on "The Lady's Walk," by one Ashton Carle, an actor, that appeared in the *Kilmarnock Standard* some time ago, is so good, and describes the place and incident so faithfully, that I may be pardoned for presenting it to my readers.

" A wild, weird look has the ' Lady's Walk,'
And the trees are stripped and old;
They solemn bend in mute-like talk,
In the twilight grey and cold.

Each gaunt and rugged sinewy root
Starts up along the way—
Memento sad of the lady's foot
That erst did mournful stray.

Ghost-like the boughs loom in the sky,
And, skeleton-like, they meet ;
The very pathway, white and dry,
Curves like a winding-sheet.

The rustling leaves that autumn weaves
In wither'd hillocks lie,
And the chilly wind soughs just behind
Like the lady's tearful sigh.

> Heavily rolls the evening mist,
>   And the rising night winds throb
> By root and shoot, just where they list,
>   Till they sound like the lady's sob.
>
> And the nightly shadows come and go,
>   And the gaunt trees bow and wave,
> Like weeping mourners, to and fro
>   Over a dear one's grave.
>
> Then this is the far-famed "Lady's Walk,"
>   And walketh she there to-night ?
> Holdeth her spirit silent talk
>   With that moon so sickly white ?
>
> I hear no sound but the rushing bound
>   Of the swelled and foaming river,
> That seems to say : I cannot stay,
>   But must on for ever and ever."

Near to the close of the Lady's Walk I come to a piece of ground between it and Dundonald Road, enclosed within a paling, and planted with shrubs and young trees. In this spot a number of people lie buried who fell victims to cholera during the prevalence of the epidemic in 1832. At the termination of the walk a couple of cannon are stationed, partly for ornament and partly to teach the Artillery Volunteers how to use such weapons. From their site a fine view of the town, of the village of Riccarton, and a wide expanse of country, is obtainable. I now cross the Public Park and arrive in the footroad that skirts the Kilmarnock Water. The stream here is both shallow and filthy in appearance, and abounding in sewage. Turning in the direction of the town, I pass the Cattle Market, enter Waterside Street—a row of old-fashioned houses—and after a short walk arrive in Saint Marnock Street. Turning to the right, I cross the bridge and enter Sandbed Street, which runs along the side of the river from Saint Marnock Street to Cheapside Street. It is narrow and not over-cleanly, and its appearance is anything but heightened by the sewer-like stream that flows below its level. Many of the houses that line it are tall, dingy, tenant-crowded blocks, but as its extremity is neared a few buildings still stand whose old walls and thatch-covered roofs speak of other days. Sandbed Street is a very old thoroughfare. It at one time formed part of the main road to Ayr, and along it the stage-coaches and other vehicles used to rattle as they passed through the town; but, like every other place in its vicinity, it is much changed, so much so that scarce a vestige of its early appearance is now left. Arriving at the Old Bridge, at the top of Sandbed, I pause to view the unsavoury scene, and mentally compare the past with the present. At the north-east side of this bridge the "Thieves' Hole" was situate. It was, as already stated, attached to the Tolbooth, and is associated with the name of "bloody Dalziel." When stationed in Kilmarnock, in 1667, it is recorded that he and his soldiery perpetrated many atrocities amongst the inhabitants, and that he consigned numbers of them to the "Thieves' Hole," "where they could not move themselves night or day, but were obliged constantly to stand upright." An old building, once an inn, that stood close to the bridge and near to where Victoria Place now stands, tradition affirmed to have been that in which the tyrant resided, and from which he issued his orders.

Crossing the bridge, I enter Cheapside, turn to the right, and once more arrive in the Cross. After having traversed the principal streets and many of the byeways of "Killie" in the course of my three excursions, what is to be learned from them? Simply this, that Kilmarnock of to-day is almost entirely a modern town. Its principal streets, as we have seen, have been opened up and built on, and all that constitutes its superiority over what it was in former times has been accomplished within the recollection of people still living. Its remarkable extension of late years may be attributed to various causes, not the least of which has been the utilisation of the resources of a district teeming with mineral and agricultural wealth, and of its being blessed with a manufacturing and commercially enterprising people. But, reader, I will now ask you to accompany me in

"My wanderings by hill and dale
Round Killie's auld dear sheltered vale,"

and I will do what I can to entertain you by the way.

RAMBLES ROUND KILMARNOCK.

―――o―――

CHAPTER I.

The Bridges connecting Kilmarnock with Riccarton, and the objects of interest in their vicinity—Caprington Castle—Riccarton Castle, its site and traditions—Traditions of Sir William Wallace—Riccarton—The Parish Church—Sandy M'Crone—The Churchyard—Old Stones—The East Shaw Street Miser—The Old Church—Village Worthies—The Village past and present—The Manse.

On a bright morning in the leafy month of June I stood in the Cross of Kilmarnock, staff in hand, for I had cast business and care aside for the day, and formed the resolution to ramble along some of the rustic highways and byeways, and explore the antiquities and sylvan scenes that intersperse the cultivated landscapes round the town. Glancing at the numerous thoroughfares which branch off this local centre, I passed down King Street, and being light of heart and limb, was well through Glencairn Street before I was aware that I was leaving the busy town behind, and that the beauteous scenery by which it is surrounded was bursting into view. Looking in front I beheld a scene at once picturesque and lovely—a scene that never fails to delight me when I look upon it. In the foreground Riccarton Tollhouse and old Bridge, behind a portion of the village, and away in the background the steep hills of Craigie bathed in sunlight.

Gaining the Tollhouse I found it situated between two handsome bridges which span the river Irvine. One of these has an ancient look, but the other is a comparatively modern structure. The river here divides the parishes of Kilmarnock and Riccarton, and forms the boundary line between the districts of Kyle and Cunninghame. The old Bridge bears the date of its erection (1726), and it is not a little curious—if Aiton is to be relied on—that the first carts used in Ayrshire were employed to convey stones for its construction. The road over the old Bridge leads through the village of Riccarton. At one time it was the highway between Kilmarnock and Ayr, but the portion on which the village stands being steep, crooked, and narrow, the new Bridge was built and a straight line of road formed some thirty years ago.

From the parapet of the new Bridge an extensive view is obtainable. In the distance are seen the cloud-capped hills of Arran and the heights of Dundonald, but as I have no desire of tiring the reader with lengthy descriptions of scenery I will merely refer to the places of interest that come within the range of vision to the west of the village. About a quarter of a mile below the bridges, the river Marnock—or, as it is commonly called, the Kilmarnock Water—mingles its leaden flood with that of its more pellucid and sprightly sister the Irvine, which winds along until it is concealed from view by the tall trees that embower the Castle of Caprington, the turrets of which peer from its sylvan retreat in impressive magnificence. This Castle is of great antiquity. It is built upon a rock that juts out near the bed of the river, and having been greatly improved and modernised of late years, it may be considered one of the finest buildings in the district. It originally belonged to a branch of the Wallace family, and according to the "Statistical Account" is mentioned in a charter bearing the date 1385, under the name "Castellum turris fortalicium de Caprington." Adam Cuninghame, the first of the Caprington family, was a grandchild of Sir William Cuninghame of Kilmaurs. He inherited Caprington by marriage with a daughter of Sir Duncan Wallace of Sundrum during the reign of James II. The estate remained in the possession of his descendants until 1829, when the death of Sir William Cunninghame, bart., occurred. That nobleman dying without issue, the Baronetcy devolved upon Sir Robert Keith Dick, of Prestonfield, but Caprington is at this date (1875) in the possession of William Cathcart Smith Cunninghame, Esq. The estate is rich in mineral, coal of the finest quality being found in great abundance, and the miners are noted for their respectability and sobriety. The houses built on the estate by the proprietor for their accommodation are commodious and neat, and seem palaces when compared to the dwellings too often provided by coalmasters for their men.

To the left, on the top of some rising ground, stands the farm-house of Yardside. It is built on the site of Riccarton Castle, but there is nothing of interest about it save some stately trees which are said to have adorned the garden of the ancient edifice. History is silent regarding this stronghold, and even Pont has failed to notice it in his topography; yet it is nevertheless certain that it was the abode of the Wallaces, barons of Riccarton, who were the early possessors of the district, and it is referred to as such in several ancient documents. Blind Harry speaks of it, and according to him it was the residence of Sir Ronald Crawford, and a favourite resort of his nephew, Sir William Wallace, the Scottish hero. It was to Riccarton Castle Wallace fled when he slew the Cumberland chief, Selby, governor of Dundee, and to it he also directed his steps upon revenging the treacherous murder of his uncle and other barons by firing the barns of Ayr.

In the hollow, a little below the water meetings, stands the farm-house of Maxholm. Near to it a thorn tree called the "Bickering Bush" stood, it was said, to mark the spot where Wallace was set upon by English soldiers while fishing. A troop happening to ride past, five of the party left the corps and demanded the fish he had taken. Refusing to comply with their request, an altercation ensued, and one dismounted to forcibly possess himself of them. Being unarmed at the time, Wallace struck him down with his fishing-rod, wrenched his sword from him, and with a back stroke cut off the fellow's head. Seeing the fate of their comrade, the others quickly dismounted to revenge his death, but two of the number met a similar fate. Blind Harry, who graphically records this incident, tells the remaining part of the story as follows:—

> "Three slew he there, two fled with all their might
> Unto their horse in a confounded fright;
> Left all their fish, no longer durst remain,
> And three fat English bucks upon the plain;
> Thus in great hurry, having got their cuffs,
> They scampered off in haste to save their buffs."

A local tradition says that when Wallace found himself master of the field he made with all possible speed to the castle and related the adventure to his uncle's housekeeper.

D

The good lady, fearing that the English would not allow such an ignominious defeat to go unavenged, persuaded him to don a gown and "mutch," and seat himself at a spinning-wheel. The disguise was perfect, but it was not effected a moment too soon, for the clattering of horses' hoofs were heard, and Wallace had scarce time to lay hold of the distaff and commence spinning when a number of soldiers dashed into the courtyard and roughly enquired if the author of what they termed "an outrage" was within. The old housekeeper met them, professed great amazement, and invited them to search the place. This they did, but failed to discover in the supposed old woman at the wheel the hero of the unequal fight.

Crossing the old bridge, I passed up the street of the village and soon arrived at the Parish Church. It is a plain building of no particular style of architecture, and is adorned with a handsome spire, which is a conspicuous object on the landscape, being discernible nearly the whole country round. The church bears the date of 1823, is built on the top of a justice-mound, and from its situation has an elegant appearance. A road leading to Hurlford separates the church from the churchyard, and while passing it I observed a man seated on a milestone at a place vulgarly called "the lazy corner." Remarking to him that the spire of the church was exceeding high, he civilly replied that it was, but added he with a grin, "High an' a' as it is, a blin' man ance gaed to the tap o't."—"A blind man go to the top of a steeple!" I said with astonishment.—"Yes, an' what's mair, he stuck a tattie on the cock's neb—ye ken there used to be a cock on't." —"But how did he get up? who and what was he?" I curiously enquired.—"Weel ye see there was a scaffoldin' roun' it at the time, for it wasna quite finished," continued my friend, with an air of a man communicating something of importance. —"But the blind man?" said I.—"Oh, ay, they ca'd him Sandy M'Crone, an' although he had been blin' frae his boyhood he was smarter than mony wi' their e'esicht, for there wasna a farm-house for miles roun' but Sandy could gang to his lane; an' what's mair, he ance fand a lark's nest, an' brocht a seein' man to see it."—"But what did he do for a living?"—"Oh, Sandy was a fiddler, sir; a grand fiddler was Sandy M'Crone, an' a' body ken'd an' liked him, for his cheery, droll ways gat him mony frien's. He belanged to Riccarton," he continued, after a pause; "an', as I said before, Sandy was a grand fiddler—he could maist gar his fiddle speak. Hech, ay (here he drew a long breath as if thinking of past pleasures) mony a waddin', an' rockin', an' merrymakin' Sandy played at; but his elbow's still noo, an' nae mair will his music put life an' mettle i' the heels o' the dancers," he said in a sorrowful tone. After this my loquacious friend began to relate a fishing exploit that Sandy figured in on the banks of the Cessnock, but it smacked so much of the improbable that I bade him a hasty good morning and pushed on my way.

Passing the house of the venerable Alexander Black, I had a desire to call upon him, but the hour being early I deferred my visit until another time. Mr. Black is hale and hearty, and although bordering on ninety can crack a joke and enjoy one. He is the oldest man in Riccarton, and I believe the oldest freemason in Ayrshire. He is possessed of an excellent memory, and graphically and with great vivacity relates the sayings, doings, and actions of a past generation.

Finding the churchyard gate ajar I entered, strayed amongst the grassy hillocks, and began to read the brief records on the tombstones—a rather solemn occupation, but one that does me good, for it reminds me that I am dust and shall to dust return. The churchyard is small; it stands some ten feet above the level of the road, and contains some curious and elaborately carved headstones which have the appearance of considerable antiquity, but the inscriptions are for the most part obliterated by the hand of time, and some are falling to pieces, although William Walker, the sexton, who is a kind of antiquary, is doing his best to unearth and preserve them. A favourite representation on several is a ploughing scene, which in every case is rudely executed. In most instances the plough is drawn by oxen, and held by a figure resembling that of a man, while another stands in front with a goad in its hand as if urging the oxen forward. Other stones are decked with heraldic designs, and a few with Garden of Eden scenes, while others have emblematical representations of the trades that the sleepers followed when in life. For instance, one has the shuttle, reed, and temples sculptured on it; another millstones, wheels, and other

gearing; while one small but curious stone has the bodkin, shears, and iron. The stone containing the oldest legible date bears that of 1641. Near the centre of the churchyard is the burying-place of the Cuninghames of Caprington, and behind it is that of the Campbells of Treesbank. Near to these there is a tablet to the memory of Sir James Shaw's father. The stone states that he died in 1796, aged sixty-seven years. Close to that, again, a plain slab announces that it is "Erected in memory of Mary Keohie, who was killed in the Low Church, Kilmarnock, 1801, aged 13 years." There are many other stones both ancient and modern that I might notice, especially that to the memory of the well-known wit, William Millar, who told the farmer's wife when she set down whey to his porridge, that she needna hamper her pigs for him, he could take milk brawly.

Among the forgotten dead, and in "a dry and comfortable corner" near to the gate, lies an eccentric individual whose death caused considerable stir in Kilmarnock, and more especially in the Holm quarter, where it occurred on the 17th July, 1817. He was named William Stevenson, was a professional beggar of miserly habits, and occupied a back house in East Shaw Street that stood near to where Mr. William Frazer's school now stands. He belonged to Dunlop, was a mason to trade, but begged his bread and lived upon charity during the greater part of his life. Robert Chambers mentions him in his "Book of Days," and from that work I cull the following particulars:—

"About the year 1787 he and his wife separated, making the strange agreement that whichever of them was the first to propose reunion should forfeit one hundred pounds to the other. It is supposed that they never met afterwards. In 1815, when about eighty-five years old, Stevenson was seized with an incurable disease, and was confined to his bed. A few days before his death, feeling his end to be near, he sent for a baker, and ordered twelve dozen burial cakes, a large quantity of sugar biscuits, and a good supply of wine and spirits. He next sent for a joiner, and instructed him to make a good, sound, dry, roomy coffin; after which he sent for the Riccarton gravedigger, and requested him to select a favourable spot in a dry and comfortable corner of the village churchyard, and there dig for him a roomy grave, assuring him that he would be paid for his trouble. This done he ordered an old woman who attended him to go to a certain nook and there bring out nine pounds to pay all these preliminary expenses, telling her not to grieve for him for he had remembered her in his will. Shortly after this he died. A neighbour came in to search for his wealth, which had been shrouded in much mystery. In one bag was found large silver pieces such as dollars and half-dollars, crowns and half-crowns, and in a heap of musty rags a collection of guineas and seven-shilling pieces; while in a box were found bonds of various amounts, including one for three hundred pounds, giving altogether a sum of about nine hundred pounds. A will was also found bequeathing twenty pounds to the old woman who attended him, and most of the remainder to distant relations, setting aside sufficient to give a feast to all the beggars in Ayrshire who chose to come and see his body lie in state. The influx was immense, and after the funeral, which was attended by a motley group of gaberlunzies, all retired to a barn that had been fitted up for the occasion, and there indulged in revelries but little in accordance with the solemn season of death."

In the centre of the churchyard stood the old church of Riccarton, a small structure of considerable antiquity which will be remembered by many of the old inhabitants of the village and of Kilmarnock, for many of them have worshipped in it, and in their turn watched the little golgotha by night to scare the resurrectionist and prevent the desecration of the dead. There is now not a vestige of the old building left. The stones which formed it were used to erect a one-storeyed house that stands near the old bridge. It was at one time a Roman Catholic place of worship, and anciently belonged to the convent of Dalmulin, but was transferred to the monks of Paisley, and remained in their hands until the Reformation. "After the Reformation," says Chalmers, "the parish of Ricardtoun was united to that of Craigie, and both were placed under the charge of one minister. But they were again disunited in 1648, and have since remained distinct parishes."

Leaving the churchyard, I regained the village street and passed on my way. The portion of the village surrounding the churchyard is very old. At the gate the houses have a quaint, old-fashioned appearance. Here is situated the principal inn, a modern building, and next to it a low-roofed, dingy, thatched cottage, with a signboard over its door displaying a crown. The house was called the Freemasons' Arms, and was kept in "the good old times" by John Morton, a village worthy who was noted for wit and wisdom, and was looked to by the villagers as an authority in matters of law and politics. For a series of years he held the honourable position of village postmaster, and although long since dead he is still spoken of with respect. At the back of this erection is a two-storeyed one, venerable in appearance and old-fashioned in construction. An outside stair surmounted by a porch leads to the second flat, which at one time was the hall of the freemasons. Here the "brethren of the mystic tie" held their meetings, and often have the old walls rung with the sounds of merriment and applause on festive occasions.

Amongst village notables of the old school, old David Templeton the bellman, and Robert Pitt the shoemaker, are worthy of notice. The first was peculiar for his dry caustic wit and droll sayings, and although long since gathered to his fathers the tall, gaunt form of the old man will be familiar to many readers. The last-named lasted his last shoe some four years ago, and now sleeps the dreamless sleep of death in the village churchyard. He was a poet as well as a wit, and during the last thirty years of his life he was a contributor to the poet's corner of various Ayrshire newspapers.

Riccarton has a population of 1889. It was created a burgh of barony in 1638, but its civic power was never exercised. Although of great antiquity it was long an insignificant hamlet, and it is only within the last seventy years that it has become of any size or importance. It is now included in the parliamentary burgh of Kilmarnock, and being a suburb of that thriving town it will doubtless increase with its prosperity. About fifty years ago weaving was extensively carried on in it, so much so, indeed, that the sound of the shuttle could be heard issuing from almost every door, but the appliance of machinery in that branch of industry has in a measure silenced it. The village is principally inhabited by miners, and I think the character given them by a late minister of the parish is very applicable. He says—" I am happy to bear testimony to the general good conduct of a very large class of the inhabitants—I mean the colliers. There are very many of them in comfortable circumstances, inhabiting their own houses, bringing up their families respectably, and seemingly surrounded with many comforts, many of them being intelligent and pious men. Indeed, I may almost say with confidence what can seldom be said of the same class of workmen, that they are amongst the most orderly, industrious, and intelligent of our parishioners."

Leaving the old portion of the village behind, I passed along the footpath that skirts the garden wall of the manse and turned into Craigie Road. The manse is at present occupied by the Rev. William Jeffrey, the parish minister. It is a plain, old-fashioned structure, and has nothing of interest connected with it save it be the mantelpiece in the kitchen, which "The Statistical Account" states is the identical one that graced the fireplace of the dining-room of Riccarton Castle.

CHAPTER II.

Craigie Road—Knowehead and its surroundings—The Buchanan Bequest—Treesbank Manor House—Scargie—John Burtt—Knockmarloch—Craigie Hill—Craigie Church—The Village—The Witch Stane—Craigie Castle—A Strange Story—A Curious Stone.

Upon entering Craigie Road, I passed some neat cottages, and a little farther on others of a humbler order, and after a brisk uphill walk gained Knowehead, an eminence over which the road passes and from which an extensive view of the surrounding country can be obtained. Pausing, my eye swam over the scene. Behind was the quaint village, with the smoke curling from the cottage chimneys; beyond it, in the hollow, old Kilmarnock, with its stalks and spires; in front the estate of Treesbank, with its manor-house peering out from amongst the trees, and the road winding over hill and dale until lost to view on a rugged range of hills over which it passes. To the right Ayr road and the estate of Caprington were the most prominent objects on the landscape; to the left, on a hilly piece of ground, stands the farm-steading of Witch Knowe. Doubtless its site was supposed to be a resort of the uncanny fraternity in times past, or perhaps some withered beldame was burned on it. The scene withal was very pleasing, and the song of the lark and the multifarious sounds that greeted the ear made it doubly delightful.

Beyond Witch Knowe is the estate of Bellfield. The mansion-house is concealed by a belting of trees which surround the beautiful garden and pleasure grounds. Bellfield House was the residence of Misses Margaret, Jane, and Elizabeth Buchanan, daughters of the late George Buchanan of Woodlands, Glasgow, who died in the order of seniority, the youngest on the 23rd April, 1875. During their lifetime they jointly executed a will, and although subject to the alteration of the last survivor it substantially remained as agreed upon, and confers the following munificent bequests:—£10,000 to the Merchants' House of Glasgow, the revenue to be applied in the same way as the funds of the House are at present, on condition that the tomb of the family in the Glasgow Necropolis be maintained in a proper order and repair during all time coming. £4,200 of reduced three per cent. annuities to the Principal and Professors appointed by the University Court of Glasgow, to found bursaries for the maintenance of two matriculated students who intend to become licentiates of the Established Church of Scotland. £30,000 to be held by the trustees on the estate and accumulated for ten years, the object being to found an hospital for the maintenance of indigent and infirm burgesses of Glasgow, of sixty years and upwards, preference to be given to those of the name of Buchanan. The trustees are to purchase two acres of ground within eight miles of Glasgow, and erect an hospital thereon, and furnish and fit it up; and on the lapse of ten years they are to hand over the hospital and all the funds which they have accumulated to the Lord Provost and Magistrates of Glasgow, the minister of the High Church, the minister of St. George's Church, and the testamentary trustees as governors.* It is stipulated that no fewer than ten burgesses will at one time have the benefits of the hospital. The lands and estate of Bellfield to be held by the trustees till Martinmas, 1885, and the rents to be accumulated during that period; part of the mansion-house to be fitted up as a library, and to be open to the public for consultation only, at such times and under such regulations as the trustees may think proper; all the portraits, paintings, books, and fittings suitable to be placed in this library; the grounds and garden to be open to the public of Kilmarnock and Riccarton at such times and under such regulations as the trustees may think proper; £5 to be paid yearly to the Ragged School of Kilmarnock out of the revenues of Bellfield; £3 yearly to the Fever Hospital and Infirmary of Kilmarnock; £130 for a missionary to be appointed by the minister of the parish of Riccarton, and £10 yearly for him to buy flannel clothing for the poor. If the trustees find the revenue to admit of it, they may fit up the remaining portion

---

* It is expected that the accumulation at the end of the ten years will be something like £12,000, which will cover the cost of the ground and of the erection and fitting-up of the hospital, and that the £30,000 will remain for the purposes of endowment.

of Bellfield House as an asylum for poor people of sixty years and upwards who have resided in the parishes of Kilmarnock and Riccarton for ten years consecutively, and for young persons who may have been permanently injured by accident. The trustees are to lease the minerals on the estate, and at the end of ten years the estate and accumulated funds are to be conveyed to the Provost and Magistrates of Kilmarnock, to the minister of Kilmarnock and the minister of the parish of Riccarton for the time being, and to the testamentary trustees, for the carrying on of the purposes above-mentioned. The balance of the revenue, after providing for these purposes, is to be divided equally between the parishes of Kilmarnock and Riccarton, to be distributed by the minister to the deserving poor not on the poor's roll, and there must always be a certain sum set apart for this object. The whole residue of the estate, after providing for these purposes, is to be paid, one half to the Glasgow Royal Infirmary and the other half to the Glasgow Asylum for the Blind.*

The nearness of Bellfield to Kilmarnock and Riccarton, and the fact of its salubrious situation and finely-wooded grounds, will render it a favourite resort to all who are desirous of retiring from the noise and bustle of the town to enjoy suburban quiet and hold communion with nature.

Rambling onward, the cool air of the morning fanned my cheek, and as I contemplated the tiny wayside flower, the stately tree, and the numerous natural beauties met with at every step, my very soul was thrilled with ecstacy and adoration—adoration to Him who has clothed the earth with verdure and filled the groves with melody.

Passing through the tollbar of Shortlees, some ruined cottages appeared on my left, and I soon arrived at a part of the road where the trees on either side intertwine their branches and form a leafy canopy overhead. Walking beneath the rustling boughs I arrived at a small bridge which spans a burn as it jinks through a small plantation by the wayside. Across the bridge there is a drive to Treesbank manor house. The manor house—which has recently been enlarged and improved—was built by Sir Hugh Campbell of Cessnock, and

---

* Condensed from "Abstract of settlement made by Misses Margaret, Jane, and Elizabeth Buchanan of Bellfield, dated 8th July, 1861, as altered by codicil made by Elizabeth Buchanan of Bellfield, 11th May, 1871."

gifted along with the estate to his second son, James, upon his (the son's) marriage with Jean, daughter of Sir William Mure of Rowallan, in 1672, and from that union the present proprietor is descended.

Leaving the purling burn, I followed the course of the road, and after climbing a steep brae, passed Scargie, a couple of thatched cottages of mean appearance standing a little off the road. Scargie is associated with the name of John Burtt, author of the sweet song beginning

"O'er the mist-shrouded cliffs of the grey mountains straying,"

And of other lyrics and lengthy pieces of verse. Although born at Knockmarloch, Burtt spent the greater portion of his boyhood at Scargie with his grandfather, who occupied the place. In early manhood he was a schoolmaster in Kilmarnock, but emigrated to America in 1817, where he became a clergyman, and was honoured with the chair of Ecclesiastical History in the college of Cincinnati.

Travelling onward, I passed Sunnyside—a neat farm house—and soon arrived at Knockmarloch. A small plantation skirts the road, and within its shade the feathered throng rendered the air vocal, for they chanted their joyous lays right merrily, and the rich shrill notes of the blackbird echoed, and the cadence died away like the last low strains of a lute. I paused and listened, for the sounds and the scenery had an exhilarating influence upon me—an influence that only those who are confined to the desk or the bench six days out of the seven can best comprehend. Turning down a bosky lane that skirts the plantation, a walk of a hundred yards brought me to a bubbling brook that purled amongst the brackens. Here, a portion of a dry-stone dyke was broken down, and up to an ivy-mantled ruin that was almost hid from view by the tall firs of the plantation, a footroad worn by the feet of the curious ran zigzag through the gowan-spangled grass. The ruin—a solitary gable which the ivy green has clasped with its tendrils and adorned with its shining leaves—is a remnant of Knockmarloch manor house, but there is nothing interesting associated with it. It was a thatch-covered mansion of the olden time, and was last used as a family residence by Major George Brown, a descendant of the Browns of Knockmarloch, a family who had possessed the estate for a hundred and fifty years. About 1800 the estate came into the market and was purchased by Robert Shedden, a relative of the Knockmarloch family, who had spent the years of his boyhood upon it. It is still in the possession of the Sheddens. They have always been non-resident, and on this account the Manor House was allowed to fall into decay. Ultimately, with the exception of the shattered gable, the walls were pulled down and the stones used to construct a couple of cottages that stand a little off the main road by the side of the plantation. About a stonethrow from the ruin there is a farm-steading, the dwelling-house of which was once the coach-house of the mansion. It bears the date 1775, and is at present occupied by a grandchild of Major Brown's coachman, who, by the bye, was the father of John Burtt, the poet.

Retracing my steps to the road, a sharp walk brought me to the base of Craigie Hill, an eminence that stands some 500 feet above the level of the sea, and although comparatively low, yet the view from its summit is extensive and beautiful. A short distance from it are the limestone mines of Howcommon, the excavations of which penetrate the bosom of the hills, and form vast caverns through which a horse and cart can be driven with facility. Being desirous to gain the top of the rugged height, I entered a field gate, but here the stillness was broken by the sound of the hammer and pick, and the snorting of a steam engine, for workmen were busily engaged in a kind of quarry, cutting away the columnar trap of which the hill is composed. Climbing the steep, I gained the verdant summit somewhat out of breath with the exertion, and sat down upon a boulder to gaze upon the landscape at my feet. Stretched before me was a panoramic view of over one hundred miles, consisting for the most part of an undulating and highly cultivated track of country. Away in the misty distance I beheld the Grampian Hills, "the lofty Benlomond," the Mull of Cantyre, the Paps of Jura, and the coast of Ireland. More near, the Frith of Clyde, and the historic Carrick Shore, with the rock of Ailsa towering above the waters like some rude monument, while along the coast lay scattered numerous towns and villages. Landward, there is a fine view of Loudoun Hill and other historically interesting places. On the plain below the hill, the town of Kilmarnock with its spires and smoky sky seemed spread out in a valley, while the estates of Caprington, Treesbank, Coodham, and Knockmarloch filled up the picture between. Among the many farmhouses dotting the landscape that of Mosshead is worthy of remark—it being the birthplace of Sir James Shaw, a gentleman who by energetic perseverance rose from a comparatively humble position to that of Lord Mayor of London.

After lingering on Craigie Hill I descended to the main road and directed my steps towards the village, which nestles in sweet retirement at the foot of the whinney ridge of which the eminence above mentioned is the highest elevation. Passing the manse, I turned down a narrow path to the left that runs along the foot of the hills and terminates at a wall that surrounds a burying ground. In its centre stands Craigie Parish Church. It was erected in 1776, and is a small old-fashioned like structure. The churchyard is overgrown with grass, and although

> "Some village Hampden that with dauntless breast
> The little tyrants of his field withstood!
> Some mute inglorious Milton here may rest;
> Some Cromwell guiltless of his country's blood,"

Yet there is no stone in it that is curious or containing any remarkable inscription. The church of Craigie that existed before the present one was very old. Paterson says —"In 1177 Walter Haso of Cragyn" (the then patron), "whose father had previously granted half a carucate of land, gave to it another half carucate, gifting the whole—church and lands—in pure alms, for the salvation of the souls of his father and mother, to the monks of Paisley," and, according to Chalmers, the property remained in their hands till the Reformation, after which the parish of Craigie was united to that of Riccarton, but was again disunited, as previously stated.

The village of Craigie adjoins the church. It consists of about eighteen neat cottages, a post office, a schoolhouse, and an inn which flourishes under the name and sign of "The Red Lion." A parish seminary has recently been erected by the School Board, and forms a handsome addition to the secluded little hamlet.

After partaking of refreshments in the village inn, and indulging in a chat with the landlord, I retraced my steps to the highway, and in doing so got into conversation with an old lady who was very loquacious and well versed in the lore of the district. Amongst other things, she informed me that once on a time the church of Craigie had a narrow escape of being destroyed by a witch who had taken umbrage at it. It seems that the hag selected a large stone, and having placed it in her apron, flew with it in the direction of the building with the intention of dropping it upon its roof. Her design, however, was frustrated by the breaking of her apron strings, for, upon nearing the object of her spleen, they gave way, and the stone fell with a crash that shook the earth. This accident seemingly so disheartened the carlin that she abandoned the destructive idea and allowed her burden to lie where it fell. The boulder lay in a field near the churchyard wall, and was known as "The Witch Stane." It was long regarded with superstitious awe by many; but the farmer on whose ground it lay being of a practical turn of mind, looked upon it with an eye to utility, and had it blasted for building purposes. Strange to relate, when broken up the debris filled twenty-five carts—a circumstance that would lead one to suppose that the witch must have been very muscular, and must have worn a *very large* apron.

On my arrival at the highway I stopped a youth who came whistling along and enquired my nearest way to Craigie Castle. "That's the shoonest," said he thoughtfully.— "Yes."—" Weel, gang alang the road till ye come to the yett next the hill, when there you'll see an auld road gaun through the parks; follow it till ye come to Smeetonrig (Smithstonridge), turn the corner o' the house an' you'll see the castle before you." After I had thanked him for the information, he resumed his whistle and passed on his way "happy as a king." Following his directions, "the yett next the hill" was soon found, and having passed through it I traversed a rudely Macadamised traffic-worn road which stretched across the open fields, and after a pleasant walk by the gowan-spangled lea—the pleasure of which was heightened by the cry of the peesweep and the song of the lark—I arrived in a farmyard, and most unexpectedly found myself face to face with a watch-dog that did its best with voice and gesture to frighten the life out of me. Expecting every moment to be torn in pieces, and not knowing whether to go forward or turn back, I was relieved from embarrassment by a middle-aged woman appearing upon the scene. Having stated my difficulty to her, the goodwife of Smithstonridge—for such the lady proved to be—invited me forward and in the kindest manner conducted me to the end of her house and showed me the object of my search in the hollow. From her I learned that the old Tarbolton Road, a portion of which winds over a neighbouring hill and is now covered with brambles and wild brier, passed by the farm, and that it was the remains of it I came along. After a kindly goodbye to Smithstonridge I struck through the fields in the direction of Craigie Castle.

Viewing the ruin from a distance, it seems destitute of that hoary appearance that is so inviting about shattered places of strength, but upon nearing it I was agreeably surprised to find it alike magnificent in situation and architecture, and if not so noted and extensive as other buildings in a like condition, it at least displays a degree of military science and skill rarely to be met with. The ruin stands upon a knoll between what appears to have been two marshes, and probably ditches were cut between them when the castle was in its entirety. This being the case it would be isolated from the mainland, and an insurmountable barrier raised to besiegers at the period when gunpowder was unknown, and when no missile, save from a height, could be thrown at any great distance with effect. Two crumbling gables, portions of walls, and shreds of battlements yet remain in tolerable preservation, also several underground vaulted chambers are entire, although partly filled with rubbish. In these the fox has now its lair and the bat its abode, and wreck and decay are the chief characteristics of the pile. Picking my steps amongst solid blocks of masonry that lay as time had hurled them from their position, I gained what appeared to have been the principal apartment. The roof had fallen in, but from the appearance of the walls it seems to have converged at the top and been supported by fluted columns. Here lay a shattered and dismantled cornice; there, partly hid by rubbish, pieces of sculpture that bore testimony to the skill and taste of the designer, while stunted trees and shrubs grew in places once trod by the mirthful and gay. To me it is a spirit-depressing task to stray through an old ruin, for each crumbling stone is a monitor that speaks of death and decay, and points to the futility of all human labour. At this ruin I met with a natural curiosity in the shape of an old tree. Against it lay two huge blocks of masonry that have toppled off the rampart; the trunk was bent and distorted as if the plant had done its utmost to support or throw off the encumbrance, and curious enough, in spite of it, the growth had continued and imbedded portions of the burden in its wood.

Craigie Castle was long the residence of the descendants of the Wallaces of Riccarton, but when or by whom it was built cannot be ascertained with certainty. Previous to that family one of the name of Lyndesay possessed the lands; but the race terminating in a daughter, who became the wife of John Wallace about 1371, the property passed to his family. In 1588 they removed to the Castle of Newton-upon-Ayr, and left the Craigie mansion, which doubtless being tenantless got out of repair, and in the course of time became ruinous.

Amongst the many traditions connected with this Castle, perhaps that of how it became ruinous will interest the reader. It is told by Woodrow, and from that indefatigable writer I quote the following strange story:—"The Lairds of Craigie wer none the best affected to the gospell. . . . . When the ministers wer very strict in discipline, the Laird of Craigie had either some tenants or servants who brought some horses laden with carriages from some distant place, and travelled openly upon the Sabbath day, throw many parishes. The ministers of the places wrote to Mr. Inglish about such ane open and scandalous breach of the Sabbath. He spoke to the Laird of Craigie, and he huffed, and told it was done by his orders, and he would support them in what they had done! The minister caused cite the persons guilty to the session; but being supported by their master they would not compear. When noe other way was left, Mr. Inglish took occasion to bear testimony against it very plainly in a sermon. The Laird was in the church, sitting in his seat before the pulpite, and the minister fell upon it soe flatly that Craigie's malice and spite was soe raised that he rose up, and took up his whinger (a short sword) and threw it at him, when in the pulpite! Mr Inglish, when he perceived him draw it and going to cast it, gote down in the pulpite and escaped it. The whinger went over his head, and stuck in the backside of the pulpite. After he had risen and composed himself a little, he addressed himself to Craigie, and said—' Sir, you have put ane open affront upon God and his ordinances in what you have aimed at me, and now I will tell you what God will doe to you. Your great house, in this place, shall be reduced to a heap of stones, and he that offers to repair it shall lose his pains; and your son now, whom you have such great hopes of, shall die a fool." And none of Mr. Inglish's words fell to the ground. His son was then in England, in the army, and was at that time a youth of great parts and expectation. Whether by a fall or sickness, within a little time turned fatuous and silly, and died soe. His great house of Craigie fell to be some way out of order, and either he or his son went to repair it, and when the workmen were at it a great part of it fell down and had almost buried them all; and its now, indeed, a ruinouse heap!" About a portion of the castle falling while undergoing repair is borne out by tradition, but the other part of the story is unsupported. Sir Hugh Wallace, the laird referred to in the foregoing, was knighted by Charles I. He was most liberal in his ideas, fought with Montrose at the Battle of Philiphaugh, and was amongst the vanquished insurgents. He died about 1650.

After straying among the ruins of Craigie Castle I crossed the field in which they stand, and soon arrived in the farmyard of Craigie Mains. Here, built into a wall is a curious old stone with some grotesque figures cut on it. It was found amongst the ruins of the castle, and the design was considered by the peasantry to represent wild men engaged in a game of draughts. At first glance it is not unlike a thing of the kind, but upon closer inspection the initiated in heraldic designs finds it to be the arms of the Wallaces of Riccarton and the Lyndesays of Craigie quartered—a circumstance suggesting that a portion of Craigie Castle was built during the lifetime of John Wallace, who, as already stated, married the Craigie heiress.

CHAPTER III.

From Craigie to Barnweill—Barnweill Kirk and Graveyard—The Wallace Monument—Fail Castle—The Warlock Laird—Tarbolton—Willie's Mill—Peden's Pulpit and Cave—Through the Fields to Ayr Road—The Halfway House—The Estate of Coodham—Peace-and-Plenty—Back to Kilmarnock.

FROM Craigie Mains a short walk along an avenue landed me in the highway that runs between Bogend Toll, Craigie, and other places. Turning to the left, I took the first road to the right and directed my steps to the Wallace monument, which is a prominent object on the heights of Barnweill and discernible from a great distance. The road was somewhat steep and rugged, but I liked its rustic appearance, and fairly revelled in the rays of the mid-day sun, as I paused now and again to listen to the rich notes of the lark, or view the wayside flowers as they nodded on their slender stems in the balmy breeze. When nearing Underhill—a small hamlet consisting of a wright's shop and a few detached houses—I observed a well in a shady spot on the dusty highway and sat down by its brink to rest. Producing a drinking cup I dipped it, and quaffed a bumper of cool spring water. How it refreshed—how it invigorated, and made me grateful to the Creator for one of His best and most bountiful blessings! After lingering by the liquid treasure, I ascended Barnweill Hill, pausing now and again to view the monument and surrounding scenery. While thus engaged my attention was attracted by the ruin of Barnweill church, which stands within a belt of trees that enclose a small burying-ground on the north-west side of the hill. Over a field gate, which on trial I found locked, I saw that of the graveyard opposite. By the worn appearance of the rails it was evident that the curious had found admittance by climbing over the barrier; therefore, following their example, I vaulted across, traversed the field, and entered the churchyard, the situation of which is truly picturesque. Reverently treading over the grassy graves I advanced to the ruin, which seems when entire to have been a moderately-sized one-storied building, and entered the roofless sanctuary by a broken-down doorway, but alas! there was nothing of interest to be seen. All was wreck, the floor being covered with rubbish, out of which grew nettles and rank grass. The outside is more cheerful. The two gables, which are pretty entire, are almost covered with ivy. Up to a recent date a bell hung in one of them, but it is now removed, and in the keeping of a gentleman in the neighbourhood. Little is known regarding the old church of Barnweill. It was, previous to the Reformation, a Roman Catholic place of worship, and at one time within the ruin there was to be seen an inverted holy-water font. At the suppression of the parish—which Paterson states took place in 1714—the church doubtless would be deprived of its minister, and very likely, being unoccupied, it gradually became ruinous. Be that as it may, the worshippers have long departed, and

"Where of old there stood
The altar and God's shrine, so loved and treasured,
Comes now the blackbird's ceaseless, gladsome hymn,
Poured forth with gratitude and joy unmeasured."

The stones in the churchyard are few and scattered, and merely contain the simple announcement that the individuals whom they are meant to commemorate lived and died. One tablet bears the date 1661, but there are other stones on which the records are unreadable that have every appearance of being anterior.

Taking leave of the secluded spot, I gained the road by the same means that I left it, and after walking up the steep ascent for a short distance turned to the left. Here I entered what had the appearance of being a piece of waste ground, for portions of rock and loose stones lay confusedly about, and made the surface most uneven. Advancing to the brow of a hill that rises abruptly from the north, and from which a gorgeous view of a great portion of the district of Cunninghame is obtainable, I rapturously gazed upon the scene as it lay spread out like an unrolled map. Tradition states that this height was used by the lords of Craigie Castle as an outlook station, and that it was the site of an old fortress, which doubtless has been the case, for the appearance of the ground indicates that the foundations of a building lie buried beneath the soil, and even the moat that surrounded it can be traced with facility.

After lingering awhile to view the expanse of country I returned to the road and continued the ascent of Barnweill Hill, and ultimately, after considerable exertion, reached the summit whereon stands the Wallace monument, and on which, tradition states, the Scottish hero paused in his flight to view the lurid flames that consumed the Barns of Ayr, which he had fired in revenge for the murder of his uncle and other noblemen. He must have watched the scene with intense interest, for, as the flames shot heavenward, he exclaimed, "The Barns o' Ayr burn weel!" —a pithy saying from which it is said the place takes its name.

The monument—which was built to commemorate the above act—is surrounded by trees, and stands in an enclosed ornamented piece of ground. It consists of a square tower about twelve feet at the base, and fully sixty feet high. It has a castellated appearance, and is surmounted with turrets topped with sculptured thistles. It contains a spiral stair, and above the entrance the Wallace arms are blazoned in bas-relief. On three sides there are indented tables bearing the following inscriptions :—

I.

"Erected MCCCCLV., in honour of Scotland's greatest national hero, the renowned Sir William Wallace, born MCCLXX., who after performing numerous exploits of the most consummate bravery in defence of the independence of his country was basely betrayed into the hands of his enemies, by whom, to their everlasting disgrace, he was unjustifiably put to death on the XXIII. of August, MCCC. Centuries have not dimmed the lustre of his heroic achievements; and the memory of this most disinterested of patriots shall through all ages be honoured and revered by his countrymen.

"A soul supreme, in each hard conflict tried,
Above all pain, all passion, and all pride,
The frown of power, the blast of public breath,
The love of lucre, and the dread of death."

II.

"Sir William Wallace, Regent of Scotland, MCCXCVII. In

resistance to treacherous invasion, and in defence of the laws and liberties of his country, he fought against fearful odds the desperate battles of Biggar, Stirling, Blackearnside, and Falkirk, and between these actions, in little more than a year, he stormed and took from the invaders every fortress, castle, and town which they had seized in the kingdom. Though worsted at Falkirk by overwhelming numbers, aided by fatal dissensions in his own army, he continued warring with the oppressors of his native land until his foul betrayal, seven years after that disastrous battle, by the execrable Monteith."

III.

" ' At Wallace name, what Scottish blood
But boils up in a spring-tide flood!'

Ever honoured be the memory of the matchless Sir William Wallace, the first of his countrymen who in an age of despair arose and

'Dared to nobly stem tyrannic pride,'

throw off the yoke of foreign oppression, and maintain the independence and nationality of Scotland; and who, by deeds of surpassing valour and stainless patriotism, has glorified this his native land, and imperishably associated his name with the defence of national rights and the liberties and immunities of freeborn men. From Greece arose Leonidas, from Scotland Wallace, and from America Washington— names which shall remain through all time the watchwords and beacons of liberty." Such is the eulogium bestowed on "the matchless Sir William Wallace."

" Had he fought for Greece of old,
His urn had been of beaten gold,
The children of his native land
Had hewn for him with cunning hand
A mountain for a monument,"

and not allowed centuries to elapse before they raised a stone to his memory; however, in my opinion, stone, lime, and "tall talk" make but a poor monument to a national benefactor. The memory of the great and good of any nation is best preserved when enshrined in the hearts of their countrymen, and when their names and deeds are handed down from generation to generation by an appreciative people.

At the gate of the plot wherein the monument stands there is a neat lodge, at the door of which I tapped after viewing the exterior of the pile. It was opened by a middle-aged woman, who upon being made aware of my wish to examine the interior kindly sent a boy along with me, who proved a capital cicerone and withal very polite and obliging. Opening the door of the monument, we entered, and my young friend began to ascend the spiral stair with alacrity. I followed, but " such a getting up stairs I never did see," and it was not until after considerable exertion that the battlemented roof was reached. The scene that met my vision was gorgeous. Far above the tree-tops I looked down upon a splendid natural panorama, and ecstatically viewed the variegated scene. Cut on the stonework I observed the words, " The Barns o' Ayr burn weel." This caused me to look in the direction that "the saviour of Scotland" is supposed to have done, and was delighted to find auld Ayr the most prominent object on the landscape. Backed by Carrick hills, and with the woods of Rosemount intervening, its spires glistened in the sunshine, and the smoke that curled from a thousand chimneys hung like a pall over the ancient burgh. To the left of the scene is Tarbolton, and near to it are the woods that surround Montgomery Castle, a spot rendered classical by the genius of Burns, for it was there he took the last farewell of his sweet Highland Mary, as he so pathetically states in immortal verse. To the right is the Frith of Clyde, decked with many a sail; in the distance Arran hills; and along the coast lie scattered Troon, Irvine, and other towns; inland, Dundonald hills and the old grey ruins of the castle, while peering from a dell are the spires of Kilmarnock, and on the rising ground beyond them the quaint village of Fenwick is distinctly seen. But the scene is too expansive to be described, and the reader to form an idea of its grandeur must view it for himself, and I can assure him that the prospect will amply repay the journey from the town, irrespective of any traditional or historical association the place may possess.

After some conversation with my youthful guide, who seemed shocked when he found me somewhat sceptical regarding the supposed origin of the name Barnweill,* I descended to *terra firma*, entered my name in "the visitors' book," and departed highly delighted with my visit to the monument.

Pausing in the roadway, it struck me that a portion of a monastic building called Fail Castle stood in the vicinity. Calling to my aid my topographical knowledge of the district, I crossed a stile, traversed several fields in the direction of Tarbolton road, and upon arriving in that thoroughfare observed the ruins—which consist of a gable and part of a side wall—in a stackyard near Fail toll. These remains are all that are now left of an extensive monastery. When entire the shattered remnant is said to have been the residence of the prior or chief minister of the institution. Fail monastery was founded in 1252, and was dedicated to Saint Mathurine. The Red Friars to whom it belonged were styled "Fathers of Redemption," because they devoted their lives to redeem captives from slavery, yet notwithstanding the sacredness of their mission they seem to have been a jolly lot of fellows, if the following stave of an old ditty is to be relied on:—

> "The Friars of Fail
> Gat never owre hard eggs or owre thin kail;
> For they made their eggs thin wi' butter,
> An' their kail thick wi' bread;
> An' the Friars o' Fail they made gude kail
> On Fridays when they fasted,
> An' they never wanted gear enough
> As lang as their neighbours' lasted."

Fail Castle, as the remnant of the manor-house of the monastery is generally termed, has many weird associations, its last occupant being a notorious warlock, who, to use the words of an aged friend, "wrocht mony cantrips in his day," and at whose death, tradition states, the castle was blown down in a storm that Satan had raised to celebrate the event, it being the consummation of their compact. A fine old ballad entitled "The Warlock Laird o' Fail" tells how that worthy revenged himself upon a farmer's wife who had

---

* "It is evident that the name of Burnwell, derived from an alleged speech of the celebrated Wallace, is an unsupported vulgar tradition. In the old charters, and in the records of the kingdom from the earliest period extant, it is spelt Barnweill or Barneweill; in no single instance that I have ever seen is it spelt Burnwell."—*History of the County of Ayr*," page 460.

refused him a drink. Slipping "the merry pin" (a magic instrument that he was possessed of) into the thatch above the door, the gudewife, who was churning and late with the dinner, instantly left off her work and began to skip and dance about the floor in a very happy manner. The reapers in the field being curious to know why dinner was so late, came one by one to ascertain the cause, but they had no sooner passed under "the merry pin" than they became frolicsomely inclined, and danced and sang with great glee. When they had danced for some time the warlock withdrew the pin and the whole company fell down with exhaustion. Many other tales of the Warlock Laird are extant, and form subjects to while away the long winter evenings at many an ingle in the country. Often have I listened to them and watched the young people

" A' cour wi' dread as they'd list to the crack,
An' start gin a rattin e'en squeaked in the thack."

But such legends are of the past. They are of a time when superstitious ignorance ascribed to tottering age supernatural power, and peopled glades and old buildings with ghosts and hobgoblins.

Adjacent to Fail Castle there is a cluster of rustic cottages and about a mile distant from them on the top of a hill stands Tarbolton, a small town with a diminishing population which at present numbers 829. Its trade consists of weaving and boxmaking. Tarbolton is associated with the name of Robert Burns, the ploughman poet. When residing at Lochlee—a farm in its vicinity—he wrote many of his best poems, and was initiated into the mysteries of masonry in the local lodge. The scene of "Death and Doctor Hornbook" is laid at "Willie's Mill," a place near the town. The mill referred to by the poet has been pulled down, and a new one erected. On the face of the brae near to the mill two stones are yet pointed out as those upon which "Robin" and Death "eased their shanks" when they held their memorable conversation about "Jock Hornbook o' the clachan."

The Rev. Alex. Peden was schoolmaster in Tarbolton before he entered the ministry. In Coilhome wood there is a ledge of rock called "Peden's Pulpit," and further up the river Ayr there is a cavity in the face of a cliff called "Peden's Cave," in which it is said the good man often concealed himself during the troublous times of the Persecution. The "Pulpit" overlooks a level piece of ground which is enclosed by lofty banks and precipitous cliffs, and when he preached *on it* his auditory sat on the green sward with their firelocks and broadswords over their knees, a necessary precaution at the period, as many of the churchyards in Ayrshire abundantly testify.

After lingering some time in the vicinity of Fail Castle, and being desirous of reaching home before

"The sun was out o' sicht,
And darker gloamin' brocht the nicht."

I retraced my steps along Tarbolton road, entered a "slap" by the wayside, followed the course of a cart-track, and after a stiff walk arrived at the farmhouse of Rotten Rock, and once more on the summit of Barnweill Hill. Going round to the back of the monument I crossed a fence at a place well worn by the feet of near-cut-seekers, and followed a beaten path through a field skirting the kirkyard of Barnweill.

Arriving in an old road I followed its intricate windings through a farm-steading and down the face of a brae until I came to Underhill, the cluster of houses already mentioned. Striking into a stile road that runs along the edge of several fields, I arrived at the Pow Burn and strayed along its bank until I came to a rustic bridge by the side of a ruined mill. This I crossed, and in a short time reached Ayr road at a point where a road branches off to the village of Symington.

From the Wallace Monument to Ayr road through the fields is one of the most picturesque and secluded byeways in the district. While descending the heights a wide track of country lies before the pedestrian, and the scene is enhanced by the thousand natural beauties that fringe the path as it winds along the wimpling burn that purls through the glen.

Turning my face homeward I passed what is termed "the half-way house to Ayr," a favourite halting place where pleasure parties to and from "the auld toun" generally stop to water their horse and partake of refreshments. At its door were two machines laden with a happy rollicking lot of lads and lasses who seemed to enjoy themselves immensely, for they laughed and joked right merrily, and looked as if they had had a pleasant day of it somewhere.

At Bogend Toll I paused to decipher a milestone and discovered that it was 4¾ miles from Kilmarnock, a circumstance that gave me very little concern, for Ayr road is one of the best and most picturesque highways I ever traversed. At this bar there are a few neat cottages and an entrance to Coodham, a handsome estate, well wooded, and for the most part walled in. Passing through the gateway a pleasant walk along the carriage drive brought me in front of the mansion house—a massive square building, at the back of which there is a lake with an island in its centre. The island is covered with shrubbery and contrasts beautifully with the sylvan scene that surrounds the margin of the water.

Coodham is at present the residence of W. H. Houldsworth, Esq., who purchased it some three years ago. Since it came into his possession he has expended large sums in improving its appearance and in rendering the mansion more commodious and comfortable. On the occasion of my visit the foundation of an extensive wing was laid, and a large conservatory, and a small but neat chapel (both connected with the mansion) were all but completed.

Formerly this estate belonged to a family named Fairlie. In 1826 Mrs. William Fairlie, the widow of a wealthy Calcutta banker, purchased it, and it is said expended £20,000 in improvements. The mansion house was built by this lady, the cost of which is included in the above sum. Following the course of the carriage drive—which passes through the estate—I found its terminus adorned with a handsome pillared gateway and neat lodge, and situated in Ayr road a mile nearer home than the Bogend entrance.

Trudging onward I soon reached Spittal Hill, and, with Riccarton steeple and the spires of Kilmarnock in full view, I rejoiced that my ramble was drawing to a close, for the day was far spent, and the western sky wore a crimson tinge that betokened rest to man and beast, and hush of toil.

Passing the finely wooded entrance to Treesbank estate I came to Peace-and-Plenty—a place that derives its name from a roadside public house that once flourished under that title, it being the custom of the landlord to supply his customers with bread and cheese when they purchased a dram. Here are situated a row of neat cottages, with gardens behind and flower-plots in front, tastefully laid out and decked with choice flowers. The dwellings are scrupulously clean, and to judge by their appearance and that of their occupants a commendable rivalry seems to exist as to who can have the neatest plot and the most comfortable home. These cottages were built some years ago by the proprietor of Caprington for the accommodation of his workpeople, and the experiment has been so successful that that gentleman has been induced to build another row of similar dwellings nearly opposite the entrance gate of his estate.

Leaving Peace-and-Plenty behind I soon passed Caprington gates, and after a brisk walk arrived at the village of Riccarton. Passing the long row of one-storied houses that line Campbell Street, I crossed the new bridge and entered Kilmarnock, delighted with my ramble, and feeling better from having held communion with Nature.

CHAPTER IV.

Wild Flowers—The Macwheelan Murder—The Cairn—Symington—The Church and Graveyard—Witherington—Old Sandy Neil—"Laird" M'Pherson—"Jock o' the Whalps"—The Glen.

My first ramble having wakened both curiosity and interest, I gave myself to the delight of visiting in my leisure hours the many scenes and antiquities in the vicinity of the town that are consecrated by history and hallowed by tradition. This being the case, I selected a sunny Saturday for my second ramble, and equipped with a walking-stick I passed through the Holm, crossed the new bridge at Riccarton, and sped along Ayr Road. Leaving the village behind I soon gained Peace-and-Plenty, and paused to admire the neat flower-plots in front of the miners' cottages, but as they were already familiar to me I moved on, for

"The wayside flowers, sequestered from the throng
  In Nature's quiet lanes,"

are dearer to me than the gaudy plants of the garden. Yes,

"There seems a bright and fairy spell
  About their very names to dwell;
And though old Time has marked my brow
  With care and thought, I love them now.
Smile if you will, but some heart-strings
Are closest link'd to simplest things;
And these wild flowers will hold mine fast,
Till love, and life, and all be past;
And then the only wish I have
  Is that the one who raises
The turf-sod o'er me, plant my grave
  With buttercups and daisies."

About a quarter of a mile from Peace-and-Plenty a road to Dundonald branches off to the right. Turning into it I crossed a bridge, beneath which a burnie purled as it jinked on its way through the fields. A little beyond the bridge I entered a road on my left which is known as Fortacres Road. Like most old roads it is rugged and undulating, but nevertheless it is very pleasing, because from its heights the eye sweeps over a wide range of landscape. Following its course for half-a-mile or so, I came to a part where it takes a sudden turn and passes on to Fortacres and other places.

At the turn on the left hand side there is a cairn or heap of stones, formed by every passer-by so inclined adding one. It marks the spot where one of the most cold-blooded and heartless murders that ever stained the annals of our country was committed, for there one in the dawn of early manhood welled out his heart's blood, and stained the highway with the crimson tide. He was named James Young, was in the eighteenth year of his age, and a native of Riccarton. On the evening of Dudd's-day, 1848, he left the farm of Fortacres, where he was serving, promising to return the same night. About seven o'clock he arrived at his father's house at Knowehead, Riccarton, and remained in the company of his father and mother and other members of the family until half-past ten, when he left to return to his master's house. That house he never reached, for his body was found by two young men about four o'clock next morning at the spot indicated lying in a pool of blood, with a ghastly wound in the neck that had been inflicted with a carpenter's chisel. When found the body was cold and stiff, and both hands were filled with earth and grass that the poor fellow had clutched in the agony of death. A small bundle lay beside it. The pockets had been rifled, and a silver watch that the victim wore was gone, showing clearly that the murderer had stained his soul with blood for the sake of plunder. The authorities were soon at the scene of the crime, but a clue to the murderer was wanting. An Irishman named Macwheelan had been seen lurking in the vicinity on the afternoon of the day of the murder, and as he was suspected, but having disappeared, a description of his person was sent to the various police stations throughout the country, and this circumstance led to his apprehension. While passing a toll-bar between Beith and Paisley, a farmer observed a suspicious-like character leaving the toll-house. He thought nothing of the circumstance at the time, but shortly afterwards, upon hearing that £35 and a silver watch had been abstracted from it in the absence of the occupant, it struck him that he knew the thief, and he at once mounted a horse and rode post-haste after him. He overtook the object of his search near Paisley, dismounted, laid hold of him, and unaided took the watch and money from him, after which he detained him and handed him over to the Paisley police. Finding that the description of their new prisoner tallied with that of the man wanted in Kilmarnock, they communicated with the authorities there. He proved to be Macwheelan, was brought to Kilmarnock, and link after link of evidence was formed until a chain was made that convicted him. It was found that he arrived in Beith on the Saturday after the murder, and that he gave the watch of his victim to an acquaintance to pawn, and after the proceeds had been squandered in drink he had set off to Paisley. All this and more was proved against him at the trial. Suffice it to say he was sentenced to death, and that he suffered the extreme penalty of the law at Ayr, dying impenitent, having denied the crime to the last.

As I stood by the spot where the earth had drank a brother's blood I thought on the present barbarous state of society, and wondered when the great federation of mankind would take place. Eighteen hundred years have rolled away since the angelic host on the plains of Bethlehem announced the "good tidings of great joy," and proclaimed "peace on earth and goodwill toward men;" but alas! that blessed state is still far distant, and will remain so, so long as men disregard the laws of their being and allow a spirit of selfishness to predominate over their duty to God and themselves.

Throwing a stone on the cairn—not with a feeling of superstitious reverence, but as a mark of my abhorrence of the crime—I descended the hill and at Fortacres toll entered a road that turns off in the direction of Symington. It is one of the old country sort, rugged, hilly, and winding, but it passes through a varied and beautiful country, and as I traversed it I was charmed with the view of Dundonald hills, the old grey ruins of the castle, and many other beauteous scenes that stud the landscape.

A walk of two miles or better brought me to the secluded village of Symington, a small place with some 300 inhabitants, who are nearly all engaged in agricultural pursuits. It is beautifully situated. In and around it there are very many fine old trees, whose giant arms and luxuriant foliage give to the place a picturesque appearance and to the visitor a favourable impression. The houses are nearly all one-storeyed, and for the most part are built near the church—a quaint, old-fashioned, low-roofed structure, with an old-fashioned-like clock on its front, and a bell, the rope of which dangles by the side of the building. It stands in the centre of a small burying-ground, which is surrounded by a wall and shaded by tall trees. The date of its erection is unknown. Chalmers says—"The church of Symonstoun was granted to the convent which was founded at Feil, or Faile, in Kyle, during the year 1252, and it continued to belong to that convent till the Reformation. .The cure was served by a vicar pensioner who had a settled income and a glebe, and the minister and brothers of Faile enjoyed the remainder of the tithes and revenues." In 1797 the church was repaired, and a wing added to it, but at this date it is in an excellent state of preservation, and likely to serve for many generations.

Being desirous to inspect the burying ground, I tried the gate, but found it locked. Climbing to the top of the wall I dropped inside and stepped with reverence upon the grassy mounds, and in the quietude of the place spent an hour of sad reflection rambling among the tombstones. Many of these are very old and curious, and have, when new, been masterpieces of art in the eyes of the villagers. Near the church door there are several elaborately carved, and bearing curious devices, in which the plough, the spade, the skull, and cross bones are very prominent. There are several very chaste stones and monuments of recent erection, amongst which that to the memory of the Rev. Thomas M'Cracken is the most attractive. It bears the following inscription :—"Erected by the Free Church congregation of Symington in affectionate remembrance of the Rev. Thomas M'Cracken, A.M., M.D. Born 2nd November, 1836; ordained 11th May, 1865; died 31st May, 1869. He fell asleep." From the churchyard I gained the roadway by crossing the wall at a corner where stands the ruins of a cottage, and found myself opposite an entrance to the manse, It was built in 1786, and is at present occupied by the Rev. Mr. Davidson, the parish minister.

At the foot of the village is situated the Free Church, and adjacent to it the schoolhouse of the body. The church is a small building entirely destitute of architectural adornment. It bears the date 1843.

At the foot of the village also, and in a field off a road that branches towards Ayr, an individual named Witherington was executed in 1815 for highway robbery. This place was the scene of the crime. He was tried in Edinburgh, and from that city was brought under a strong escort. When passing through Kilmarnock the cortege was followed by a vast crowd to the place of execution. When the revolting spectacle had been gone through the body of the culprit was cut down, conveyed to the town, and buried in the Low Churchyard.

Although Symington is mentioned in records dating as far back as the reign of Malcolm IV. and William the Lion, yet there is little of interest connected with it, the church being the only antiquity in the district. Symon Loccard held the lands under Walter, the first Stewart, in 1165, and from him they are said to have derived the appellation of *Symonstoun*. This Symon also held a manor in the upper part of Lanarkshire which bears the same name.

Symington cannot boast of having given birth to any "eminent characters," although it has produced several droll ones. The most prominent of these was old Sandy Neil, the minister's man—or, in other words, beadle, bellman, and gravedigger. He was a droll character in every sense of the word, and will be long remembered for his eccentric habits and witty sayings. There is a story told of him in connection with the church clock. It seems at one time to have got out of repair and would either go too fast or too slow. Several clockmakers had tried their hand at it but had failed to regulate it. Sandy latterly took the wayward machine in hand, and under his care it kept excellent time. A villager meeting him one day said—"Man, Sandy, the clock does brawly noo since ye took it in hand; hoo do you manage?" "Weel," replied Sandy, "when she gangs owre fast I just throw a shoolfu' o' gravel intae her; an' when she gangs owre slow I just tak' a pickle oot."

One Sabbath a goat found its way into the churchyard during divine service, and finding the churchdoor open walked in. The intruder being observed, Sandy's attention was called to it. Going up he stroked its back with great kindness, and gently pushed it towards the door, but when he got it there he kicked it into the churchyard, and as he did so, exclaimed—"Out the house o' God, ye brute! out the house o' God!"

I might relate other anecdotes of old Sandy did space permit, for there are many good things told of him; but he has passed away with all his peculiarities, and now sleeps

> " Where the cottar and the laird
> Lie side by side and slumber
> In the auld kirkyard."

"Laird" M'Pherson was another well-known character. He was a shoemaker, and was dragged into fame against his will, being chosen by Thom, the sculptor, as the model of his Souter Johnnie. The likeness is very striking, and any one who knew the "Laird" cannot fail to recognise him in the figure at the Burns' monument.

The road that passes through Symington proceeds north-westward by Dundonald. When passing up that portion on which the village is built, I was amused to see the occupants of the primitive-like cottages looking after me. Doubtless they speculated as to who and what I was, and what would be the purport of my visit. At the outskirts of the hamlet the road makes a quick descent. Here I stopped at a well to drink from the pitcher of a village maid with bare feet and unkempt hair. Her laughing countenance spoke happiness and contentment, and as I drank I longed to be as void of care as she. The well is an open one. It is neatly built in, and bears the date of 1821. Making good use of my stick I sped onward and soon left the village behind. The road is very picturesque, and winds over gently rising grounds. On either side are sloping fields with numerous enclosures, clumps of planting, farmhouses, and gentlemen's residences. The mansion house of Townend and the woods and lawns that surround it have a fine appearance from the road. This estate is delightfully situated, and being greatly improved of late years, is one of the finest in the district.

Arriving at a very romantic portion of the road where a craggy eminence is covered with trees and decked with brambles and creeping ivy, I turned into a roadway that leads to Clavin farm. Proceeding along it for a short distance I came to an excavation in the face of a mound, on the top of which there is a plantation. The place is called "Jock o' the Whalps," and is so named from the circumstance that a hermit-like personage bearing that title lived in a wretched hut built against the face of the rock, with his wife, a pig, a cow, and a number of fowls. The hut has long been in ruins. John Vallance was the proper name of this "charicter." He is said to have received the appellation of "Jock o' the Whalps" from his having taken a number of moles to Ireland and sold them to the *green* natives as the pups of a peculiar species of the dog tribe. He was an individual of very filthy habits. Sharing the apartment in which he lived with a pig was not his worst fault, for it is affirmed that if a cow in the neighbourhood died of disease he would watch the place where the carcase was buried, disinter it by night, carry it piecemeal to his dwelling, and convert it into hams, but for what purpose can only be conjectured.

About a quarter of a century ago a favourite walk was to Jock's residence, and many pranks the youths of the town played upon him. He was a native of Stranraer, but when very young settled in the parish of Symington. In early manhood he is said to have been well-to-do in the world, but how he came to adopt the strange mode of life that he led during his latter years seemingly no one knows. Over twenty years have passed away since he lived, but he is still remembered and his name has become a household word in the district.

Returning to the highway, I held onward until I came to a spot where the road takes a sudden bend. Here I entered an avenue, and having passed through a field gate began to ascend a steep hill-side. The sward beneath my feet felt soft and carpety, and the blooming heath perfumed the air with its fragrance. At my approach numerous rabbits timorously scampered off to conceal themselves in their burrows beneath the furze, while the linnet chirped its alarm as it flew from bush to bush. Gaining the top of the eminence I reached a plateau, which is of circular form and surrounded by the ruins of a wall supposed to be of Roman origin, and to have enclosed an encampment or look-out station—a purpose for which the height is eminently adapted, for it commands a wide range of the Frith of Clyde and of the surrounding country. Seating myself on a boulder, I gazed with delight on the scene—a scene the like of which cannot be witnessed from an equal elevation in any other part of the country. Looking eastward a glimpse of the Emerald Isle is obtained, and the dark hills of Arran are seen standing out in bold relief, forming a fine background to the waste of waters that lie between them and our shore. Along the coast are several towns with wreaths of smoke hanging over them, while the view inland is said to comprise " portions of fourteen counties." Reluctantly withdrawing my gaze from the delightful prospect, I descended the hill in the direction of the farm of Harperscroft, and having gained Troon Road turned my face towards Dundonald, and sped onward at a brisk pace.

Arriving at the entrance to " The Glen," I paused and listened to the flood of song poured forth by the feathered inmates of the wood. There is a neat gateway here, and near it a board fixed to a post with the polite request, " Please shut the gate," painted thereon. Entering, I complied with the modest demand, and walked down the pathway, shaded from the sun's rays by the wealth of foliage overhead.

"The Glen" is a pass through the Clavin Hills, is used as a foot-road to Troon, and is much resorted to by pedestrians and picnic parties during the months of summer. The sward is of a mossy nature, and feels soft and elastic under the feet; and here and there in the pathway I observed names and initials, the letters being formed by the removal of the turf. The plantation through which "The Glen" passes is thickly wooded. The tall trees in some instances stretch their arms over the path and form a leafy canopy, while Flora has scattered her flowery gems around in rich profusion. In the wood the foxglove, the harebell, and the tall fern grow in wild luxuriance, and enhance the beauty of this truly picturesque place. Directing my steps to the farm of Hallyards, I entered the garden in quest of the ruins of St. Mary's Chapel; but alas! time and the many improvements made by the tenant have nearly obliterated all traces of this ancient religious house. With some difficulty I managed to trace a portion of the walls, but did not meet with anything calling for special note. About one hundred yards or so from the site there is a well of excellent spring water which is still known as St. Mary's well, but like the chapel its history is shrouded in oblivion. Seating myself by its brink I mused upon "the days that are gone"—dark days, when superstition strangled science and retarded the progress of the human race. Producing a drinking cup, I dipped it, and as I quaffed the dripping bumper I felt thankful that my lot was cast in an age and in a land where science is nurtured and where intellectual and political freedom is the birthright of every citizen.

CHAPTER V.

The House of Auchans—Dundonald Castle—The Village and Parish Church—Extracts from the Parochial Registers—Smuggling—Tam Fullarton—Newfield—"Fairlie o' the Five Lums"—Old Rome—Home again.

Leaving ecclesiastical haunts, I entered a path in the wood, and after following its intricate windings through the glade arrived at Auchans Castle, as it is called, but strictly speaking it is nothing more than a mansion-house of the olden time that has been built for defensive purposes. The building is extremely plain, is constructed for the most part of whinstone, and forms two sides of a square. One wing bears the date 1644, which infers that it is an addition to an earlier portion, and possibly the erection of Sir William Cochrane, who acquired the lands of Dundonald in 1638, and those of Auchans in 1640. Previous to the ancestor of the Earls of Dundonald coming into possession, the house of Auchans was the residence of a family named Wallace, the last of whom was a Colonel James. He was a devoted supporter of the Solemn League and Covenant, and headed the rising at Pentland. Through the unfortunate scientific speculations of Archibald, ninth Earl of Dundonald, Auchans came into the possession of the Eglinton family. The last individual of distinction who occupied the venerable mansion was Archibald, eleventh Earl of Eglinton, and his gifted mother, the Countess, to whom Ramsay inscribed his "Gentle Shepherd." That gentlewoman died in it in 1780, in the ninety-first year of her age. Boswell, in his "Journal of a Tour to the Hebrides with Dr. Johnson," in 1773, states that he along with the celebrated lexographer visited her ladyship, while she resided in the house of Auchans, and gives a spirited account of the interview, and states that when going away she embraced her distinguished visitor and said, "My dear son, farewell!" The ground apartments of the building are at present occupied by foresters on the estate, but the greater part of the interior is in a ruinous condition, and curious enough the most recent portion of it has suffered most. Ascending the stair of a tower situated in the corner of the courtyard, I was struck by the devastation that time and neglect has wrought. Many of the apartments were in a hopelessly irreparable condition, and looked as if they had been bombarded by artillery. The floors in several had fallen through, and in others rotten rafters and portions of walls hung so loosely that I expected every moment to see them crash into the rooms below.

Leaving the sombre-looking building I crossed the grass-covered courtyard and entered the garden, which is still under cultivation. In the orchard grew the parent tree of the Auchans pear, which was brought from France at an early date, and was the first of its kind in this country. It was blown down in 1793.

From the garden I passed through a wicket and strolled along a footway that runs along the bottom of a thickly-wooded bank. In some parts the light of day was almost excluded by the wealth of foliage overhead, and in others

> "The birch rock-rooted drooped
> And draped with lightsome shadows from its leaves
> The lone path, and burn that sang a song unheard."

At a neat gate the romantic footway merges into an old road that passes beneath the shade of some fine old trees. Following its course for a short distance I arrived at a low wall that surrounds the rocky mound on whose summit stands Dundonald Castle, roofless and shattered, yet in decay, looking stern and defiant from its commanding position, and bidding fair to brave the elements for many years to come. Crossing the wall I began the ascent, greatly to the amazement of a number of cows quietly browsing on the scant herbage that clothes the hillside, for they looked wonderingly at me as if half inclined to resent the intrusion. Reaching the ruin without mishap, I began my explorations, but lack-a-day! it bore ample testimony that wreck and decay had long held unchecked revelry within and without, for blocks of masonry lay as they had toppled from the walls, and melancholy silence pervaded the place. The courtyard—a portion of the walls of which are still standing—was covered with debris and rank grass, and like its surroundings had an abandoned and desolate appearance. The castle is not extensive; it is a rectangular building, two storeys high, but tradition states that it was at one time three, and that the stones of one were used to build the house of Auchans. Its architecture is very plain, and the walls, which are of great thickness, contain gun ports and arrow slits. On the western wall the royal arms of Scotland and other devices in *alto relievo* are still discernible, although much disfigured by time and weather. The interior consists of one spacious chamber with an arched roof of rubble work, a portion of the keep, a cell of which is entire, and several underground vaults, which are for the most part filled with rubbish. Round the conical eminence portions of a moat can be distinctly traced. This would render the stronghold almost impregnable prior to the introduction of artillery, and would make it worthy of the royalty that history and tradition ascribes to it.

Following the example of some boys, I climbed to the top of the castle by the aid of some rusty-looking nails that some one had driven into the wall; but I near came paying dearly for my foolhardiness, for a portion of the masonry gave way, and I was within an ace of coming down faster than I went up—a circumstance that most likely would have been the means of furnishing my family with mourning dresses.

Beyond a small chamber there is nothing of interest to be met with on the top of the building save the extensive prospect. I was fairly enchanted with it, and remained up some time to enjoy it. Towards the north-west a wide expanse of sea glistened in the afternoon sunlight, and inland an expansive view of the fertile district of Cuninghame lay before me. At my feet, as it were, the pretty little village of Dundonald, with its line of street and neat parish church, was in itself a picture of rustic neatness. Behind the castle, and at the foot of the eminence, there is a truly picturesque scene which consists of a precipitous cliff clothed with wood. It looked dark and gloomy. Around it swooped flocks of dark-plumaged birds, which kept up a discordant noise as they screamed forth their harsh notes of pleasure or alarm.

Having performed the somewhat dangerous and difficult task of descending from the top of the building, I strolled down the face of the hill and left the shattered remnant of the castle to crumble and decay beneath the heavy finger of time. The mound on which the castle stands is the only piece of ground in the district that now belongs to the Dundonald family, and it is stated that the Earl takes his title from it, and will retain it so long as the walls of the castle hold together.

When or by whom the castle of Dundonald was built is unknown, but judging by the style of its architecture and the construction of its walls it is probable that its erection dates as far back as the twelfth or thirteenth century. Tradition states that a fortlet of a much earlier date occupied the site, and a popular rhyme of great antiquity makes mention of it as follows:—

> "There is a castle in the wast,
> They ca' it Donald's din;
> There's no a nail in it ava,
> Nor yet a timmer pin."

"The first historical notice we have of the place," says the *Statistical Account*, "is in the time of the third Walter the Stewart, who was styled 'of Dundonald,' and was made Justiciary of Scotland by Alexander II., at St. Andrews, in 1230. It is said, however, by Chalmers that the manor and parish belonged to Walter, the son of Allan, the first Stewart, who held the whole of the northern half of Kyle, in the beginning of the reign of William the Lion, and that it might have been granted to him by David I. or his successor, Malcolm IV. Nothing more is known or even conjectured regarding it until the reign of Robert II., who appears, by several charters dated at Dundonald, to have made it the place of at least occasional residence from 1371 till the time of his death in 1390. This latter event is particularly mentioned by the Prior of St. Serf's Inch, Lochleven.

> ' The secownd Robert of Scotland Kyng
> As God purwaid maid endying
> At Dowdownald in his countrie.
> Of a schort sickness thare deyed he."*—Wynton, B. ix. C. 10.

That his gentle but ill-starred son and successor, Robert III., died in the same place, is also asserted by the same author;

---

* When Dr. Johnson visited the ruin, Boswell states that he was "very jocular on the homely accommodation of 'King Bob,' and roared and laughed till the ruins echoed."

and though his authority on this point is disputed by Pinkerton and Fourdon, there are others of no mean authority, such as Ruddiman and Macpherson, who stand up in defence of the testimony of the poet. But, be this as it may, there cannot be a doubt of his continuing to reside here sometime after his father's death; and it is probable that it was honoured by occasional visits from his royal successor till the time of James IV. From the predecessor of this monarch, James III., Allan, first lord Cathcart, obtained the custody of the castle, with the dominical lands, in 1482, and with this family they may be supposed to have continued for some time. The next account we have of it is in 1527, the date of a charter from James V., confirmatory of one probably given in his minority, and granting it in right of possession to a person of the name of Wallace, a cadet, in all likelihood, of the family of Craigie." This family probably built the original part of the house of Auchans when the castle began to be ruinous. From the castle hill I strolled through the village of Dundonald, and found it to be neat in appearance and picturesque in situation, being embosomed in a hollow at the foot of one of the Clavin hills. Its vicinity is well wooded, and the sombre ruins of the castle that frown from the height near it makes it doubly romantic. The houses are all modern in construction, and form a line of street about a quarter of a mile long. The inhabitants are cleanly in their habits and very tasteful about their dwellings—in fact, the whole place has an air of bien respectability and comfort. It contains two inns, a commodious schoolhouse, and two churches—the one Established and the other Free. The Established, or Parish Church, stands at the head of the village in front of the graveyard, and is a plain square building with a handsome spire, in which there is a clock and bell. It was built in 1803, and occupies the site of a very ancient religious edifice that belonged to the monks of Paisley previous to the Reformation. In it was interred the mortal remains of William, first Earl of Dundonald. He died in 1686. The bell that belonged to it is an antiquarian curiosity. It is in the possession of the Free Church of Dundonald, and bears the following inscription:—
" SANCTE EGIDIE ORA PRO NOBIS ANNO DNI. M.CCC.LXXXX. V to. X," which being translated, signifies—"Saint Egidius pray for us. In the year of our Lord Jesus Christ, 1395."

During the construction of the new church this relic was suspended between two trees in the churchyard, and was rung to summon the congregation to attend the ministrations of a clergymen who preached from a tent. The graveyard contains many gravestones, but there are none very curious or interesting. The oldest is dated 1737.

"The Statistical Account," in mentioning the Parochial Registers, says—"The oldest volume, containing the records of session, and bearing date 1602, is tolerably entire; nay, strange to say, much more so than any of the succeeding ones. It extends over a period of forty years, comprising a silent interval of sixteen years, and contains a great deal of parochial information that is curious and interesting. Among other entries of this kind are minutes of the trial of Patrick Lowrie, warlock, and Catherine M'Tear, demite of witchcraft. These seem to have been cases of peculiar interest and considerable judicial difficulty, from the minute detail of evidence adduced, and the length of time they appear to have been under trial. The attention of the session was more or less occupied by them for nearly five years—a term which would now-a-days do no small honour to a chancery lawsuit. Notwithstanding all this trouble, however, matters seem to have been left just where they began, no decision being recorded. The volume contains a record of a different, and to Scotchmen at large, of a more interesting kind—namely, the Solemn League and Covenant, to which are added no fewer than 222 signatures. But of these, which is a lamentable proof of the low state of education at the time, 179 are subscribed by proxy, because, as is stated, 'they could not wryt themselfs.' It appears, however, that the eyes of the public were beginning to open to this defect, as we find them making arrangements two years afterwards, in 1640, for forming what may be considered the first parish school." The following extracts may be interesting to the reader :—

"17th March, 1605.—John Fergushill, younger of Haly, deferrit ane slanderous taill spoken to him by Agness Lyoun, spous to Petir Renkin in Parkheid; she aledgand upon George Lachland her author, as the said George Lachland aledgit Symon Muir his author—'That the late minister of Kilwinning now departit this life was eardit with his mouth down, and that he confessit that the minister of Ayr and Irvine, and he, had the wyt of all the ill wedder this year.' "

"10 July, 1608.—The quilk day Isobell Turnbill, in Lones, comperand before the session, was accusit of the sclandler of ane superstitious doing by her. Declared that she was sent for anes or twys be Catherine Walker, spous to John Dook, in Chamber in Lonis, and that when she cam to her she took ane auld left scho of the husband's, and therein thrust the said Catherine's sair pap, and cast the said scho over the balk; and that she thrust her pap in the scho, and cuist it over the balk twys or thryse, and thereafter she grew seik."

"8 November, 1629.—The quhilk day the minister publicklie out of the pulpit, by the authority of the Presbytery, did inhibit and discharge all sorte, of charming, and resorting to charmes, consulting with wizards, sorcerers, and uthers of that sorte, certifeing all and sundrie who did so in time cuming, they should be chalengit criminallie thairfore, and followit and persewit with death, as for the crime of witchcraft."

"16 May, 1642.—The Session ordained that no woman be suffered to sit in the Kirk in the tyme of sommer with plyds upon their heids, because it is a cleuck to their sleiping in tyme of sermon, and desyred the minister to exhort them gravelie the next day to the observance of the same."

The above are taken from several curious entries which throw considerable light upon the manners and customs of the people in byegone days, and upon the stringent measures the church adopted to enforce morality. Notwithstanding her vigilance, however, cases of illegitimacy frequently occurred, and the cutty stool was too often in requisition to be consistent with ethics.

Smuggling was extensively carried on in Dundonald in the olden time, and very many stories are related regarding those engaged in it. The nearness of the village to the coast, and the hilly nature of the country, facilitated the contraband trade considerably. It was carried on extensively from the year 1700 until 1819, when the stringent measures then adopted by the Government put a stop to it. From what I have learned concerning smuggling exploits in the parish, the men engaged in the illicit traffic must have been a brave lot of fellows, fearless alike of danger and law. When on business each man carried what was called a "kent;"

this was a stout stick about four feet long, and very often loaded with lead. But many carried more effective weapons, and were not slow to use them when hard pressed by an enemy. A detachment of infantry were generally stationed at Irvine for the purpose of protecting the revenue officers in the discharge of their duty, and many an encounter occurred between them and the smugglers; but the latter, armed with the "kent," were often more than a match for the soldiers. Upon one occasion a ship arrived in Troon bay ladened with brandy, which was successfully landed and carted across the hills under the shadow of night. A considerable quantity found its way to the Holmes and was secreted, but by some means the excise officers were apprised of it, and arrived most unexpectedly, accompanied by a strong body of infantry. Making a seizure the booty was placed in carts, and triumphantly marched in the direction of Ayr. When passing Rosemount plantation a party of smugglers dashed out, "kents" in hand, and attacked the military. The fight was short, sharp, and decisive, and ended in the defeat of the revenue party, who being routed, left the field and the prize to the victors. I have often heard the name of Tam Fullarton mentioned in connection with many smuggling raids. Tam was a harum-scarum sort of a chield, a kind of a dare-devil, who was as fond of a fight as any Irishman could be. Upon one occasion Tam was accompanying a string of carts laden with contraband goods through a pass in the hills near the village, when an outlook espied a party of soldiers drawn up in the way to intercept them. Tam, however, was equal to the emergency, and being a good general, he acted at once. Advising his companions to retrace their steps, and to drive as fast as whip and rein would permit, he added, "I'll keep yon lads in check till ye're out o' danger." Turning their horses, they set off at full gallop, while Tam ascended a precipitous cliff, on which was a drystone dyke. Placing himself behind it he roared defiance. The soldiers, supposing that a party of smugglers were about to offer battle, advanced and attempted to attack the place whence the sounds proceeded. Tam kept his position, and hurled down stones with such regularity and precision that the soldiers had to retire. Deciding upon a new mode of attack, they proceeded to take the enemy in the rear. Tam observing this, and knowing that his friends had sufficient time to be out of danger, gave a shout of triumph and dashed into the wood. The soldiers being unacquainted with by-paths, and not relishing Tam's peculiar warfare, relinquished the undertaking and returned to the turnpike road. I might continue the narration of smuggling stories—for I have collected many—but I trust the above are sufficient to convey to the reader a faint idea of the fearless class of men who trod the hills long ago, defiant alike of law and revenue officers. Crags and caverns, known only to themselves, were their store houses, and in time of emergency the vaults of the Castle have concealed many a keg of brandy and bale of silk.

From the village of Dundonald I turned into the Kilmarnock road, and started on my homeward journey. From the hamlet it rises to a considerable elevation, then strikes off along an almost dead level. On the height, I paused and looked back upon the village and the frowning ruin, then sped onward. On my right I passed Newfield, the seat of William Finnie, M.P. The mansion house is situated on the top of some rising ground a short distance from the road, and is almost hid from view by trees. Of late years it has been greatly improved and additions built, and it is now a handsome residence. Near to it in a marshy piece of ground is said to be the remains of a Roman bath or reservoir. The place is nearly always flooded with water, and it is only in very dry weather that the relic can be seen. Passing through Damdyke toll-bar, I soon arrived at "Fairlie o' the five lums," as Fairlie House is locally termed. It is at present occupied by Captain Tait, a relative of the Caprington family. It stands off the road some considerable distance, and is approached by a broad carriage drive, at the gate of which there is a neat lodge. Beyond, on the brow of a steep brae, where the road swoops down and crosses a fine bridge that has recently been erected over the Irvine in place of the old structure, I passed Old Rome, a row of ruined cottages of mean appearance that were at one time occupied by a colony of colliers, who left the place when the pits in the neighbourhood became "worked out." The prospect from the bridge is very pleasing, and I need not say that I lingered sometime to enjoy it. The river comes sweeping round a bend after washing the bank of the beautiful estate of Caprington and turning the wheel of Cambuskeith Mill; it is then skirted by a hanging wood, passes the remains of Old Rome distillery, purls beneath the bridge, and rolls round a curve on its way to the sea. Leaving the pleasing scene, I followed the course of the road, which, a short distance from the river, crosses a line of railway and enters Gatehead, a small village that has sprung into existence within the last fifty years. It has a railway station, but no feature of interest, being possessed of neither kirk, market, mill, or smithy.

From Gatehead the scenery is very tame, and it was only at a turn where the road crosses a railway bridge that I had a glimpse of the picturesque. The gloaming had set in, and the western sky was tinged with the glory of sunset. Nature seemed hushed, but the stillness that reigned was at intervals broken by the lowing of cattle and the notes of a blackbird that piped its evening lay. In the hollow flowed the Irvine. The turrets of Caprington Castle peered over the tree tops, and, in the receding distance, Kilmarnock and the quaint village of Riccarton loomed in the fading twilight.

Passing Gargieston tile-works, and the entrance to the Mount, the handsome residence of Mrs. Guthrie, I gained Pointhouse toll, and turned down a narrow lane that runs to the edge of the Kilmarnock water. Crossing a wooden bridge I passed up West Shaw Street, and arrived in the Holm Square, none the worse of my long walk.

CHAPTER VI.

Beansburn—Dean Castle—Its situation and appearance—The Castle besieged—Destroyed by fire—A Tradition of the Persecution—The Boyd Family—From the Dean to Craufurdland—Craufurdland Castle and Grounds—Craufurdland Bridge—Up the Stream to Fenwick.

SELECTING a pleasant morning for my third ramble, I equipped myself for the road, and set out staff in hand. Passing up Portland Street, a brisk walk brought me to Beansburn Toll. Here I paused to view the beautiful scene that the valley to the east of the road presents. The view is not extensive, but the background being well wooded it has a romantic appearance, although somewhat disfigured by the unsightly buildings that cluster together at the Foundry Holm. Passing Dean Hill, the pleasantly-situated family residence of the late Bailie Craig, and numerous villas and cottages of a less assuming order, I arrived at Beansburn Smithy—or rather the works of Messrs. M'Kerrow, the noted agricultural implement makers. Before them lay many curious machines for the tillage of the ground that would have astonished our grandfathers, who knew none other than the plough, the harrow, and the roller. Turning into Dean Road, which branches off at Beansburn,* rises to a gentle eminence, then descends the side of the valley that I looked down on at the toll, a short walk brought me in sight of the ruins of Dean Castle, which are approached by a neat roadway. The ruins look hoary and grey in the distance, nor do they improve in appearance upon nearer inspection, although every care is taken to preserve them from the ruthless assaults of time. Near to the west wall is the handsome residence of Mr. F. J. Turner, the much-respected factor to his Grace the Duke of Portland. It is surrounded by a neat garden, and being under the shadow of the frowning ruin its situation is romantically picturesque. On the right hand side of the roadway there is a large mound—seemingly artificial—called

---

* So named from an insignificant burnie that falls into the Kilmarnock Water near Tam's Loup. Tradition states that it was originally called Bienie's Burn, a girl of that name having drowned herself in one of its pools.

"Judas Hill." I have heard it asserted that men slain in battle are buried beneath it, but am of the opinion that it is nothing more than one of those justice hills so common in this part of the country, and doubtless was used in days of feudalism, when the life of the offending vassal depended upon the whim or caprice of his lord.

By the side of the ruin, and winding zig-zag through the valley, the Kilmarnock Water flows on its way to the Irvine. The breast of the hill to the east is draped with wood, and the Dark Path—a roadway among the trees well known to the lads and lasses of the town—looks picturesque and inviting. Near the ruin the grounds are neatly laid out, and the bank on the west side is ornamented with shrubs and young trees, which lighten the frowning appearance of the pile and throws a cheerful aspect over the relic of "hoar antiquity." While viewing the shattered remnant of feudalism I was accosted by a gentleman, who proved to be Mr. Turner, the factor. Inviting me to inspect the interior, I complied, and accompanied him through a small gateway into the courtyard ; but had scarce time to look about me when he presented me with a bunch of keys, and after telling me that the old place was at my service left me to my own meditations.

The courtyard is spacious and partly enclosed by a remnant of the rampart wall. The buildings of the castle, which form a kind of angle, consist of two massive square towers of unequal height, with a lesser building intervening. The lesser tower and building seem to have been an addition to the higher, which, judging by the thickness of the walls (9 feet), masonry, loopholes, and construction, dates back to a very remote period. Above a doorway in the lesser building there is a crumbling stone tablet, on which is sculptured the arms of the Boyd family, and an inscription that the finger of time has obliterated. The higher tower is a sombre-like building, with an outside stair leading to a low doorway. Ascending the steps, I applied a key to the lock. The bolt shot back and I entered a spacious hall, with an arched roof of rubble work, which must have been a splendid apartment when decked and furnished. Through a large oblong window at the far end the sunlight streamed across the floor and lit up the wreck of former greatness, and cast a hallow over the shattered abode, wherein the voice of mirth had ceased and where oppressive silence reigned profound. My very tread echoed throughout the ruin, and sounded like a voice from the dead, resenting the inspection of a sad memento of an unfortunate family. In a corner of the apartment I came upon a spiral staircase, but the steps were gone, and in their stead a ladder was placed to facilitate ascent. Mounting, I rambled through the apartments in the upper storeys, but as they contained nothing of interest a description is unnecessary; one with a large window looking northward is said to have been the chapel. The roof of the tower fell in many years ago, but lately it has been replaced by one of wood. Through an opening the top of the walls are reached. Upon them there is a walk some four feet broad, and also the remains of a battlement and watch-tower. The view is very extensive, and comprises not only the town of Kilmarnock, but a panoramic scene extending over many miles of country. At the foot of the staircase there is a small doorway, and a narrow stair that led to the dungeons below. These are now turned to a more useful account, one being used as a milk-house and the others as cellars. At the foot of this stair the entrance is said to be to a subterranean passage that communicated with Craufurdland Castle, for, like all old buildings round which an air of mystery hangs, the Dean is not without its secret means of egress. There is a tradition concerning it to the following effect:—Once on a time—very far back, I fear—the castle was besieged by the English, who being unable to take it by force or stratagem surrounded it with the intention of compelling the garrison to capitulate. Patiently waiting for three months daily expecting a surrender, to their surprise one morning the besieged hung a quantity of new-killed beef over the battlements, and jeeringly asked the English if they were in want of provisions, for they had and to spare. Being unable to solve the mystery, the general raised the siege, and left the field fully persuaded that the garrison's resources were inexhaustible. The entrance to the subterranean passage is now closed; but proof of its existence is said to have been found upon the late modification of Craufurdland Castle—a passage being discovered that tradition and supposition pointed to as the communication connecting that house with Dean Castle.

Leaving the high tower, I directed my attention to the

lesser and to the building connected with it, which consists on the ground floor of what has been a spacious kitchen and two or three rooms, with arched ceilings. The second floor seems to have been a large room. It contains a row of modern-like windows facing the south. It is roofless and much decayed, and appears to have been the principal dwelling of the family. The tower contains a staircase, the steps are much worn, and several towards the top have fallen through, and curious enough, though it and its ruinous associate are the most recently constructed, they seem to suffer most from the ravages of time.

The last occupant of Dean Castle was William, fourth Earl of Kilmarnock. When returning from the Continent, in 1735, he observed in a newspaper that a castle in Scotland named the Dean had been destroyed by fire. Hastening home, he found the statement too true. The catastrophe formed a strange prelude to that unfortunate nobleman's tragic end. After the destruction of the castle the Earl resided in Kilmarnock House, and allowed the home of his ancestors to become a ruin, and as such it has braved the blast for a hundred and forty years, and now stands a sad memento of the fallen house of Boyd. Tradition states that the conflagration was occasioned through the negligence of a servant-girl, who had left some flax she had been sorting too near the fire.

An enumeration of the plenishing of Dean Castle at the death of Thomas, fifth Lord Boyd, in June, 1611, may interest the reader. "It was found," says Paterson, "among the Boyd papers," and is as follows:—"Twa cowpis of siluer, every ane of thaim vechtan ten unce of siluer; ane lang carpet, half worset half selk; ane schort carpet for the chalmer buird; ane lang green buird claithe, the length of the haill buird; twa schort green buird clathis for the chalmer buird; four cuschownis of tripe veluit; four cuschownis of carpet ruche vark; thric schewit cuschownis of the forme of coweriug vark; four cuschownis of rushie vark; twa lang buird claiths of flanderis damis; saxteine sernietis of damis; ane lang dornick buird claithe; ane lang damis towell; ane cower buird claithe of small lynying; ane duson of dornick seruietis; ane braid dornick towell; twelf lang lyning buird claithis; four duson and ane half of lyning scruetis; fyve buird claithis of grit lyning; fyve duson of round lyning seruetis; aucht towells of roun hardine; four drinking clathis, twa thairof sewit with selk, and the ither twa paine; twa lyning drinking clathis; ane copbuird clath; ane down bed; aucht feddir beddis, with aucht bowsteris offering thairto; auchteine codis, pairtlie filed with downs and pairt with feddirs; auchteine pair of dowbill blankettis; fyve cowerings of ruchie vark; ane rallow caddow; sevin houshaild cowerings; saxteine pair of lyning scheittis; twa pair of heid scheittis of small lyning, schewit with black selk; ane pair of plaine heid scheittis; sax pair of heid scheittis; ten codwaris of small lyning, schewit with black selk; sax codwaris of small lyning, unschewit; ane stand of spampit crambassie vorset courteinis, with ane schewit pand offering yrto; ane stand of greine champit curtains, with ane pand offering yrto; ane ither stand of gray champit vorset curtains, with the pand offering yrto; ane stand of greine pladine curtains, with offering yrto; ane stand of quhyet schewit curtains; ane pair quhyet vowen curtains, with the pand offering yrto; seventie pewdir plaitis; ane duson pewdir trunchoris; ten cowries of pewdir; seventeine saisceris; twa new Inglis quart stowpis; two new quart flacownis; thrie ale tyne quart stowpis; twa ale tyne quart flacownis; ane tyne pynt stowp; twa new chalmer pottis; four new tyne chandilieris; fyve grat brassin chandilieris; ane grit morter of brass, and ane iron pester; twa tyne bassings, with ane lawr of tyne; five grit brass panis; thrie meikle brassin pottis, and ane lytill brassin pot; twa iron pottis; ane grispan of brass, and ane pair of grat standard raxis; fyve lang speittis; ane grit iron tank; ane meikill frying pan, and ane grit masking fatt; thrie gyll fattis; twa meikill barrals; four lytill barrals; ane burnist, and twa grit iron chimnays; twa pair of taingis; ane chalmer chimnay; twa lang hall buirds; thrie furmis; ane schort hall buird; twa chalmer buirds; twa chyris of aick; ane copbuird of aick; sax buffet stuills; ane meikill bybill (bible); twa meikill meill gurnells of aick; thrie cofferis; twa grit kistis of aick, for keiping of naipparie; four less kistis, and ane candill kist; twa stand bedis of aick."

Dean Castle is associated with the name of "bloody Dalziel." During a period of the Persecution it was his headquarters in Ayrshire, and many atrocities were committed by him and his soldiery in its neighbourhood. Upon one occasion several troopers observing a man running across a field, gave chase, but the individual being fleet of foot avoided them, passed through the entry of a cottage and concealed himself in a pool of water in the garden. Entering the cottage the pursuers found an old woman its only occupant. Laying hold of her, they threatened her with instant death if she did not deliver up the man. Pleading ignorance of his whereabouts, she was dragged to the Castle and thrown into one of the dungeons, where, tradition states, she was allowed to die of starvation.

At what period any portion of Dean Castle was built is a matter of conjecture. Pont, who topographized Cuninghame about 1608, speaks of it as being " veill planted, and almost environed with gardens, orchards, and a parke," and of being " the cheiffe duelling almost for 300 zeirs of ye Lords Boyde;" while Captain Grose, who visited and made a drawing of it in 1789, supposes it to have been built about the beginning of the fifteenth century.

Paterson hazards an opinion that it was built about 1316, the lands, according to a charter granted by Robert the Bruce, having passed from John Baliol to Sir Robert Boyd at that date ; and M'Kay, the local historian, frankly states that " the period at which either of the towers was erected is unknown," which I daresay is tantamount to the truth.

Dean Castle was the residence of the Boyds, lords of the barony of Kilmarnock, as far back as authentic history can trace. They were ever loyal to the cause of Scotland. One fought at the battle of Largs in 1263, and by his prowess so distinguished himself at Goldberry Hill, an eminence near to the scene of the action, that a grant of land in Cuninghame was conferred upon him. His descendants, from that incident, emblazoned the word " Goldberry " upon their family shield. Another aided Wallace and Bruce to emancipate Scotland from the thraldom of the English, and many more rendered their country good service. William, the fourth and last Earl, forfeited the lands, and perished on the scaffold for the part he played in the rebellion of 1745. These were again restored to his son, Lord Boyd, in 1752, but were afterwards sold to the Earl of Glencairn. The Glencairn family died out in 1796. The lands were then, or previous to that event, purchased by a Miss Scott, who became Duchess of Portland. They now belong to her descendant, the Duke.

Leaving the courtyard of the Castle, I passed through a kind of farm-yard and marched down a little avenue to the sonorous notes of a chained mastiff that barked until I was out of sight. Arriving in the roadway I found myself at a little bridge, and near to the spot where the Borland and Craufurdland unite and form the Kilmarnock water. The scene is possessed of much sylvan beauty. The Craufurdland dashes itself into foam as it dances down its rocky bed to wed itself to its more placid mate that murmurs round its perverted course as if anticipating the embrace.

Holding along the bank of the Borland, I passed near to the edge of Dean Quarry—an excavation sometime abandoned, and now filled with water. Arriving at a kind of glen where the streamlet is crossed by a bridge, I deviated into a bypath, ascended Assloss brae, and on past the farm and mansion-house of that name. On the face of the brae I leaned over a fence and looked down upon Dean Castle, and through the valley that lies before it, upon the town in the distance and the hills of Craigie in the background. In this scene the past and the present are beautifully blended. The old ruin represents feudalism and the cloggish systems of the *past;* the busy town beyond, with its schools and churches, its workshops and factories, represents the *present* progressive system of society, and shows what can be attained when a people are unfettered by absurd laws and restrictions. The spot is well worth a visit, the view of the town being good—perhaps the best to be had in the district.

In Assloss farmyard there are the remains of a fortlet, supposed to have been erected by a Jacob Auchinloss, who received a charter of the land of that ilk from Queen Mary in 1543. His descendants occupied the estate for a lengthened period. The family were of no great influence, but they are now extinct. The present proprietor (Miss Parker) is a descendant of the family of John Glen, merchant in Kilmarnock, who obtained the lands by purchase in 1725. The mansion-house is delightfully situated on the top of a thickly wooded bank overlooking the Borland water.

Pacing along the secluded highway, I drank in with open

eyes and ears the glorious sights and sounds of nature. The hum of the treasure-ladened bee smote my ear as I paused now and again to listen to the rich melody of a lark that appeared like a speck in the sky, for

> " Wild was the lay and loud,
> Far in the downy cloud
> Love gave it energy, love gave it birth."

I enjoyed its song; in fact, it had such an exhilarating influence upon me that I tripped lightly on my way and soon arrived in Craufurdland road, and in an amazingly short time at the gate of the beautifully wooded grounds which surround Craufurdland Castle, the seat of the Craufurds, but at present the residence of Alex. Cochrane, Esq., merchant, Glasgow. I walked along the carriage drive under the leafy shade of trees through whose umbrageous foliage as through a leafy screen I espied glimpses of the deep blue summer sky. The walk was a pleasant one, but it was doubly so when I rounded a turn and beheld the castle before me. It stands on the top of a gently rising bank, and is surrounded by scenery distinguished for its sylvan beauty. The building is large and commodious. The right wing has the appearance of considerable antiquity—in fact, it is said to have been built " prior to the days of William the Conqueror," and originally was a strongly-fortified square tower. There have been several additions made to this tower, which have to all appearance been erected at different periods; but, nevertheless they agreeably harmonise. The centre portion was erected by the late William Houison Craufurd, Esq., and is a beautiful specimen of Gothic architecture.

Many of my readers will have sunny memories of *Glen Saturday* (the third Saturday of April) and Craufurdland Castle. On that day it was and still is customary for the children of the town to go in droves to the castle to gather "glens"—as they term the yellow daffodils that grow in great abundance on a lawn behind the mansion. The late Mrs. Craufurd of Craufurdland delighted to welcome the little people, and to load them with bouquets of the coveted flowers. None were sent away empty handed, the crop being often so abundant that hundreds more could be supplied.

While viewing this ancient residence a gentleman approached me from the castle, and in the most kind and affable manner enquired if he could do anything to oblige me. Stating the purport of my visit he kindly pointed out the ancient and modern portions of the building, and other objects of interest connected with it; then, bowing, took leave, and left me to meditate and view the place at my leisure.

The Craufurds of Craufurdland trace their descent from a person named Sir Reginald de Craufurd, who was Sheriff of Ayr during the early part of the thirteenth century. He married the heiress of Loudoun. The first "Laird" was a grandson of Sir Reginald's, and flourished in the reign of Alexander II., King of Scotland.

Among the Craufurds there were several who were not afraid to unsheath the sword in defence of national rights and liberties. In 1297 a James Craufurd of Craufurdland followed the valiant Sir William Wallace, and assisted to wrench our native land from the grasp of the invader. Other members of the family distinguished themselves in battle, and one (John Craufurd) fell on the disastrous field of Flodden in 1513. For a long period a feud existed between the Mures of Rowallan and the Craufurds of Craufurdland, which was carried on with considerable bitterness by the respective barons. The Craufurdland estate at one period nearly became lost to the family by the eccentric conduct of John Walkinshaw Craufurd. Paterson, referring to this member of the family, says that he "early entered the army. In August, 1761, he was appointed Falconer to the King for Scotland. He was an intimate friend of the unfortunate Earl of Kilmarnock, who suffered with others for the attempt to restore the house of Stuart. He attended him to the scaffold, and, it is said, held a corner of the cloth to receive his head; he afterwards performed the last sad office of friendship by getting him interred. For the public exhibition he then made he was put to the bottom of the army list. He rose to be major—commandant of the 11th Regiment of Foot, and latterly to the rank of lieutenant-colonel in the army. He was present at the battles of Dettingen and Fontenoy, where he distinguished himself, He died at Edinburgh, unmarried, aged 72, Feb. 1793, settling his estate, by a deed made on his deathbed, upon Thomas Coutts, banker in London. His aunt and nearest heir (Elizabeth Craufurd), however, instituted an action of reduction of this settlement, and after a long litigation, carried on by her and her successor, the deed was reduced by a decree of the House of Lords in 1806, by which the succession to this ancient estate returned into its natural channel." Passing in front of the castle, I entered a carriage drive that winds through a thickly wooded portion of the estate. The trees on each side intertwined their branches and formed as it were a triumphal arch of green boughs. Strolling beneath the leafy shade, I passed on my left a beautiful sheet of water on whose bosom several snow-white swans glided gracefully along. In winter the "roaring game" is carried on with great spirit upon its frozen surface, and the stillness which usually pervades the scene is then broken by loud voices and merry peals of laughter, which "viewless echo" takes up and reiterates again and again.

Arriving at the termination of the shady path, I passed through a gateway and entered a rustic road. Turning to the right, a short walk brought me to Craufurdland bridge, a plain one-arched structure, in the vicinity of which the scenery is remarkable for its picturesque loveliness—so much so, indeed, that the muse of the poet has been awakened by it, and the painter and photographer have celebrated it by their art. The stream which the bridge spans is called Craufurdland water. It takes its rise in the moors beyond Fenwick, and to use the words of Burns—

> " Whyles owre the linn the burnie plays,
>   As through the glen it wimples;
> Whyles round a rocky scaur it strays,
>   Whyles in a wiel it dimples;"

until it bickers down the rocky declivity at Dean Castle. Entering a private road that leads to the residence of Captain Picken, I passed through a "slap" and held along the bank of the streamlet, which was swollen by recent rains, and as it poured its mossy flood along it dashed its waters against fragments of rock that impeded its progress, as if peevish at the obstruction. The scenery was very pleasing, but walking was rendered toilsome by the moist, clayey nature of the soil, and at every step I sank ankle-deep in mire. Struggling onward for more than a mile, consoling myself with the thought that bad roads like bad fortune were probationary and possessed of no great duration, I arrived at an old cart-road on the face of a hill, and having entered it found more solid footing. A short walk brought me to the farm of Dalreath, and having passed it a sharp downhill pedestrian feat landed me at a rickety wooden bridge spanning the Craufurdland. Crossing it I beheld at a short distance the farm of Midland, a spot that reminded me I was treading on ground once trod by the sons of the Covenant, who thought it better to suffer and die than that tyranny should reign.

After lingering awhile on the bank of the Craufurdland I struck into a disused cart-track, and directed my steps to Low Fenwick, an ancient but unassuming hamlet that tops the rising ground to the west.

CHAPTER VII.

Low Fenwick—Old John Kirkland—"The Kirk-town"—The erection of the Parish and origin of the name—The Parish Church and Burying-Ground—The Rev. William Guthrie—The Burial Place of the Howies—Captain Paton.

ARRIVING at a bridge spanning the Fenwick water I crossed over, passed up the "waterslap," and entered the highway between Kilmarnock and Glasgow. On each side of it, forming a kind of street, stands Low Fenwick, which for the most part consists of a few primitive-like one-storeyed houses. Besides these there are a few modern erections of the plainest architecture, the most noteworthy of which is the mansion of Mr. John Graham, a gentleman connected with a banking firm in Glasgow. The place being isolated and possessed of neither "kirk nor market, mill nor smithy," it is entirely unprogressive. The inhabitants are mostly engaged in weaving and agricultural pursuits; work at the former is very difficult to obtain, and wretchedly remunerated when it is procured.

Mr. John Kirkland, a minor poet, is a native and a resident of Low Fenwick. This venerable bard has wooed the muse for well nigh half a century, and; like some of Scotland's great song writers, though bred to the loom, poesy has been to him an oasis from which he has drawn pleasure and solace in many a lone hour. He was a contributor to *The Ayrshire Inspirer* and other publications, but since age and its attendant infirmities have began to tell on him his harp has been somewhat neglected. Perhaps it may not be out of place to append a few verses from his pen, therefore I make the following brief extract from a long poem entitled

AN OLD MAN'S ADDRESS TO THE MOON.

" Hail, lovely orb of tranquil light,
  Whose soften'd radiance makes the night
    Seem fairer than the day;
  Before thy presence in the sky
  The stars and planets fade and die,
    Their glory melts away.

> Vain of thy charms the sky we view—
> Unfolds her ample field of blue
>   Thy beauty to display;
> With youth immortal on thy brow,
> And queenly mien and grandeur thou
>   Rejoicest on thy way.
>
> No frailty with increasing years,
> But fresh and vigorous thou appears,
>   As when the Almighty's finger
> First touch'd thee into being bright,
> And filled thy lamp with quenchless light—
>   Nor dost thou pause or linger."

* * * * * *

Passing through Low Fenwick, a walk of half-a-mile brought me to High Fenwick, or as it is more commonly called "the Kirk-town." It is situated on the Glasgow road, four miles north-east of Kilmarnock, and consists of a respectable street and a number of lowly cottages that cluster round its quaint but highly interesting parish church, which stands in a hollow a short distance from the highway. It has a population of 469. Its trade is very meagre, and consists of handloom weaving and such crafts as are incidental to all rural villages where the scream of the locomotive whistle is unheard, and where the inhabitants retain much of the rustic artlessness of their forefathers. Besides an inn and several public-houses, the place though small contains no less than three churches. The first—a large building belonging to the U.P. body, and erected in 1830—I passed on my right as I entered the village, and the second—a small structure erected in 1844, and inscribed "The Guthrie Church"—I found situated next to the inn and nearly opposite a lane leading down to the *real* Guthrie Church, for evidently the title conferred by the Free Church body upon their little tabernacle is a misnomer, the parish church being the Guthrie Church proper, the eminent divine of that name having laboured in it for twenty years.

Previous to 1642 the parish of Fenwick was included in that of Kilmarnock. Upon the disjunction it was termed *New Kilmarnock*, but Fenwick—which according to Chalmers is a word of Anglo-Saxon origin and signifies the village of the fen or marsh—being the name of the first-mentioned hamlet, the inhabitants persisted in calling the parish by the same cognomen, and in course of time the appellation, which is appropriately descriptive of the boggy nature of the greater portion of its soil, came to be universally recognised.

The year after the erection of the parish of Fenwick its celebrated church was built. Houses gradually sprang up around it, and the Kirk-town, although comparatively modern, has become the parochial centre of commerce and divinity, but there is nothing of interest connected with its history beyond what is purely ecclesiastical.

After straying through the quiet village I turned down a lane and soon arrived at the gate of the little burying-ground that surrounds the parish church. Finding it unfastened, I opened a rusty leaf and entered, and as it closed with a clank behind me I felt as if the world was shut out, and I,

"Far from the madding crowd's ignoble strife,"

left in solitude to muse upon the sons of the Covenant—the bold, undisciplined peasantry who buckled on the sword for conscience sake and battled to the death against tyrannical diction.

The church is a low-roofed, old-fashioned-like building, with a small steeple or belfry. By its side the *juggs* still dangle at the end of an iron chain. They consist of a hinged circular iron collar about six inches in diameter, and were used in the olden time to punish individuals guilty of petty offences. The collar was padlocked round the neck of the culprit, and he or she was left to be stared and jeered at by every passer by for a given number of hours. The punishment was much dreaded. The interior of the church—into which I had the good fortune to obtain admittance—is neat and comfortably seated, and contains three small galleries, the fronts of which are of carved oak. The pulpit, which is also of oak, is the same in which the eminent William Guthrie, first minister of the parish, preached, and on this account is greatly prized. By its side, on an iron stand, there is a half-hour sand glass. Preaching by the sand glass is a very ancient custom, and one that is still observed in this little church. When the minister begins his discourse the beadle turns it, and a glass to a glass and a half is considered to be sufficient for a sermon. The second turning gives the speaker a hint to draw his remarks to a close. The church was erected in 1643. Its site is said to have been chosen by the Rev. William Guthrie and a number of the parishioners, and it is recorded that he preached in it before it was finished, so anxious was he to begin his labours. Near to the church and opposite the gate there is a handsome tombstone to the memory of this distinguished divine. It bears the following inscription :—" In memory of the Rev. William Guthrie, first minister of this parish, and author of *The Christian's Great Interest.* Born, 1620; ordained, 1644. Ejected by prelatic persecution, 1664; worn out by labours and sufferings, he died, 1665, and was interred in the church of Brechin. His active and self-denying ministry, through the Divine blessing, produced a deep and lasting impression. This stone is erected, 1854, as a token of gratitude by the Christian public.

> 'With heavenly weapons I have fought
> The battles of the Lord;
> Finish'd my course, and kept the faith,
> Depending on His word.'"

The Rev. William Guthrie was a native of Angus, and the eldest son of the laird of Pitforthy. He studied philosophy at St. Andrews University, and took the degree of Master of Arts. After this he studied divinity under the famous Samuel Rutherford, and was licensed to preach. In order that worldly cares would not interfere with the ministry to which he had dedicated himself, he handed over his right of succession to the family estate to a younger brother, and energetically applied himself to his profession. He was for some time tutor to Lord Mauchline, eldest son of the Earl of Loudoun, and while in that position he preached on a preparation day in Galston. Several people from Fenwick being present, they were so taken with his forcible style that they resolved to induce him to become their minister. He accepted the call, but the difficulties he had to contend with in the new parish at first was most disheartening. Many of the parishioners had accustomed themselves to loiter about the fields, or pass the Sabbath shooting, fishing, or playing at games. Some would not be spoken to, and others refused him admittance into their houses, but being a man of tact he tried stratagem, and was ultimately successful in gaining their confidence and making a change in their morals. He very often disguised himself as a traveller, and called at the houses of the most profane and careless in the dusk of evening, and begged a night's lodging. If admitted he tried to make himself agreeable by telling racy stories and engaging in general amusing conversation, and gradually introduced subjects of a more weighty nature. By this means he procured the attendance of the most obstinate, and endeared himself to the people of the parish. As time went on, Mr. Guthrie's fame spread, and he came to be a most popular and successful preacher. People came from Glasgow, Paisley, Hamilton, Lanark, Kilbride, Glassford, Strathaven, Newmilns, and many other places to hear his eloquence. It was the practice for such to come on Saturday and spend the greater part of the night in prayer and conversation, attend public worship on the Sabbath, dedicate the whole day to religious exercises, and go home on Monday—"travelling," says his biographer, "ten, twelve, or twenty miles, without grudging in the least the long way, or the want of sleep and other refreshments. Neither did they find themselves the less prepared for any other business through the week." Such popularity did not go unnoticed, and although by the influence of Chancellor Glencairn and the Earl of Eglinton he had been allowed to occupy the church for four years after the restoration, the Archbishop of Glasgow determined to suspend him. The curate of Calder was nominated to serve the notice. He arrived in Fenwick with a dozen soldiers, and having delivered a short address and declared the church vacant, started on his homeward journey. Woodrow says:—"I am well assured he never preached any more after he left Fenwick; he reached Glasgow, but it is not certain if he reached Calder, though but four miles from Glasgow. However, in a few days he died in great torment of an iliac passion, and his wife and children died all in a year or thereby, and none belonging to him were left." Mr. Guthrie continued in Fenwick for a year after his suspension, but he never preached more. The death of a brother called him to Angus to look after the paternal estate that had again devolved upon him, but when there, he was seized with a violent disease, and after lingering a short time died in the 45th year of his age.

There is not another graveyard in Ayrshire that contains

so many mementoes of the persecution as that of Fenwick. Several who "wandered in deserts, and hid in mountains, and in dens and caves of the earth," have found a balm for their sorrow and suffering in the Lethe of death, and slumber forgetful of their wrongs in this little golgotha. To the north of the church is the burial place of the Howies of Lochgoin. There, 'neath a flat stone, lie the remains of James Howie, who suffered much during the persecution. The rythmical inscription the stone bore was obliterated some years ago, and a prosaic one substituted. Though lengthy it is far inferior in my opinion to the former one. In these matters, being somewhat of a Conservative, I beg to present the reader with the old epitaph. It is preserved in the appendix to the "Life of John Howie," and is somewhat of a curiosity.

> " The dust here lies under this stone
> Of James Howie, and his son John
> These two both lived in Lochgoin
> And by Death's power were called to join
> This place. The first, November twenty one,
> Years sixteen hundred ninety one
> The second, aged ninety year
> The first of July was brought here
> Years seventeen hundred and fifty-five,
> For owning truth made fugitive
> Their house twelve times, and cattle all
> Was robb'd, and fam'ly brought to thrall
> All these, before the Revolution
> Outlived Zion's friends 'gainst opposition."

"And he said unto me, these are they which came out of great tribulation."—Rev. vii., 14.

> " The voice said cry, What shall I cry ?
> All flesh is grass, and so must ly
> As flow'er in field with'reth away
> So the goodliness of man decay."

Alongside this stone there is another with a list of names and dates which covers the remains of other members of the Howie family. Amongst these moulder all that is mortal of the gifted author of "The Scots Worthies." The inscription briefly refers to him as follows:—"Also of his son John, who lived in Lochgoin, author of the 'Scots Worthies,' and other publications, who died Jan. 5, A.D., 1793, aged 57 years."

To the east of the church, and close to the side walk, there is a handsome monumental tombstone. It bears the device of a drum and flag, cross swords, etc., and also the following inscription :—" Sacred to the memory of Captain John Paton, late of Meadowhead, of this parish, who suffered martyrdom in the Grassmarket, Edinburgh, May 9th, 1684. He was an honour to his country ; on the Continent, at Pentland, Drumclog, and Bothwell, his heroic conduct truly evinced the gallant officer, brave soldier, and true patriot. In social and domestic life he was an ornament; a pious Christian, and a faithful witness for truth in opposition to the encroachments of tyrannical and despotic power in Church and State. The mortal remains of Captain Paton sleep amid the dust of kindred martyrs, in the Greyfriars Churchyard, Edinburgh. Near this is the burying-place of his family and descendants.

> " Who Antichrist do thus oppose,
> And for truth's cause their lives lay down,
> Will get the vict'ry o'er their foes,
> And gain life's everlasting crown."

Captain Paton was one of the most heroic of the worthies who suffered during the persecution. His life was an eventful one, and the closing scene tragic. In early manhood he exchanged the sickle for the sword, went abroad and joined the army of Gustavus Adolphus, King of Sweden, and was for some valiant deed advanced to the post of Captain. His stay abroad is supposed to have been brief, for in 1645 he was called out to assist in opposing Montrose's insurrection. He was present at the battle of Kilsyth, and behaved with great bravery, as did all the Covenanting leaders ; but nevertheless Montrose's daring purpose and superior generalship carried the day, and the little army was driven into a bog. Howie—from whom I condense—relates the following extraordinary achievement: —" In this extremity, the Captain, as soon as he got free of the bog, with sword in hand made the best of his way through the enemy, till he had got safe to the two Colonels Hacket and Strachan, who all three rode off together ; but they had not gone far till they were encountered by about fifteen of the enemy, all of whom they killed except two who escaped. When they had gone a little farther, they were again attacked by about thirteen more, and of these they killed ten, so that only three of them could make their escape. But, upon the approach of about eleven more, one of the Colonels said, in a familiar dialect, 'Johnny, if thou dost not somewhat now, we are all dead men.' To whom the Captain answered, 'Fear not; for we will do what we can before we either yield or flee before them.' They killed nine of them, and put the rest to flight." Making good their retreat, the three friends separated, and the Captain returned to Fenwick.

The year following this event the Rev. William Guthrie, accompanied by Captain Paton and a number of friends from Fenwick, went to Mauchline to meet with a party of Covenanters who had agreed to celebrate the Lord's Supper. When engaged in their devotions, General Middleton and a company of soldiers surprised them. Middleton ordered his men to fire into the worshippers, but the Earl of Loudoun, who was one of the party, begged of him to allow the people to depart in peace. This he did, but coming upon them the next day he commenced hostilities, and a skirmish ensued. In it the Captain is said to have killed eighteen of the enemy.

After joining the expedition to oppose Cromwell's entry into Scotland, he returned home, settled at Meadowhead, and married. His life was now peaceful. He sat under the ministry of the Rev. William Guthrie, and became a member of his session, but in November, 1666, being invited to join the Covenanters of Galloway, who had taken up arms against Sir James Turner, "he behoved to take the field again, and commanded a party of horse from Loudoun, Fenwick, and other places." Having joined others who had collected forces, they marched to Lanark, renewed the Covenants, and from thence to Rullion, a place near the Pentland hills. The little army, numbering some 900, was attacked at this spot by General Dalziel, who commanded 8000 men. The position the Covenanters occupied was favourable, and they kept their assailants successfully at bay for some time, but ultimately overwhelming numbers forced them to retreat. During the engagement Captain Paton behaved with great bravery, and fought hand to hand with Dalziel, who knowing him tried to take him prisoner. Each fired a pistol at the other. The Captain observing his ball to "hoop down," supposed the General to be proof against lead, and with the intention of breaking the spell slipped a piece of silver in his remaining pistol. The General observing the movement retreated behind an attendant to avoid the shot. In this he was

H

successful, for when the Captain fired the man fell dead. Paton was amongst the last to leave the field. Finding himself and two horsemen from Fenwick surrounded by the foe, he cut a way out, and along with them escaped. Dalziel being still intent upon his capture sent two troopers after him. As they neared his companions cried, "What will we do now?"—"What is the fray?" cried the Captain; "there are but two of them." Wheeling about he met the foremost rider, and with a stroke of his sword clave his head, then cried to the other to take his compliments to his master, for he would not be with him to-night. He afterwards returned to Meadowhead, but was now a marked man. Hunted from place to place, and compelled to lurk about the moors, he had often to make the cold heath his bed. Yet in all his wanderings and hairbreadth escapes he drew consolation from his Bible, and from the thought that he would receive an imperishable reward for his suffering in a life beyond the grave. After the battles of Drumclog and Bothwell Bridge, in which he acted a gallant part, his position, if possible, became worse, and he turned weary of life and unresistingly allowed himself to be taken prisoner by five soldiers who visited the house of Robert Howie in Floack, in the parish of Mearns. His captors did not know him, and supposing him to be some old minister they conveyed him towards Kilmarnock. At Muir Yett, a farm-steading on the Glasgow road, a farmer standing at his door gave vent to his astonishment at seeing the Captain in custody by exclaiming, "Alas! Captain Paton, are you there?" The soldiers thus learning his identity well knew the value of their prize. On being conveyed to Edinburgh he was met by Dalziel, who remarked that he was both glad and sorry to see him. "John," said he, "if I had met you on the way before you came hither I should have set you at liberty, but now it is too late. But be not afraid, I will write to his Majesty for your life."—"You will not be heard," replied the Captain.—"Will I not?" said Dalziel vehemently. "If he does not grant me the life of one man I shall never draw sword for him again." Dalziel kept his word, petitioned the King, and obtained a reprieve; but the document having to pass through the hands of Paterson, Bishop of Edinburgh, it was designedly delayed until the sentence passed on the Captain had been put into execution.

CHAPTER VIII.

The Churchyard continued—John Fulton—King's Well—Lochgoin: its Traditions and Relics—Duntan Cove—Back to Kilmarnock.

> " By yon rudely-lettered stone,
>   In the auld kirkyard,
> Bend thy spirit's holiest tone,
>   In the auld kirkyard;
> Where the long grass rankly waves
> O'er the holy martyrs' graves,
> Pour the solemn meed it craves,
>   In the auld kirkyard."

Following the advice of the poet, I strayed among the grass-covered mounds in quest of less assuming mementoes of persecuting times. The first of these I met with was a plain upright slab bearing the following inscription:—" Here lies the body of James White, who was shot to death at Little Blackwood by Peter Inglis and his party. 1685.

> ' This martyr was by Peter Inglis shot,
> By birth a tiger rather than a Scot;
> Who, that his monstrous extract might be seen,
> Cut off his head, and kick'd it o'er the green.
> Thus was that head, which was to wear a crown,
> A football made by a profane dragoon.' "

James White was one of twelve men who met one night for prayer and religious conversation in Little Blackwood, a farm-house on the estate of Grougar, a mile and a half to the east of Fenwick. Being surprised by a party of soldiers commanded by one Inglis, they entered the spence, but White, who was possessed of a firelock, the only weapon of the kind in the house, stationed himself in the lobby between the front and back doors, and when the soldiers appeared he fired. Unfortunately for him his gun burned priming, and the light thus occasioned revealed his person to the enemy, who poured in a volley and shot him dead on the spot. Two of his friends escaped through a hole in the thatch, and one named Gemmell in the darkness ran into the arms of a soldier, who laid hold of him. Gemmell being a powerful man dashed his opponent to the ground, but being dragged with him a dreadful struggle ensued to obtain the mastery. Finding himself overmatched, the soldier drew his bayonet with the intention of ridding himself of his antagonist, but Gemmell wrenched it from him and buried the weapon in its owner's body. Freeing himself from the quivering grasp of his foe he started to his feet and made off, but his flight was abruptly stopped by a sentinel. Rushing at the man he knocked him down with a well-directed blow, and before the prostrate son of Mars could gather himself up he dashed into the darkness and escaped. The cries of the wounded soldier brought his companions, who finding him writhing in agony lifted him up, conveyed him into the house, and threw him into a bed among three little children, who were terrified at his bloody appearance and the unusual scene enacting before them. The fugitives along with the master and mistress of the house, who had sought refuge in the room, durst not leave lest they might be murdered, but the good woman hearing the voice of Inglis recognised it, and implored him for the love of God to give them quarter. With an oath he asked who she was that knew his name. She replied that she was the daughter of William Wylie of Darwhilling, in whose house he with others had been quartered for six months some years previous. Sending her soul to perdition, he ordered her to come out. Obeying, he told her that owing to the kindness he had met with at the hands of her father he would grant her friends quarter on condition that they would crawl out of the room on their knees. This they consented to do, and having approached the tyrant in the humiliating position submitted to be bound, and while thus rendered helpless one of their number was deliberately stabbed in the thigh by a soldier who carried a fixed bayonet. This piece of brutality Inglis passionately rebuked, and cursed the man for inflicting a wound upon a prisoner to whom he had given quarter. Having secured their victims, the soldiers next set about plundering the house, which they did so effectually that they did not leave "so much as a spoon or the worth of it" behind them; and to consummate the whole one of the band—whom Sir Walter Scott, who was no great admirer of the Covenanters, has described as "a monster"—chopped the head off the corpse of White with an axe, and conveyed it to Newmilns, where it was used the next day as a kickball on the public green.

Close to the spot where the ashes of James White repose are the graves of three of Lieutenant Nisbet's victims. The spots are marked by simple, rudely-carved slabs, and bear the following inscriptions :—

I.

"Here lies the dust of John Fergushill and George Woodburn, who were shot at Midland by Nisbet and his party. 1685.

> 'When bloody prelates, once these nations' pest,
> Contrived that cursed self-contradicting test,
> These men for Christ did suffer martyrdom,
> And here their dust lies waiting till He come.'

Renewed by subscription 1829."

II.

" Here lyes the corpse of Peter Gemmell, who was shot by Nisbet and his party, anno 1685, for bearing his faithful testimony to the cause of Christ. Aged 21 years.

> 'This man, like holy anchorites of old,
> For conscience sake was thrust from house and hold;
> Bloodthirsty red-coats cut his prayers short,
> And even his dying groans were made their sport.
> Ah, Scotland! breach of solemn vows repent,
> Or bloody crimes will bring thy punishment.' "

It was on a Saturday evening in November, 1685, that the sons of the Covenant mentioned in the above inscriptions met in the old farm-house of Midland, which stood in the vicinity of the village, a short distance from where the modern house and offices now stand. They along with John Nisbet of Hardhill were engaged in devotional exercises when a party of dragoons commanded by Lieutenant Nisbet were observed approaching the house. Escape being impossible, the worshippers set about concealing themselves, and at the same time agreeing in the event of discovery to resist capture as they best could, for they well knew that if they fell into the hands of the soldiery in all probability they would be put to death—an Act being then in force which made it a capital offence to be present at a conventicle. The troop drew up in the farmyard, and made a formal examination of the premises, and lingered about for an hour without suspecting that the prey they were in search of was so near at hand. When riding away they were met by two individuals, one of whom jeeringly cried, "You are guid seekers but ill finders." Acting upon this hint they returned and renewed the search, which resulted in the finding of the fugitives. Being armed, the wanderers fired three shots upon their assailants, and in return received twenty-four, which seemingly did little damage, for they rushed from their concealment and with clubbed guns closed with the foe. The struggle was fierce, and although the dragoons evinced much firmness they had to recede before the desperate men, and ultimately, finding that they could not prevail, a cry was raised amongst them to fire the house. Retreating to the outside of the building, they were closely followed by the four heroes who thus far had bravely defended themselves; but their success was of brief duration, for Nisbet of Hardhill, who had received six wounds, became weak, and he and his friend were soon overpowered, disarmed, and taken prisoners. Gemmell, Woodburn, and Fergushill were taken into a field about a stone-throw from the house and shot (the spot is still pointed out), but Hardhill was too valuable a prisoner to be despatched so hastily, the Council having offered a reward of 3000 merks for his apprehension. With their prisoner the Government butchers rode to Kilmarnock and lodged him in the Tolbooth. Thence he was conveyed to Ayr, and from Ayr to Edinburgh, where after a short imprisonment and hurried trial he was sentenced to be taken to the Grassmarket and executed, and his "lands, goods, and gear to be forfeited to the King's use." He suffered on the 4th of December, 1685, appearing on the scaffold "with a great deal of courage and Christian composure, and dying in much assurance and with a joy which none of his persecutors could intermeddle with."

Woodburn was tenant of Loudoun Mains, a farm about a

mile and a half north-west of Newmilns. He was at the Battle of Drumclog, and for that was a marked man, and from it to the day of his death he was nearly always in hiding. Upon one occasion a dozen troopers who were in search of him came to the Mains, and after fruitlessly examining the premises left, but when a short distance from the house one of the number returned and strictly charged the guidwife to tell George to cover himself better the next time he hid, for he had seen one of his feet sticking through the straw. This traditional anecdote infers that the callousness ascribed to the soldiery was not so general as some writers would have us believe. Woodburn's descendants still occupy the Mains, and a very interesting heirloom in the family is the martyr's sword, an "Andrea Ferara," forty and a half inches long. It is a piece of excellent steel: lately the point was bent to the hilt, and when released sprang back to its wonted straightness.

Peter Gemmell, whom the second stone commemorates, was an ancestor of the mother of Robert Pollock, author of the "Course of Time," and doubtless this fact suggested to her gifted son the pleasing covenanting tale entitled "Ralph Gemmell."

When nearing the churchyard gate I observed a stone indented in the wall to the memory of Robert Buntine and James Blackwood, natives of Fenwick, who were executed for taking part in the rising at Pentland. Buntine was hanged with two others at Glasgow on the 19th December, 1666, and Blackwood passed through the same ordeal at Irvine on the 31st of the same month and year, along with another man named M'Coul. Woodrow states that the two latter were visited a few days before their execution by Alexander Nisbet —the commentator on Ecclesiastes—who found them much cast down; but he cheered and instructed them so in the way of salvation, that "when the day of execution came, they died full of joy and courage, to the admiration of all who were witnesses."

As I passed through the gate of the churchyard into the roadway I thought of the dark days of the Covenant, and of Scotland's noble sons who died for conscience sake, and upheld a great principle during a critical period of our country's history. They fanned the smouldering embers of liberty, they broke up the clods of oppression, and battled for freedom to the death. Yea,

> "Their hearts were firm, and nobly strong,
> To trample under every wrong;
> And stamp, in God's eternal page,
> Their fierce contempt for despot's rage.
> Peace to their ashes! honour'd dust!
> Sleep on, ye noble slumbering just!"

Strolling into Spout-mouth, I stopped before the humble cottage wherein dwelt John Fulton (born 1800, died 1853), the well-known self-taught astronomer. This remarkable genius, who was a working shoemaker, conceived the idea of constructing a mechanical illustration of the structure and movement of the Solar System, and under difficulties that would have disheartened the most sanguine enthusiast, produced his famed Orrery, a greatly admired piece of mechanism, to the construction of which for ten years he devoted his leisure hours. It is now located in the West End Park Museum, Glasgow, and consists of a central frame of movements which cover the orbicular revolutions of the planets, and of the secondary train that controls the axle rotation, and preserves all the relations both to the sun as centre of the system, and to the moon and satellites connected with them. This mechanical arrangement comprises all that had been discovered in his day, with the exception of some small planetary bodies between Mars and Venus. The whole is worked by over two hundred movements, and so admirably adjusted that motion is given with the greatest facility. From Spout-mouth I directed my steps to the highway, and entered the village inn to rest and indulge in a refreshment before starting on a pilgrimage to Lochgoin, for it had been part of my plan at the outset to visit the secluded dwelling of the Howies. Doing ample justice to the viands which the lady at my request placed before me, I started on my viarian excursion with renewed vigour, although I fain would have lingered about the isolated hamlet somewhat longer, but had no time to lose, for the day was wearing through the afternoon, and I well knew that its beauties would soon be on the wane.

From the village of Fenwick Glasgow road rises steadily over a gradual ascent that attains a height of some 700 feet above the level of the sea. It is very picturesque, is lined on either side with neatly-trimmed hedges, and skirted for about three miles by cultivated fields, many of which of late years have been reclaimed by drainage from the bleak moorland that at one time stretched in swampy sterility almost to the village. Beyond that distance the soil gradually loses its fertile appearance, vegetation becomes more stinted, and ultimately on each side of the road a dreary, marshy, barren, trackless waste, dotted here and there by moorland farm-steadings, stretches far beyond the range of vision. But to return. As I plodded onward, listening to the melodious notes of the lark, and to the humble hedge-sparrow chirping forth an accompaniment, I paused now and again to contemplate the beauties of Nature, and scent the sweet aroma that floated on the breeze. While thus engaged, the rumbling of wheels smote my ear. Turning round I observed a horse and cart approaching, and in the driver recognised an honest country chiel' whose acquaintance I had made in the village inn. He recognised me and kindly offered me a lift on the road. I was soon seated beside him, and found him to be most inquisitive; but, notwithstanding this, a very agreeable companion—in fact, one well acquainted with the district through which we were passing, and not slow to communicate all he knew about it. He was curious to know who I was, and what business brought me so far from town, but to each of his queries I gave evasive answers. Not being satisfied, he got on to a new tack, and enquired if I belonged to Kilmarnock. I replied that I did not. " Then," said he, " you'll belang here awa some place." I assured him Ayrshire was not the place of my nativity, " but since you are so anxious to know, I beg to inform you that I am a Cosmopolitan." " A Cosmo what ?" he enquired in amazement. Repeating the word more distinctly, with a perplexedly puzzled look he exclaimed—"Man, I thocht ye were a foreigner o' some kind !" At this I laughed heartily, for it was evident by his stoical gaze that he did not comprehend the meaning of the term. Apologising for my rudeness, a brief explanation made him aware that the goal of my journey was Lochgoin, and its object an examination of the covenanting relics in the possession of the Howies. This so pleased him that he began to speak of that family, and of matters connected with the district through which we were passing, and seemed well acquainted with its lore, and not unqualified to relate its gossip and traditions. Remarking the probability of the moor being the scene of many a well-authenticated tradition, he said everything connected with the Covenanters had been carefully collected; but several traditions of dark deeds which had been perpetrated in the moss were locally popular. "For instance," said he, "pointing to a hollow part of the morass, "that mosshag owre there was counted no canny langsyne." "What was the reason of that?" said I. "Because the body o' a sodger who was robbed and murdered was drawn out o't—the moss refused to conceal the awfu' crime," he replied, in a solemn manner. "I'll tell you how it was," he continued, "for I have heard the story often. A sodger used to travel this road frae Glasco' to Ayr wi' the siller to pay the troops stationed there. The last time he was seen alive was at King's Well, where he exchanged civilities wi' some folk about the door o' the auld inn. Not reaching his destination, a strict search was made for him, but nae tidings o' his whereabouts could be obtained. His horse, however, was found a short distance frae here, but the beast bore nae marks to lead to the supposition that the rider had met wi' foul play. His disappearance was a mystery, and many conjectures were formed about it at the time. Some said that he cut aff wi' the siller; while others affirmed that the siller had been the cause o' his death. Murder, they say, winna hide, and this ane came to light in a very extraordinary manner. Somebody had been crossin' the moss at the place I showed you, an' were horrified to see the hand o' a man stickin' up through the bog. Assistance being procured the body was dragged out, and from its appearance it was evident that a fearful struggle had ta'en place before he yielded his life. Suspicion fell upon a cottar body, frae the circumstance that he had become suddenly weel-to-do. The authorities apprehended him, an' ta'en him to Ayr, where he was tried for the murder; but the evidence being defective, they couldna convict him, an' he was acquitted. He returned to Finnick an' took the farm of ———. It stauns aff the Glasco road—ye nae doubt noticed it as ye entered the village. The descendants of the supposed murderer still occupy the place and are very decent folk." My friend proving excellent company, I kept the conversation in the right groove, and he rattled away at the story telling to his satisfaction and my amusement. "See you house yonder," said he, pointing in the direction with his whip; "it's maist a ruin, but was ance a farm-steading. A near-fisted body o' a farmer leeved in't; but, my certie, he was nicely ta'en to the fair by a sodger." "How did that happen?" I enquired. "Weel, ye see, he hained his meal ae dear year an' selt it at a famine price—for, as I heard my mother say, it was baith scarce and bad. But this is the way the thing happened. A poor woman came to him ae day to buy meal for her family, but when she was about to pay for it, she found hersel' a shillin' short o' the amount; an' though she begged hard for credit, yet the farmer was deaf to her entreaties, an' said that he maun either hae his meal or the shillin'. A sodger travelling to Kilmarnock happened to be at hand, and takin' pity on the puir body, he asked the farmer how muckle she was short. 'Just a shillin',' said he. 'Then, said the sodger, ' here's ane in the king's name.' The farmer took it and gied the woman the meal, wha, after thankin' the sodger, gaed hame to her bairns. The sodger continued his journey, but returned the next day wi' twa companions, and marched the farmer aff to Kilmarnock, where he had to pay the smart, having learned to his cost that caution's needfu' when dealin' wi' recruitin' sergeants."

With such tales as these my companion whiled away the time until we arrived at King's Well, where he stopped to water his horse at a trough by the wayside. Here I took leave of him, and crossed over to an old building, at one time a noted hostelry and a favourite halting place between Kilmarnock and Glasgow in the days of stage-coaches; but

"Thither no more the peasant shall repair
To sweet oblivion of his daily care,
No more the farmer's news, the barber's tale,
No more the woodman's ballad shall prevail;
No more the smith his dusky brow shall clear,
Relax his ponderous strength and lean to hear;
The host himself no longer shall be found
Careful to see the mantling bliss go round;
Nor the coy maid, half willing to be pressed,
Shall kiss the cup to pass it to the rest,"

for solemn silence pervades the spot, and the old inn is converted into a quiet farm-house. King's Well Inn was a place of considerable note for many generations. Before carts were used in Ayrshire there were no regular roads, and goods were conveyed from one place to another on the backs of pack-horses.* About twenty yards to the south of the old inn the remains of a pack-horse track can be distinctly traced for miles across the moor. During the middle of the last century, and ages before it, it was the highway between Glasgow and the west country, and strings of pack-horses passed along it daily, their drivers stopping at the inn for refreshments. Behind the old place there is a little spring called the King's Well, and a short distance from that an ugly-looking marsh called the King's Stable. Local tradition explains the origin of both names, and as it is worth relating, I subjoin it. A fray having taken place during the reign of one of the James's, the monarch determined to learn the facts and administer justice personally. For this purpose he started on a journey to Pathelly Hall, a baronial residence, some slight remains of which still exist in the neighbourhood of King's Well. After a long ride over difficult ground his horse became jaded, and being tired and hungry he determined to alight at the first house he came to and satisfy the craving of his royal stomach. It proved to be a peasant's cottage. Being more needful than nice, he threw the rein over the horse's neck and entered. The goodwife received him graciously, and having learned his desire, set before him scones and milk, the best and readiest meal she had in the house. It was homely fare to place before a king, but royalty was not so fastidious in those days, and could rough it when necessary. After resting and eating heartily he gave his hostess a piece of gold, and was about to depart when she said—" Sir, I ken ye to be the king, an' I ken what brings ye to this part o' the country. Oh! hae mercy on my man." "Who may your

---

* In 1730 the youthful Earl of Loudoun, having occasion to travel from Loudoun Castle to Edinburgh, was placed in a pannier slung across the back of a horse, and, with an attendant mounted on another horse, accomplished the journey of sixty miles in about seven days. Until the genius of Macadam made roads passable in wet weather, it was not uncommon for carriages to sink axle-deep in mud. A good story is told of a man whom a traveller found digging in the highway between Fenwick and King's Well. Upon being asked what he was doing, he replied—" I'm houkin for my horse an' cart."

man be?" he inquired. "He is ane o' the unfortunate men now lying in the dungeon of Pathelly Ha' awaiting your Majestie's pleasure," was the reply. "Being determined to put down lawless raids in my dominion," said the king, "I am afraid I cannot interfere with the course of justice." "Oh, sir," cried the guidwife pleadingly, as she threw herself at his feet; "shurely you'll never hang a man after having eaten his bread an' rested yoursel' in his arm chair." This appeal was too much for the monarch. He raised the suppliant to her feet, promised to bear the request in mind, and proceeded on his journey. When near the inn his horse stopped at a little spring, out of which it drank—hence the name *King's Well*—but proceeded only a short distance afterwards when it became bogged, and sank in the ugly-looking marsh already referred to, his Majesty saving himself with considerable difficulty. Making the best of his way to the inn, he was met by the landlord, who enquired about his horse. "It is stabled," replied the monarch jocularly, and so the swamp retains the name of the *King's Stable* to this day. From the inn the King walked to Pathelly Hall. The same evening he had the prisoners brought before him, and commenced an examination which resulted in his finding eighteen of them guilty. These he ordered to be hanged on a thorn tree, which is still pointed out and looked to from the circumstance with a kind of superstitious dread. The husband of his hostess, whom he had singled out, was admonished and dismissed with a caution that if ever he was found in a like fault all the old wives in Christendom would not save him from the wuddie.

Observing an elderly dame at the doorway of a cottage dividing her attention between me and the culinary operation of scraping a porridge-pot, I asked my way to Lochgoin, and was kindly conducted by her to a beaten track running zig-zag through the moss. Pointing across the moor to some solitary trees about a mile and a half distant, she told me they grew in the garden of the spot I was in search of, and whatever I did I was to keep them in sight, "for," said she, "gin ye loss the foot-road—as maist likely ye will—ye may wander for hours i' the contra direction." Tendering thanks, I bade her goodbye and entered the heathy wilderness, deeply impressed with the bleak desolation, yet wild grandeur of the scene. The heather waved in brown luxuriance, and its bonnie bell was a sweet recompense for the absence of the wild flowers which Nature strews so profusely over the fields and by the dusty waysides. Onward and onward I held along the mossy, heather-fringed path, listening to the varied sounds which occasionally broke the profound silence that prevailed. Now the hum of the *foggie* or moss bee would make the air musical; then the cry of the peesweep and the whirr and cock-cock of the moorfowl would be heard as they winged their aerial flight across the barren waste.

While thus revelling amid the beauties of Nature and musing on the brave men who lurked in these wilds, I forgot the instructions of the good lady at King's Well, nor did I think upon them until my progress was stopped by a broad, deep ditch—a kind of receptacle or main artery of numerous open drains which intersect the moor, for by this means large tracks are rendered comparatively dry and excellent stock reared upon them. The little path I sought, but it could not be found; it was lost and so was I, for heather-clad hills rose on each side of me, and Lochgoin standing in its solitude, which I beheld a few minutes before, was nowhere to be seen. Climbing the nearest height, I again got a glimpse of it, but despairing of ever finding the track at once struck for the solitary dwelling in as straight a line as the marshy nature of the soil would permit of. Travelling now proved both difficult and dangerous. Owing to recent rains, pools of black moss water often proved an insurmountable impediment, and I had to circumvent them by the best means possible. Sometimes in leaping I would miss my mark and go plump over the ankles in water; at other times, when seeking aid from my stick, the weight of my body would sink it to the handle in the bog—a circumstance that oftener than once brought me to grief. Persistent perseverance, however, brought this kind of travelling to an end and I to the spot which I had long been desirous of seeing.

The present house of Lochgoin is a one-storeyed, slate-roofed, plain building, internally commodious and well suited for a moorland farm-steading. It is erected on the site of an old, and from its associations a very interesting, building.

On the lintel of the door several dates are inscribed, which refer to changes which the family or their dwelling have undergone. The first of these, 1178, is said to be the year in which the first of the Howies of Lochgoin took up their abode in the fastness of the moss. The family tradition has it that they were two brothers who fled from one of the Waldensian valleys to escape persecution. Behind the house there is a small kailyard which John Howie called his "garden of herbs." It served as his study, for in a corner of it, beneath the shelter of a turf dyke, he is said to have written a considerable part of his "Scots Worthies." To the south of the house, on the edge of the moor, there is a cairn which marks the graves of two children who died of the plague in 1665. A party who came from Glasgow, where it was then raging, divided an apple between them, which they had no sooner eaten than symptoms of the disease manifested itself upon them. The inmates of Lochgoin were so terrified that they put the children in an outhouse and fled. One more courageous than the rest returned and handed food to them through a window on the end of a stick, but although death in a brief space ended their sufferings, no one in the locality could be found to give them burial, and an individual had to be brought from Glasgow to perform the rite.

Lochgoin stands nine hundred and fourteen feet above the level of the sea, and commands a magnificent view of the surrounding country. This circumstance rendered it a safe resort to the hunted, outlawed supporters of the Covenant in the days of the persecution. About one hundred yards from the house there is an artificial eminence which was used during that critical period to watch for the approach of the soldiery or other unwelcome visitors, and on several occasions warning was given by the sentinel stationed upon it to refugees in time to allow them to escape to the fastness of the moss, where it was impossible for man or horse to follow. Being delighted with the wild beauty of the landscape around the lone habitation, I ascended the mound and rapturously gazed on the vast expanse of country. Away to the west is "Auld Kilmarnock" and the romantic district surrounding it —a district that will be ever dear to my heart, and whose scenes and associations shall never be eradicated from my mind so long as reason holds its sway or memory its power. Beyond is a wide expanse of sea, backed by the lofty heights of Arran, and a little to the west of them is Ailsa Craig, a well-known rugged rock which towers from the deep. To the west the sterile moor, studded here and there with farm-steadings, stretches away in barren bleakness. Beyond it the fertile and richly-wooded district of Loudoun, and the conic form of Loudoun Hill, near which was fought the memorable Battle of Drumclog. To the north in the far distance the eye rests delighted upon the Highland hills, the most prominent of which are Ben Lomond, Ben Voirlich, Ben Ledi, and Ben Cruachan. But my description is inadequate—the scene must be seen to be *felt*.

From the mound I directed my steps to the door of the house, and timorously knocked. It was opened by the wife of the present occupant, who seemingly guessed the purport of my visit, for she invited me into the kitchen and requested me to be seated. Telling her that I had made a pilgrimage from Kilmarnock to view the interesting Covenanting relics, she smilingly expressed the pleasure it gave her to comply with my wish. "We are aye glad to see strangers," said she; "mony folk, baith gentle and simple, come here. 'Deed," she continued, "I think the feck o' the religious world hae visited Lochgoin to see the bits o' things preserved in the family—they come frae America an' a' airts. But gae awa' ben," said she, addressing a boy, "an' bring the drum but the house." In a short time I had the relics laid before me, and during a running conversation with my hostess and other members of the family examined them at my leisure. They consisted of the Bible and sword of Captain Paton, a drum and drum-stick which are said to have been at Drumclog, and a flag which waved over the same field; also a number of silver coins.

Captain Paton's Bible is a small 24mo, dated 1653, and contains the hero's autograph on the blank side of the title-page. It is encased in a small box with a glass front, this precaution being necessary to prevent visitors pilfering the leaves, several of them being carried away. Curious enough the book ends with Rev. xii. 11, "And they overcame him by the blood of the Lamb and by the word of their testimony; and they loved not their lives unto death." On the outside of the cover is the following inscription:—

"Captain John Paton's Bible,
Which he gave to his wife from off the
Scaffold when he was executed for
The cause of Jesus Christ,
At Edinburgh, on the 8th of May, 1684,
James Howie received it from the
Captain's son's daughter's husband,
And gave it to John Howie, his nephew."

The *sword* is a light, basket-handled, short shabble, twenty-seven and a half inches long. It is said to contain twenty-eight gaps or notches, which represent the years of the persecution, but I saw no trace of them. It is very rusty and much worn, and altogether in bad condition, and nothing to compare to the formidable weapon in the possession of Thomas Rowatt, Esq. of Bonnanhill, Strathaven.

The *drum* has much the appearance of an extra deep American cheese-box. The sheepskin still adheres to one end of it. The frame and fastenings are of the rudest description, and bear ample traces of home manufacture; in fact, it is just such an instrument as a rude peasant with limited tools and material might be expected to produce. The drum-stick (there is but one) is neat and possessed of a modern-like appearance.

The *flag* is six feet in length by five in breadth. It is supposed to have waved at the Battle of Drumclog, but little is known regarding it save that it has been in the family from a very remote period. Repeated washings have sadly defaced it, but nevertheless it has an antiquated and time-worn appearance. It bears the following device and inscription:—On the left a rude picture of an open Bible, and on the right the form of a crown and thistle. Beneath is "Phinick for God, Country, and Covenanted Work of Reformations."

The *silver coins* are twenty-two in number; they are heavy and not unlike our five-shilling pieces. The earliest bears the date of 1597, and is inscribed, "*Deus fortitudo et spes nostra*," *i.e.*, "God is our strength and hope." They are contained in a small box, and form the greatest curiosity of the antiquities. Like everything else they have a history, and it is simply this:—When James Howie, who suffered so much during the persecution, was fleeing from the approaching soldiery he hid his purse in the ground, about fifty yards from the house, expecting to find it when his enemies departed. He never discovered it again, but a man who was serving about the place was accused of purloining it, and although he stoutly denied the charge, yet the accusation stuck to him till the day of his death. Some fifty years ago, when a son of the author of the "Scots Worthies" was driving some cows to pasture, the hoof of one slipped and disclosed something bright. Upon examination it proved to be a large silver piece. This led to a search, and others were discovered along with the remains of a purse, which cleared the mystery and the memory of the guiltless servant. Besides these relics there is one not less interesting to the antiquarian, viz., the library, which contains some curious and rare volumes and pamphlets. Several are from the pen of the somewhat eccentric author whose writings have made the remote farm-steading famous.

There is not a vestige left of the old house of Lochgoin. From age it became so ruinous that it had to be taken down, but its form and appearance will long be familiar, numerous sketches and photographs of it being preserved. It was under its thatch-covered roof that the celebrated John Howie, author of the "Scots Worthies" and other works of less note, was born. The event occurred on the 14th November, 1735. His great work was written during the intervals of labour and in hours snatched from sleep. The first edition appeared in 1774, and a second, greatly enlarged, in 1785. The "Scots Worthies" is a work that has long been popular with all classes of society, and, like the "Pilgrim's Progress," it will be treasured by the religious world so long as Presbyterianism continues to influence the minds of the Scottish people. John Howie, after an uneventful life distinguished for its humility and piety, died in the spring of 1793, and is interred, as already stated, in the churchyard of Fenwick. In an entry in his diary, written shortly before his death, he humbly reflects upon the vanities of life, and sums up his existence in few words. He says—"When I look back upon my short and despicable life I find it altogether made up of deficiencies, faults, and imperfections." We may all say amen to this, for the good we do is the least of our lives. At the period of the persecution drainage was not practised, and from its situation Lochgoin was almost inaccessible. Horsemen could only approach it from the east, and that at the risk of being bogged, while no foot passenger unless well acquainted with the locality could reach it from any other quarter without endangering his life, the bog being so soft in many places that a dog could not cross it. A situation like this was invaluable as a place of resort to Covenanters, and to it the utmost vigilance of the dragoons was naturally directed. Twelve times was the house plundered, and as often did the inmates escape. The winter after the rising at Pentland, about twenty persons, amongst whom was Captain Paton, met one night at Lochgoin for the purpose of fellowship and godly conversation. The old man of the house being unwell went to bed, fell asleep, and dreamed that he saw the troopers approaching. Wakening, he told the dream to the company, and advised them to disperse. They did so, but were only a short time away when the soldiers entered. Upon another occasion the Captain and several others were sheltering in the house, and were all but taken prisoners. At the time, a party of troopers were scouring the country for suspected persons. Going to Meadowhead they did not meet with anything of a suspicious nature, and next rode to Croilburn, a sequestered house in Fenwick Moor. Being disappointed there also, they set off to Lochgoin—five men, under the command of one Sergeant Rae, being sent forward. The night—a stormy one—favoured their approach upon the unsuspecting wanderers, who had been watching the most of the night. At break of day a man named Woodburn left the house to reconnoitre, but being more prayerful than watchful he did not observe Rae and his companions coming stealthily along. He had scarce returned when the Sergeant presented himself at the door and cried out, "Dogs, I have found you now." Mrs Howie, supposing he was alone, cried to her friends to "run to the hills and not be killed in the house." Then running at the intruder she gave that pompous individual such a push that he went sprawling on the broad of his back in the mud before the door. While he was star-gazing in this humiliating and unsoldier-like position, the fugitives got out and ran into the moor. Regaining his feet, he fired his gun; but one, John Kirkland, stopped in his flight and returned the compliment, firing so surely that his bullet took off the knot of hair on the side of the wrathful functionary's head. Captain Paton and his companions made for Eaglesham Moor at their utmost speed, pursued by the whole troop. Two of the Covenanters who were armed brought up the rear, and kept the troopers in check by now and again firing upon them. Kirkland, kneeling, aimed so well that he shot a Highland sergeant through the thigh. This had the effect of stopping the pursuers and allowing the fugitives to gain ground. Arriving at the moor of Eaglesham, they caused the Captain, who was old and not able to keep up with his companions, to take a route by himself. This he did. Meeting with a horse in a field he took the liberty to mount it, and was enabled to get out of the reach of the enemy by its aid. Meeting with a party of dragoons coming from Newmilns he saw that flight was useless; so, making the best of matters, he rode slowly past them, and got off undiscovered. The horse being set at liberty returned home and he concealed himself in one of his lurking places. The troopers, foiled of their prey, returned to Lochgoin and set about wrecking and plundering the house. Coming upon a Bible, it is said that "they burned it in the fire in a most audacious manner." They next drove off the cattle, and left behind a ruined habitation. There are accounts of many other raids on Lochgoin, but these will suffice to give the reader some little idea of what brave, unselfish men suffered in those troublesome times for liberty and truth.

After chatting pleasantly with the inmates of Lochgoin and listening to several local traditions of the Covenant, I made known my intention of departing, being desirous of reaching home before the red streaks of sunset tinged the western sky. The announcement was met by the kindly request of "rest you a wee," but that was impossible; go I must—therefore I siezed my hat and stick with the air of a man not to be turned from his purpose, and after a brief conversation by way of preface to departure, was accompanied to the door by my newly-found friends, all of whom urged me to return at an early date and "hae a crack," especially since a cart road was made to the very door, and the danger attending the crossing of the moss had become unnecessary. Thanking them for their kindness I took my leave, struck through the moss in a southerly direction, and after a toilsome journey of a very long hour reached the farm of Duntan, which stands close to the bank of a mossy and not unpicturesque streamlet. On its eastern bank, close to the farm, there is an aperture in a rocky precipice called Duntan Cove, which afforded shelter to Covenanters during the troublous times of the persecution. I with difficulty entered it and found it to be a small natural cavern capable of accommodating half-a-dozen individuals, but containing no feature of interest. Often the wanderers made the Cove their lair, and found shelter within it from the pitiless storm and the rage of their persecutors. Tradition tells how two men who ran before a company of troopers for their very lives dashed through the stream, scaled the rock, and sought refuge in its bosom; and how the ruffians rode up and discharged their carabines into the aperture, believing that instead of an asylum the fugitives had found a grave, but it was otherwise. They crouched in the farthest recess and frustrated the diabolical purpose of their assailants. From the Cove I strayed along the bank of the stream, and after passing a number of houses clustering round a wool mill, a walk of about two miles through a district in which the bleak moor was gradually blended into fields which spoke of culture and gave promise of a rich harvest, brought me to Midland, the farm on which three of Lieutenant Nisbet's victims were shot. They lie in loving nearness in Fenwick churchyard, and of the incidents attending their murder the reader has already been made acquainted. A little below Midland I crossed the "Kirk-town" bridge, passed up the lane already noticed, which runs in the vicinity of the little churchyard wherein "the martyrs soundly sleep." From High Fenwick a sharp walk brought me to Laigh Fenwick, where, feeling tired and exhausted, I entered the house of Agnes Scott, who retails provisions and a good dram, to rest and partake of refreshment, for walking had become a toil, and the road between me and my home a matter of serious consideration. However, it is wonderful what a "wee drap o' the barley bree" can do when judiciously administered, for I got over the road wonderfully, and arrived in Kilmarnock as the shades of night were closing over the old town, after a pleasant journey to scenes rendered famous by the Covenanters.

CHAPTER IX.

The influence of sunshine—Glasgow Road and its scenery—An Adventure—Specimens of Kilmaurs cutlery—The Reservoir—From it to Rowallan Castle—The situation and appearance of the Castle described—The interior of the building—The garden—A fox story—Traditions.

"I say, wife! bring my heavy boots and walking-stick, the morning is delightful, it is a pity to remain indoors upon such a day as this is likely to be. I will take a turn in the country, so you may expect me home in the afternoon." Twirling my staff and bidding the children "ta-ta," I sallied forth in quest of adventure and curiosities. Passing along the street I could not help noticing the effect that a sunshiny morning has upon men and things in general. The thatched cottages which are so primitive and dingy-looking during inclement weather appeared snug and somewhat picturesque in the sunshine. Mirthful sounds of youthful voices were borne upon the breeze, and fell upon my ear like sweet music, as the little men and women who will take our places in society gamboled in the sheen of the bright orb. Sour-visaged people jostled each other on the pavement, and looked as if the sunshine had caused them to forget their crotchets and crosses for a space. In fact, the very dogs seemed to trot along more cheerfully and bark their congratulations to each other as if they really enjoyed themselves. Passing through the Cross —that centre for business, and loungers of all grades—I ascended Portland Street, passed under the railway bridge, and straight ahead. Arriving at Beausburn Toll, I looked down upon the Foundry Holm and upon the Forge and other buildings which stand black and unsightly in the valley below. To the right, on the top of a steep bank clothed with wood, is the handsome family residence of the late Bailie Craig. The place is called Dean Hill. It is finely situated and commands an extensive view of the town and country. Passing some neat villas on my left, I strayed onward admiring the scenery, which presents an agreeably diversified landscape of gentle rising grounds, sloping fields, numerous enclosures, and clumps of planting, until I came to a part of the road where the top of Dean Castle, roofless, time-shattered, and ruinous looms from the hollow, and reminded me of the following lines of Turnbull:—

> " See where the Dean her ruin'd fabric rears!
> A mournful scene her naked wall appears;
> The clasping ivy shades her tottering towers,
> Where night-owls form their melancholy bowers.
> Prone from the top, huge ruined fragments fall;
> The howling wind sounds dreary in the hall;
> No more the voice of mirth is heard to sound,
> But melancholy silence reigns around."

Passing Wardneuk, a small farm-steading on the left, a fine view of Assloss House and romantic surroundings is obtainable. It stands on the top of some thickly-wooded rising ground, at the foot of which, in a hollow a short distance from the road, flows the Borland Water, limpid and unpolluted, with trees laving their branches in its liquid, and trout sporting in its channel. A sharp walk soon brought me in sight of the Reservoir and South Craig, a neat farm-house that stands off the road to the left. Having heard that the occupants of North Craig—which lies at the back of South Craig—are in the possession of some cutlery of Kilmaurs manufacture, I determined to visit the farm, and if possible get a sight of the relics. For this purpose I turned into a bye-road on the left, but had not proceeded far when I found myself confronted by a powerful sheep-dog, which seemed inclined to dispute the passage, for it growled and showed its teeth, then barked furiously, as if it meant mischief. Fearing that the animal might mistake my leg for a marrow bone, I grasped my stick firmly and dealt it a whack across the nose that left a striking impression on its memory, for it dashed through the hedge and tore over a field at the top of its speed, howling forth an apology in a most unearthly manner, and leaving me master of the situation. The coast being clear I proceeded on my way, and without further adventure arrived at North Craig. This farm is at present occupied by the widow and son of the late Daniel Thomson. Here I met with a cordial reception. They expressed the pleasure that my visit afforded, and seemed glad to see strangers, and happy to submit to the curious the small specimens of Kilmaurs cutlery they are possessed of. Having seated myself in the spacious kitchen, which was scrupulously clean, Mrs. Thomson produced from a leather case the relics. They proved to be a small silver-mounted knife and fork of very plain make, but having the appearance of considerable antiquity. The knife is worn in the blade and stamped near the handle with the letters A and B, which is affirmed to stand for Alexander Bigger, the maker. The fork is two-pronged and has much the appearance of a miniature hay-fork, the make and finish being most primitive. These specimens of ancient cutlery belonged to the great-grandmother of the late Mr. Thomson, by whom they were greatly prized; but I am sure not more so than they are by the present owner, who values them highly, not for their intrinsic value, but as relics that link the present with past generations of the family. I have no doubt of the authenticity of the specimens. In proof of it I may mention that a Kilmarnock gentleman who is well known for his antiquarian knowledge was so anxious to possess them that he tempted the proprietor with a round sum; but it was respectfully declined. Bidding North Craig good-bye I entered the property of the Kilmarnock Water Company to view the reservoir and filtering basins. Mr. Reid, the superintendent, received me kindly, conducted me over the works, and explained the process through which the water passes before it is rendered fit for domestic purposes. After a little conversation, I ascended a wooden stair and reached the top of an embankment which surrounds what appears to be a lake of considerable extent. The position is commanding, and from it an extensive view of the surrounding country is obtainable. This sheet of water is the reservoir from which the inhabitants of Kilmarnock draw their supply after it passes through the filters. It stands about 250 feet above the level of the town, and covers over twenty imperial acres of land. When full it holds 900,000 square yards of water, which is equal to 65,000,000 gallons. Its tributaries are burns, which for the most part take their rise in Fenwick Moor, every precaution being taken to exclude moss water and other impurities. The Kilmarnock Water Company was formed in 1850. To it the inhabitants of the town are indebted, for at a small cost they are supplied with water of uniform purity, which not only serves for domestic purposes, but purges cesspools, sewers, etc., of disease-engendering ingredients, and in a great measure assists to preserve the health of the townspeople. Thanking the worthy superintendent for his kindness, I bade him goodbye, and leisurely strolled along the bank of the Reservoir until I came to a stile road. Following its course I passed Tannahill, a neat farm-steading, and soon arrived in the road which runs between Kilmaurs and Fenwick.

Turning to the right, a short walk along the dusty highway brought me to the gate of the avenue leading to Rowallan Castle, the shattered stronghold of the Mures, an ancient Scottish family, the last male representative of whom died in 1700. Passing through the gateway, a pleasant walk brought me to the edge of a dark wood. Here, upon turning to the right, a delightfully picturesque scene burst upon my vision. Giant trees stretched their arms over the path, and flowers of various hues bloomed in wild luxuriance along the wayside. In the wood the feathered throng poured forth a flood of song, and all seemed combined to lift the mind " from nature up to nature's God," and say—

> " Fair nature's face before thee lies,
> Her coverlet the rainbow dyes,
> Whilst up to thy delighted eyes
> Her varied beauties start.
> There's summer in each sight and sound,
> There's God and glory all around !
> Then let no wintry feelings wound
> The gladness of thy heart."

Walking leisurely along the rustic avenue, enjoying its beauties, I ultimately came to the end of the wood, and looked down upon Rowallan Castle. The scene was delightful, and amply compensated my walk from the town. Rowallan is not, strictly speaking, a castle; it has more the appearance of an ancient manor-house, and doubtless is a good specimen of the fortified feudal residences in the olden time. The building, viewed from the roadway, looks hoary and venerable, and wears a mouldering, deserted appearance. It is situated in a hollow, and is environed with trees, many of which have braved the blast for centuries, and still wave their branches as majestically as they did in days of yore, when knights and ladies gay walked beneath their shadows.

Near to the venerable building flows the Carmel, a mossy stream. It is spanned by a bridge, and takes a fine curve as it flows past the old place, after dancing through dusky glens and over rugged rocks. Crossing the stream, I aimlessly strayed through the grounds, and noted each gnarled tree and object of interest. While thus engaged I was accosted by the gamekeeper—a burly Englishman—who, finding me a stranger, conversed freely, and told me all he knew regarding the venerable pile and its surroundings. He also proffered to introduce me to the people who have charge of the castle, so that I might view the interior as well as the exterior of the edifice. Accepting his invitation, I met with a kindly reception from Mrs Dale, who along with her husband occupies a room in the building, and whose untiring industry and cleanly habits gives to the place a charm, and robs it of that dreary, sad appearance so peculiar to deserted half-ruinous buildings. Rowallan Castle has the appearance of having been built at different periods. The oldest and most dilapidated portion seems to have been erected upon the top of a rock, or crag, and probably has been surrounded at some period by a lake. The marshy nature of the ground near its base goes a considerable way to support this supposition. The ground chambers of this portion only remain, and are in a very ruinous and crumbling condition, portions of their roofs having fallen in. Historians assign it as the birth-place of Elizabeth Muir, the beloved wife of Robert II., king of Scotland. The more modern building faces the south, and is divided from the older by a loopholed wall some forty feet long. In it there is an ornamented gateway, above which the date 1666 is still legible. The front of the building has a very imposing appearance, and bears many sculptured devices. To the principal door—which is of oak, and studded with iron—there is a flight of broad stone steps. Over this entrance the family arms, surmounted by the Royal Arms of Scotland, are cut in stone. In execution the sculpture is somewhat rude, but even at this day it looks well, although chipped and disfigured. Above these devices is the crest of the family—a Moor's head—which, doubtless, is allusive to a war-like exploit performed by some member during the crusades against the Saracens. Above all, and at the top of the building, there is a small tablet with the following inscription:—" JON. MVR. M. CVGM. SPVSIS. 1562." To the right and left of the tablet, the armorial bearings of John Mure, of Rowallan, and his lady, Marion Cunningham, are quartered. From this it may be inferred that this portion of the building was erected by them at the above date. There are many other sculptured adornments, dates, and devices, but the above are most noteworthy, and are sufficient to induce the antiquary, and the lover of the picturesque, to visit this really interesting castle. Passing up the stairs, and through the doorway referred to, the visitor finds himself in a small courtyard and surrounded by architecture, the style of which ranges from the fifteenth to the end of the seventeenth century. Near the centre of the court grows a sombre yew tree, which accords in a manner with the ruinous and deserted appearance of the building. The first indication that the place is partly inhabited is a neatly whitened step in front of a finely carved oaken door. This is the entrance to the apartment occupied by the keeper, and, in fact, to the interior of the castle. There are a few relics of past greatness preserved. In the old dining-room there is an elaborately-carved sideboard and an old arm chair which bears the date of 1617. These are of oak, and very interesting. In a small room, called "Lord Loudoun's sleeping apartment," there is a beautifully carved wardrobe in oak. The room door and pannelling are of the same material, and chastely ornamental. The next room of interest is at the top of the building, and is called "the auld kirk." Here are shown several fragments of kirk stools, which are for the most part moth-eaten and rotten. In this apartment the distinguished William Guthrie of Fenwick is said to have occasionally preached, and the pious Sir William Mure to have met with his tenantry to worship the God of their fathers. In almost every room throughout the building every available portion of space on the walls is covered by names and addresses. Though hundreds have been wiped off, yet visitors resort to all manner of schemes to make their mark. Some have burst into poetry, and recorded their visit upon the walls in verse. I attempted to transcribe a rhyme written in a neat hand, but the lines limped so badly that I left them to the obliviating dishclout of Mrs. Dale. Among the signatures, initials, and addresses pencilled upon the walls,

I noticed the names of several Kilmarnock celebrities; but the most conspicuous was that of a popular clergyman, whose name and place of worship were recorded in large letters. At the back of the castle there is an old garden, but it does not contain anything of historical interest. There are some fine old trees about it, and altogether it is worthy of the visitor's attention. I may mention in passing that at that time there was a zoological curiosity in it. Foxes abound in the district, and two of these animals had taken up their abode in the old place. One of them had made its lair under a bush, while the other—contrary to the habits of the animal—had taken up its quarters in the branches of a fine old tree, and looked down from its hiding upon all passing below. The fox is proverbial for its cunning, but there was something in the conduct of these two that almost amounted to reason. Mrs. Dale, like all thrifty housewives in the country, kept a goodly number of hens, but it was curious that she never missed one, although they frequented the garden, and fed within a few yards of where the foxes were secreted. These animals seemed to discriminate between her property and that of other people, and to understand that if they molested the poultry they would require to shift. If food were scarce, however, I am afraid that they would not observe this distinction. Upon one occasion the occupant of the tree while out on its rambles, crossed the path of a pack of hounds, and started for home with the whole at its heels, greatly to the delight of the huntsmen. Being hotly pursued, it with difficulty reached the castle, bounded over the garden wall, and, to the astonishment of the dogs, disappeared. The huntsmen came up, and were equally puzzled, and would have gone in search of another of Reynard's kindred, had not a keeper climbed up the tree and dislodged the occupant. Leaping into the middle of the pack, the fox got off unscathed, and ran in the direction of Fenwick. Its adventures by the way are unrecorded; but to the surprise of every one, it was back to its old quarters the next day, peering down from among the branches as if nothing particular had happened. In spite of props and screws, the walls of Rowallan Castle are fast going to ruin. Time, the inexorable tyrant, is playing sad havoc with the building, and is imperceptibly but surely crumbling it to pieces. As in the case of other buildings in the same condition, tradition has twined itself around that of Rowallan, and many tales, probable and improbable, are related in connection with it. The great enemy of mankind is said to have visited the place upon several occasions and done his utmost to destroy it and its occupants. It has long been noted as the haunt of ghosts, witches, and things uncanny ; but these chimeras of the brain have fled before the fearless spirit of investigation now abroad, and the ploughboy can pass the venerable pile at night, without

"Whistling up Lord Lennox' march
To keep his courage cheery."

I will now relate two or three of the popular traditions of Rowallan Castle, which I trust will be sufficient to gratify the reader's curiosity and his love for folk-lore. The tradition of how Rowallan derived its name is very prettily told by the Rev. George Paxton, a Secession Church minister of Kilmaurs. He was pastor in the ancient village from 1789 to 1807, and the author of a volume entitled "The Villager, and other poems." In some verses to the Carmel he refers to the tradition in the following beautiful language :—

"A Scottish chief in days of old,
As hoary-headed sires have told,
 Was tossed upon the main;
Small was the skiff, the tempest blew,
The trembling chieftain urged the crew
 The distant shore to gain.

'Row! Allan, row!' the baron cried,
'High on the foaming surges ride,
 And bear me safe to shore;
A rich domain on Carmel side,
O'er hill and dale extending wide,
 Is thine for evermore.'

The quivering oar bold Allan stretched,
The solid land the baron reached,
 And Allan won the prize;
Adorned with ropes of twisted stone,
Long on thy banks Rowallan shone,
 And still the storm defies."

I have heard the tradition related differently, but I think the above is its most pleasing and poetic form. The next tradition to which I will draw attention refers to no less a personage than his satanic majesty. A minor poet of Stewarton has thrown it into verse, and indeed the subject, though a little sulphurous, looks best in that form.

> " 'Tis said, one wintry night of yore
> Were met a happy throng
> Within Rowallan's festive hall,
> Where all was mirth and song;
> When, crashing through the nestling trees,
> Auld Nick came in a blue-shot bleeze,
> By witch-wife conjured, to affright
> For grave abuse or cutting spite.
> But little ken'd that sinner warm
> That in the castle lay a charm
> Which Auld Nick's magic could dispel,
> And send him baffled hame. Ah! well,
> Will he go in ? he takes the road.
> 'Avaunt thou, in the name of God!'
> The parson cried, and then brought down
> His Bible whack on Auld Nick's crown.
> As when the hunter's well-aimed dart
> Strikes through the savage tiger's heart,
> Sudden he leaped, and gave a roar
> That rent the stair and burst the door,
> Then, like a rocket through the night,
> In flame of fire passed out of sight."

If the reader has any doubt of the above he had better go to the castle and examine the stair leading to the principal door. He will find it rent. The crack is best seen in wet weather. Tradition says that the stair was split by the hoof of the devil under similar circumstances to those embodied in the above metrical relation. If the tradition be true, then "the old boy" has a powerful pair of legs. Near to the castle, and on the top of a steep bank clothed with wood, overlooking a chasm through which the Carmel gurgles, is a stately tree with spreading branches and wealth of foliage. It is known by the name of "the marriage tree," and the bank on which it grows is called "Janet's Kirn." Beneath this monarch of the wood (tradition says) Dame Jean Mure, of Rowallan, was married by a curate to William Fairlie of Bruntsfield, an estate near Edinburgh, somewhere about the year 1700. The lady being sole heiress to the castle and estate of Rowallan, had many suitors for her hand and fortune. Amongst them was her future husband, Fairlie. Some obstacle now unknown stood in the way of their union, and she eloped with him. Tradition adds further that the lady left the castle by a window in the courtyard, which is still pointed out, and met her lover, who had a clergyman in readiness to perform the marriage ceremony. The spot where the marriage is said to have taken place is not more than a stone's throw from the road leading to the house of the gamekeeper. It is romantically picturesque, but is forbidden to visitors. I will notice one more tradition and pass on. The visitor to Rowallan will notice two bridges in front of the castle. One spans the Carmel and the other what is known as the Mill Lade. This lade or burn is a branch off the Fenwick Water. Long ago it used to turn the wheel of Rowallan Mill, but the mill is now in ruins, and the wheel no longer performs splashing music on the bank of the mossy stream. I have heard the following tradition related in connection with it:—Once on a time the cutlers and tinkers of Kilmaurs, finding the Carmel insufficient to supply their wants, petitioned the King to grant a greater supply of water. The King (it does not matter which) replied that he would grant as much from the Fenwick river as would flow through the leg of a boot. This they gratefully accepted, and formed an artificial stream between it and the Carmel. The lade is said to be that stream; it flows through a beautiful track of country, and in some parts retains traces of artificial construction.

CHAPTER X.

The origin and descent of the Mures of Rowallan—A letter from Queen Mary to Sir John Mure—Sir William Mure: his writings and version of Psalm xxiii.: events in his life—The last of the Mures—The late Countess of Loudoun's attachment to the Castle—The Grounds the resort of pleasure parties—An Address to Rowallan—A ride into the town.

I WILL now as briefly as possible glance at the history of the Rowallan family, and bring this ramble to a close. The source from which I principally derive my information is a curious volume entitled "The Historie and Descent of the House of Rowallane, by Sir William Mure, knight of Rowallan. Written in or prior to 1657." The manuscript of the above work, together with a number of poetical pieces from the pen of the same author, was found among some old family papers in one of the rooms in Rowallan Castle some fifty years ago. The book is both interesting and curious, and throws considerable light upon the manners and customs of our forefathers in bygone ages, when might was right, and when a strong arm and a bright blade were often the only title to broad acres. The style of the book is simple, and the editor has retained all the peculiarities of the manuscript, which greatly enhance the value of the work. Rowallan, according to this authority, had been in the possession of the Mures "from unknawne antiquity," but this is questionable; for it is the opinion of various writers that Polkelly was the first inheritance of the family, and that Rowallan was acquired by the marriage of Isabella, daughter of Sir Gilchrist Mure, during the reign of Alexander III. The Mures of Rowallan (the writer of "The Historie" states) were descended from the ancient tribe of O'More in Ireland. The surname of Mure in Scotland, Moore in England, and More in Ireland, are synonymous, all having sprung from the same source. The earliest member of the family spoken of is the Sir

Gilchrist Mure already referred to. He was dispossessed of the house and living at Rowallan by the strong hand of Sir Walter Cuming, and compelled to keep close in his castle of Polkelly until the King (Alexander III.) raised sufficient forces to subdue Cuming and his adherents. In 1262 Sir Gilchrist fought at the Battle of Largs. His friends and retainers, led on by himself, behaved with such bravery that the King conferred upon him the honour of knighthood, and "reponed to him his whole inheritance." For the sake of peace, and for his own security, Sir Gilchrist married his daughter Isabella to Sir Walter Cuming. At the death of Cuming Sir Gilchrist "secured not only title and full possession of his old inheritance, but also in his border lands quherin he succeeded to Sir Walter foresaid within the Sherefdome of Roxburgh, being sensible and mindful of the deserving of his friends and followers in time of his troubles, deals with all of them as became a man of honour, bestowing freelie vpon each some parcell of land, according to his respect, interest, or (happly) promise to the persone," etc. Sir Gilchrist seemingly greatly increased the possessions of the Mures. He died about the year 1280, nearly eighty years of age, and was interred in the Mures' Isle, Kilmarnock. Sir Gilchrist was succeeded by his son Archibald, who was slain in battle near Berwick in 1289. He is described as being a man "wt much discreation & judgment," and capable of holding his own "in the turbulent times qurin he lived." Sir Archibald was succeeded by his son and heir, William, who, according to the "Historie," died about the time King David, after his return from France, was taken prisoner at the Battle of Durham. This battle was fought upon the 17th October, 1346. During the early part of this knight's lifetime Scotland was brought "to a verie lo ebb, being deserted by the nobilitie, till by the valour of William Wallace it was set againe upon the feet, and after his death established by Robert Bruce, who, having outwrestled many sad calamities, did (after) successfully sway the cepter." Sir William was succeeded by his son Adame— a shrewd man of business, who greatly improved and enlarged the family inheritance. His eldest son was named after himself, and his daughter Elizabeth was "made choyce of (for her excellent beautie and rare vertues) by King Robert

K

to be Queen of Scotland." Sir Adame died in the year 1332, and was succeeded by his son Adame, who seemingly was a hanger-on about court, and an expectant of its favours. This Sir Adam died in 1399, and was succeeded by his son Archibald, who "died in battell against Ingland, 1426." Robert succeeded his father, Sir Archibald, and was Sheriff-Depute of Ayrshire in 1430. Archibald succeeded his father, Sir Robert, and is supposed to have been slain at the Battle of Sark in 1448. Robert succeeded his father, Sir Archibald. He was called "the Rud of Rowallane," being of large stature, great strength, and not disinclined to a fray. The author of the "Historie" mentions that "the King in his bearne head proponed to round wt him, and as he offered swa to doe dang out his eye wt the pang of ane cocle-shell. He was a man reguarded not the weil of his house, but in following court, and being unfit for it waisted, sold and wodset all his proper lands of Rowallane, qlk may be ane example to all his posteritie. he married Margerie Newtoune daughter to the laird of Michael hill in the Merse. ane drucken woman & ane waistor man, qt made then this house to stand but the grace of God." "The Rud" resigned in favour of his son John. During his lifetime a protracted feud existed between the houses of Rowallan and Ardoch (the ancient name of Craufurdland) which was the cause of a great deal of bloodshed. It is recorded that the evidents of both families were destroyed, and that John Mure and others were summoned before the Chief Justice of Scotland for breaking the King's peace against Archibald Craufurd. John, son of the above, succeeded to the title and estates. He was married to a mistress of James IV. The author of the "Historie" says— "This Johne was ane very worthie man and died at flowdone field wt King James the fourth. . . . the year of our Lord 1513." Mungo succeeded his father, Sir John. The historian says—"He bigged the hall from the ground and compleated it in his awne time. He was a man of singulare valour and verie worthie of his hands, qrof he gave good proofe in divers conflicts. He died in battell at the Black Satterday In the yeare of our Lord 1547." The editor of the "Historie" adds a note to the notice of Sir Mungo Mure; it is a quotation from the Rowallan family tree, and is as follows:—"This moungov muire raisit ye hall vpone four vouttis [vaults] and laich trance and compleitit the samen in his awne tyme; he deceissit in battell fechtan agains Ingland in pinkie feilde: 1547." John succeeded his father, Sir Mungo. He seems to have passed his life in peace, having further improved the castle and estate. The following is another quotation from the Rowallan family tree :—" This Johne Muire 3 of yat name delytit in policye of plainteing and bigging, he plaintit ye oirchzarde an gairdein, sett ye vppir banck and nethir banck ye birk zaird befoir ye zett, he bigit ye foir vark frome ye grounde ye baknall and vomanhous, he leuit graciouslie and deit in peice anno 1591: of aige 66." This Sir John Mure had a seat in Parliament, and early embraced the reformed doctrines. In the appendix to the "Historie" there are copies of three letters addressed to him. One is from Mary Queen of Scots, soliciting aid after her escape from prison. As it will doubtless interest the reader, I beg to submit it. It is as follows :—

"Traist Friend, We greit zou weil. We believe it is not unknawin to zou the greit Mercie and Kyndness that almythie God of his infinit gudness hes furthschevin towart us at this Tyme in the Deliverance of us fra the maist straitless Preson in quhilk we ware Captive of quhilk Mercy and Kyndness we cannot enough thank & therefore we will desire zou as ze will do us acceptable Service to be at us with all possible [speed] on Settirday the aught of this month be aught hours afternone or sooner gif ze may well accompanyt with zour honourable Friends and Servantis bodin in feir of weir to do us Service as ze sall be appointit because we knaw zour Constance at all Tymes. We neid not mak longeir letters for the present bot will bit zou feir weil—Off Hamilton the 6 of May 1568 and that ze with the folks bait on fute and horse be heir on yis next Sunday at the fordest.

"MARIE, R."

It does not appear that Sir John responded to this summons. William succeeded his father, Sir John. He is spoken of by the historian of the house as being "of a meik & gentle spirit, & delyted much in the studie of physick, which he practised among the poor people wt very good succcesse. he was ane religious man and died gratiouslie in the yeare of his age 69, the yeare of our lord 1616." William succeeded his father,

Sir William. He is described as being "ane strang man of bodie & delyted much in hounting and halking. He died in the year of his age 63, and of our lord 1639. William succeeded his father Sir William. In my opinion he was the most illustrious member of the family. He was the author of the "Historie," from which I have gleaned the above interesting notices. At the close of the work he modestly speaks of himself thus—" This Sir William was pious and learned, and had ane excellent vaine in poyesie; he delyted much in building and planting, he builded the new wark in the north syde of the close, and the battlement of the back wall, and reformend the whole house exceedingly. He lived religiouslie and died Christianlie in the year of (his) age 63, and in the year of (our) Lord 1657." How Sir William came to record the exact date of his death is somewhat curious. It could not have been inserted by the editor of the work; for he says he has retained the exact orthography, contractions, and punctuation of the MS., making no alteration whatever. " Sir William Mure, knight," as he styles himself, deserves a somewhat fuller notice than space has permitted me to give of his ancestors. He seems to have received (for the period in which he lived) an excellent education. He early acquired a taste for literature, which he assiduously prosecuted throughout the whole course of his life, and from which he derived peculiar pleasure. When a youth he wrote some Latin verses on the death of his grandfather. "His manuscript poetry," says the editor of 'The Historie,' "is considerable. Among the larger pieces is a translation of Virgil; a religious poem which he calls 'The joy of Tears,' and another, 'The Challenge and Reply.'" Several of his pieces have been published. In the "Muses' Welcome," a collection of poems and addresses made to King James on his visiting Scotland in 1617, there is a poetical address to the king at Hamilton written by Sir Wm. Mure of Rowallan. In 1628 he published a poetical translation of the celebrated "Hecatombe Christiana," of Boyd of Trochrig, together with a small original piece called "Doomsday." In 1629 he published "The true Crucifixe for true Catholikes," and wrote a version of the Psalms of David, which, had it been submitted to the Assembly, would doubtless have been adopted, its merits being highly spoken of by competent judges. A specimen of his skill in verse may not be out of place here. Therefore I submit the following version of

"PSALM 23.

1. The Lord my scheepherd is, of want
  I never shal complaine.
2. for mee to rest on hee doth grant
  green pastures of the plaine.

3. Hee leads me stillest streams beside,
  and doth my soul reclame,
  in righteous paths hee me doth guide
  for glorie of his name.

4. The valey dark of death's aboad
  to passe, I'l fear no ill,
  for thou art with me Lord ; thy rod
  and staffe me comfort still.

5. For me a Table thou dost spread
  in presence of my foes
  with oyle thou dost anoint my head,
  by thee my cup overflows.

6. Mercie and goodness all my dayes
  with me sall surelie stay,
  and in thy hous, thy name to praise,
  Lord I will duell for ay."

Although devoted to literature, he took part in active public life, was a "member of the Parliament held at Edinburgh in June, 1643, and of the committee of Warre, for the sheriffdom of Air, 1644." He was present at the siege of Newcastle, and fought in several engagements between the Royal and Parliamentary forces. In a postscript to a letter addressed to his "loving sone," and dated from Tyneside, before Newcastle, he says :—"I bless the Lord I am in good health and sound every way. I got a sore blow at the battle upon my back wt the butt of a musket, which hath vexed me very much, but specially in the night, being deprived thereby of sleep, but I hope it shall peece and peece weare away, for I am already nearly sound. I thank God for it." Being a man of piety, Sir William befriended the Covenanters, and as much as possible protected his tenantry from the tyranny of the troopers who scoured the countryside at the period. He was intimate with the Rev. William Guthrie of Fenwick, who, as already stated, preached upon several occasions in the "auld kirk" of the castle. Sir William was succeeded by his son William, who walked in the footsteps of his pious parent, and suffered much for his religious opinions. Conventicles were held by him in the castle, and permitted to take place upon the estate. For this, he fell under the suspicion of the Government, and on several occasions suffered imprisonment. He died about 1686, and was succeeded by his eldest son, who shared in the persecution directed against his father. He was the last male representative, and died in 1700, leaving one daughter. Dame Jean Mure succeded her father and married William Fairlie of Bruntsfield. This is the lady who was married under the "marriage tree." The fruit of the romantic union were three daughters, one of whom (Lady Jean Mure) succeeded to the estate, and married Sir James Campbell, youngest son of James, second Earl of Loudoun. At this stage of the history of the Mures, the estate passed into the hands of the Loudoun family, and is still retained by them. The late Countess of Loudoun was greatly attached to Rowallan. She often visited the castle, carefully inspected the rooms, and expended considerable sums on repairs to prevent the old place from falling to pieces. But she has gone the way of all the earth, and left the old fabric to battle with the elements and fall a victim to the ravages of time and decay, a fate to which it is bound to succumb, for it now totters beneath a crushing weight of years. I need not dwell further upon the beautiful scenery in the neighbourhood of Rowallan Castle. Numbers visit the place, and many pic-nic parties of lads and lasses, during the months of summer, enjoy themselves beneath the spreading trees in front of the castle, and merrily foot it upon the green sward. I spent some hours about the old place so pleasantly that I was loath to leave the scene, and turned round again and again to have a look at the relic of feudalism in the valley below when departing. While retracing my steps to the highway I composed the following verses, which find a place here not on account of any merit they may contain, but because they describe the old building *as it is*, and the state of my mind on the occasion of my visit :—

ROWALLAN.

Farewell unto thy rocky steep,
Thy crumbling walls and ruined keep ;
In thy decay I read a page
That tells me of a bygone age.
No more does mirth or laughter sound,
Or footsteps through thy halls resound :
Now all is still, all's bleak decay,
And Ruin wrecks thy fabric grey.

Thy knights and vassals sleep in dust,
Their blades are now consumed by rust ;
Vacant thy rooms, upon their walls
The spider weaves its web ; for all's
Now wreck within, without, around,
And solemn silence reigns profound.
Time moulders wall and winding stair
Once trod by knight and lady fair.

Farewell, Rowallan ! fare thee well !
Adieu unto thy bosky dell,
Thy ruined keep and shattered tower,
Thy winding stream and leafy bower,
For each memento seems to say
That all on earth must pass away—
That all must change and parted be,
And crumble and decay like thee.

Entering Kilmaurs road my reverie was interrupted by the rumbling of wheels. Looking in the direction I observed a medical gentleman with whom I am intimate driving at a brisk pace. Observing me, he drew up, and offered to convey me to Kilmarnock. Availing myself of the speedy mode of reaching home, I was soon seated beside him, and arrived in town as the clocks tolled forth the hour of four, after to me a short but pleasant drive. Jostling through the throng I directed my steps homeward, where I met with a gleeful reception from my little folks, and a scolding from my wife for stopping until dinner was " entirely spoiled." Somehow or other I never ate a better than I did that Saturday afternoon. Country air sharpens the appetite, and makes one relish anything savoury.

CHAPTER XI.

From Kilmarnock to Stewarton—The Parish and its Boundaries—The town: its Buildings, Trades, and Eminent Characters—Corsehill Castle and its Traditions—The Parish Church—The late William Cunninghame of Lainshaw—The Churchyard—The Viaduct—Lainshaw Castle—The Murder of Hugh, fourth Earl of Eglinton.

It is delightful on a radiant summer day to stroll along a country road and mark with ecstatic joy the form and features of the landscape, or recline on some gowan-spangled lawn and gaze at the sun through barred fingers. It is a perfect luxury when

"Deep in
The many-bladed grass the vi'let springs,
The lily and the humble primrose grow,
The hare-bell and the cowslip knit their heads,
And scented thyme and modest daisy, wrapt
In low obscurity, crowd on the sward,
And send their odours, like the captive's sighs,
Or prayers of saints, to Heaven upon the breeze."

Ah, how I love the country! I delight to gaze on Earth's ample page, and adore the Mighty Architect of the Universe through His works.

"I love not man the less, but Nature more,
From these our interviews, in which I steal,
From all I may be, or have been before,
To mingle with the Universe, and feel
What I can ne'er express, yet cannot all conceal."

I never enjoyed myself or Nature's beauties to greater advantage than I did when walking between Kilmarnock and "the auld toun o' Stewarton." My way lay along Kilmaurs road —a road whose scenery for a considerable distance is very tame, so much so that I did not feel myself thoroughly in the country until I turned into the old Stewarton highway which branches off some mile and a-half from the town. This road— like all old ones—is very undulating, and the pedestrian while traversing it finds himself either climbing a brae or descending one until he attains an elevation from which he gets a glimpse of the greatest bonnet-making town in Scotland, and of a wide expanse of country stretching for miles around him. I might have gone to Stewarton by the train on this occasion, as I have done on many others, but I didn't. Travelling by rail is too speedy a method for a rambler. He delights to stroll along quietly, feasting his eyes on the landscape, as he listens to the cadence of the lark pouring forth its hymn of praise away up in the sky at the very gate of Heaven. The flowers too—the wild flowers—have a charm, and combine to woo him from the town when he can snatch a holiday.

A five mile walk from town along the hedge-bordered highway brought me to Stewarton, which is situated in a valley on the bank of a streamlet named the Annick. It flows from White Loch in the parish of Mearns, and joins with the Glazart at a place called the "Water-meetings," some three miles below the town. The ground round the town has a fine sloping appearance, and is withal well wooded. It gradually rises from the south-west to the north-east, and ends on the limits of Renfrewshire. From these heights the admirer of the picturesque can witness a splendid panoramic view. On the north is the cloud-capped Benlomond, so beautifully referred to in one of Tannahill's songs; on the south, in the misty distance, the hills of Dumfries and Kirkcudbrightshire stand prominently out, while the spectator has the bright waters of the Frith of Clyde lying at his feet. Stewarton is situated in the centre of the parish, which is bounded by the parishes of Neilston and Mearns, in Renfrewshire, on the north-east; Fenwick on the east and south-east; Dreghorn on the south; Irvine and Kilwinning on the west, and Dunlop on the north-west and west. It was erected into a separate lordship in 1283, and vested in the family of James, high steward of Scotland, hence the name "Steward's-toun." The town of Stewarton contains a population of 3299. It traverses a line of street some three-quarters of a mile long and terminates in a portion of the town called Darlington. From this long street several smaller ones branch off. The principal building in the place is the Cunninghame Institute. It is situated in Avenue Square, and has an imposing appearance. It was gifted to the town by the late

William Cunninghame of Lainshaw, and consists of a reading-room and recreation-room up stairs, and a school-room called "the Academy" on the ground floor. The banking establishments are three in number. The Union is a very fine building, and the Clydesdale and Royal are very chaste in design. There are five places of worship, all of which are well attended. They are as follows :—The Established or Parish Church, of which more hereafter; the Free Church, the United Presbyterian Church, the Wesleyan Methodist Church, and the Congregational Church. It is worthy of note that the last-named place of worship was instituted by the late William Cunninghame of Lainshaw in 1822, and that with the forethought and liberality so characteristic of him he has left to the members the commodious and comfortable place of worship, a manse for their clergyman, and a suitable endowment to maintain both.

From a very remote period the staple trade of Stewarton has been the manufacture of bonnets. So early as the twelfth century knitted bonnets were made at Bloak and Cutstraw. When the trade was in a primitive condition they were made in farm-houses, and once a year sold at fairs in the neighbourhood. It was then the custom for females to spin the yarn in their spare time, and to while away the hours of the long winter nights knitting it into bonnets. But as time sped on, and as civilization advanced, the trade got into the hands of families, or rather a small community, who monopolised it, and framed laws to protect and retain it in their own hands. Some of these laws were curious. For instance, all privileges were carefully guarded, and no outsider was allowed to work at the trade. A son of a bonnet-maker was allowed to marry whom he pleased, but a daughter was denied that privilege, and *compelled* to choose a husband in the trade. These laws at this day are null and void, and bonnet-makers and bonnet-knitters are married and given in marriage to all classes of the community. The bonnets made fifty years ago were principally those substantial head-dresses known as the "Rab Rorison," or braid Scotch bonnet. Now the manufacture consists of "Glengaries" and "Balmorals." Large quantities of these are exported, and vast numbers supplied to the army and navy.

The next craft of importance to bonnet-making is that

of spindle-making. This branch of industry is extensively carried on by Mr. David Skeoch. The business was established by one of his ancestors some hundred and twenty years ago. The spindles manufactured are used for machinery in mills, and are made of steel. Like Kilmaurs, Stewarton at one time was famous for its hardware.

Among the men of note of whom Stewarton can boast may be mentioned Dr. Robert Watt, the compiler of the *Bibliotheca Britannica*, a standard work of great merit; also David Dale, the celebrated cotton-spinner, who was born in 1739 in a room of that house situated in the Cross, at the right hand corner of Rigg Street. His father was a grocer, and could only afford to give him a limited education. Notwithstanding this, by persistent energy he became one of the first merchants and manufacturers in Scotland. For a series of years he held the office of magistrate in Glasgow, and also officiated as pastor of an Independent Church in that city. His charity was extensive, and many in his native town partook of his bounty long after his death. He died in March, 1806, leaving £100,000. David Dale was father-in-law to Robert Owen, the advocate of Socialism and the founder of Co-operation.

John Gilmour, a poet of great promise, who died while pursuing his studies at college, must not be omitted. After his death a small volume of "Poetical Remains" was published by his parents. From that work I make the following extract:

"STEWARTON.

" O how I love thee, lovely village, where
  Our 'bonnet manufacture' boasts its rise;
For winding Annick, tuneless streamlet, there
  Received me oft o'er head, and ears, and eyes:
Aye! there I loved to lave my boyish frame,
While moments passed unheeded as they came.

" Unsung, alas! though Annick's waters flow,
  Flow thou with them, my unpretending strain;
Else may my bosom never, never know
  The raptures of celestial song again!
For there, in boyhood's first unconscious glow,
  My lot was cast among the madcap train:
But certes, far the meanest slave, I ween,
To carol in rude lays my native scene."

Stewarton is possessed of few antiquities. The parish

contains the ruins of three castles, viz., that of Robertland, and those of Auchinharvie and Corsehill. The latter is situated in a field on the Dunlop road, a short distance from the town. After strolling through the streets I paid it a visit, and found it to consist principally of a portion of a wall bearing unmistakeable evidence of recent construction or repair. Beside it there are some slight remains of foundations, but nothing to interest the visitor. The building seems to have been of no great extent, nor does it appear to have been a place of note in feudal times, little being known regarding it beyond that it was the residence of the Cuninghames of Corsehill, the first of whom was a son of the fourth Earl of Glencairn. Near to the ruin the Corsehill burn meanders on its way to the Annick, and the new line of railway between Kilmarnock and Glasgow passes close by. What history has omitted to record regarding Corsehill Castle gossip has not failed to supply, and even superstition has taken advantage of the mystery-shrouded wreck of a baronial age to people it with supernatural beings. What urchin in its vicinity has not heard of the untold wealth hid away in a dark chamber under the foundation, and of the man who was startled and almost petrified with terror while digging to discover it by hearing a sepulchral voice calling to him from the depths of the pile to "dig no more in ruined Ravenscraig." I daresay there are few Stewartonians who have not heard of the famous Fanny Howie, and of the hair-bristling sight she witnessed in the vicinity of the ruin when driving home from the fair one night at the solemn hour of twelve. When passing along the road her horse suddenly stopped, and although reminded by several sharp cuts of Fanny's whip that it was to move forward, it heeded not the lash, but stood with drooping ears and dilated nostrils as immoveable as a statue. This unusual conduct astonished the fair Fanny, and she looked around for the cause. To her horror she witnessed a funeral procession crossing the road a little in advance of her. The hearse, with its nodding plumes, was drawn by four headless steeds, the driver was headless also, and every spectral form in the procession was in the same condition. Rivetted by fear to her seat, Fanny watched the ghostly crew glide noiselessly past. With an effort she overcame the terror which paralysed her, and said, "In God's name what does this mean?" There was no reply; the mention of the sacred name was sufficient; the vision vanished, and Fanny proceeded homeward. I rather think that Fanny, like the " wee wifikie" in the old song, had gat a "wee bit drapikie," for it is the case that those who imbibe spirits generally see them.

After lingering about the ruin for some time I found my way to the Cross, and leisurely strolled along Lainshaw Street until I arrived at the Parish Church. Turning down the little lane leading to it I found the gate of the churchyard open. On entering, a strange feeling of sadness pervaded my mind, for the sight of the grass-covered mounds awakened sad recollections of near ones and dear ones who have crossed the threshold of death, and gone to a better and happier state of existence. The church stands in the graveyard, and is an old-fashioned, odd-looking structure, with a belfry and clock. The belfry seems to be an addition, for it bears the date of 1696 and the motto, "Over, fork over." Originally the building must have been very small, for it has undergone many alterations. The Corsehill and Lainshaw aisles were added in or about the year 1650, and in 1825 it was widened on the north side. Internally the church is very neat, and contains two galleries. Under the Corsehill and Lainshaw aisles are the burying vaults of the respective families. That of Corsehill was closed in 1871. On the wall opposite the pulpit there is a handsome white marble tablet bordered with black. It bears a profile of the deceased and the following inscription:—" William Cuninghame of Lainshaw departed this life 6th November, 1849, aged 73 years. Author of many works on the chronology and fulfilment of prophecy. He was a devout student, a zealous expounder of the Word of God, a laborious and successful instructor of youth, and lived daily 'looking for that blessed hope and glorious appearing of the Great God and our Saviour, Jesus Christ.'" The late William Cuninghame of Lainshaw was a philanthropist in the strictest sense of the word. He went about "continually doing good." The whole of his long life was devoted to increasing knowledge among and bettering the condition of his fellow-men. During his life he was beloved by the people of Stewarton, and deeply regretted when death closed his useful career. When a boy Mr Cuninghame was of a very pious turn of mind, and the convictions he then formed became settled principles when he reached manhood. Previous to his succession to Lainshaw he was in the Civil Service of the East India Company in Bengal. During his stay in India he became acquainted with the celebrated Dr. Carey, of Serampore, and other eminent Christians, and assisted them in their missionary labours. He often spoke of the spiritual comfort and strength that he derived from these acquaintanceships. While in India he wrote some letters on the Evidences of Christianity under the signature of "An Enquirer." These masterly epistles were afterwards published collectively for the benefit of the Serampore Mission. In 1804 he returned to his native country and took possession of his property at Stewarton, and resided upon it up to the day of his death. He was a devout Millenarian, and strongly believed in Christ's personal reign upon the earth—in fact, he daily expected His advent, and wrote several works in support of the doctrine. He also longed for the restoration of Israel, and did all in his power with purse, pen, and voice to promote Christianity among the Jews. As an author, an expositor of prophecy, and a critic on Scriptural chronology he is well known, and will long live in the works he published. He died unmarried and was succeeded by his brother.

"The Auld Kirk o' Stewarton," it is said, at one time passed through an ordeal which no other church in Scotland or any other part of the globe ever did. It seems that some bonnet-makers had been preeing the barley bree rather freely in a "public" in the vicinity of the sacred edifice. Among other matters that engaged the attention of the worthies was the fact that the kirk did not stand due east and west. They agreed that it was altogether wrong and a disgrace to the town. The more they imbibed the more they waxed eloquent upon the subject. Ultimately they agreed to turn the building round and set it right. For this purpose four of them repaired to the churchyard to shift it. Being satisfied of their ability for the task, each man laid hold of a corner and lifted with might and main. After pulling and tugging three of them announced that it would do. "Na, na, haud on a wee," cried the fourth; "lift again, lads, ye've set it down on my coat-tail.". Being unable to rise from the sitting posture he was in he fully believed it to be the case, but it was nothing more than the tail of his coat that had got under the heel of his boot. This story is laughingly told by Stewartonians. They all aver that the bonnet-makers shifted the church to their own satisfaction.

The churchyard is small and irregular in shape. One portion is separated by an iron railing, and seems to be reserved for the aristocracy of Stewarton parish. While straying through the tall grass reading the brief records on the tombstones, I observed the sexton busy throwing up spadefuls of damp, clayey soil on the side of a grave he was preparing to receive a tenant. Going up, I looked into the pit, and saw a strange-looking old man, with a low-crowned hat, and spectacles on nose, laboriously digging at the stubborn earth, and so deeply engrossed in his work that he did not seem to be aware of my presence. Thinking of the grave-digging scene in Hamlet, I was about to ask, "Whose grave is this?" when the old gentleman looked up, adjusted his "specks," and took my measure. "You are busy," said I, by way of introduction. "Oh, yes," he replied, "but this is no an ill ane; it's no sae very deep, an' it's no sae lang since it was houkit. You see," he continued, "I'm no sae far aff being doon," and, as if to prove the truth of the statement, he drew the soil off the lid of a coffin under his feet, and displayed the mountings, which appeared as fresh as though deposited in the mould the day before. "Who is to be buried there?" I asked. "Davie Currie, poor fellow," he replied. "This is his wife's coffin; she was buried about sax months' syne, and Davie, poor lad, wished to be buried beside her. Do you ken," he continued, "that there's mair o' the name o' Currie an' Picken buried in this yard than o' ony ither.—Auld stanes? O yes; there's ane yont yonder 'mang the grass; gin ye look, I think ye'll find the date o' 1410, or thereabout's on't." Leaving him to scoop out poor Davie's narrow bed, I found the relic, but the inscription was entirely gone, and the date all but illegible. Near to it I met with another in the same condition, and found it dated 1413. Many old stones are elaborately carved. A few bear rude representations of shears and implements used in the bonnet trade. Near to the back gate there is a large tablet with a long list of names. The inscription concludes thus—

"And on the left side lies John Gilmour (late student of moral philosophy) who died 14th April, 1828. Aged 18 years." This is the resting place of the youthful poet already referred to.

While straying through the old churchyard, in the direction of the gate, with solemn thoughts crowding on my mind, the following lines of Macaulay struck me forcibly :—

> " Dost thou among these hillocks stray
>   O'er some dear idol's tomb to moan?
> Know that thy foot is on the clay
>   Of hearts once wretched as thy own.
> How many a father's anxious schemes,
>   How many rapturous thoughts of lovers,
> How many a mother's cherished dreams
>   The swelling turf before thee covers !
>
> " Here for the living and the dead,
>   The weepers and the friends they weep,
> Hath been ordained the same cold bed,
>   The same dark night, the same long sleep.
> Here learn that glory and disgrace,
>   Wisdom and folly pass away,
> That mirth hath its appointed place,
>   That sorrow is but for a day."

At the gate I bade farewell to the little golgotha, passed into the highway, and turned my face towards Kilmarnock, with the intention of lingering a few hours about Kilmaurs and its neighbourhood to note and muse upon its antiquities. At the end of the town the viaduct crosses the road and spans a kind of glen through which the Annick flows. It is a stupendous erection and consists of ten arches. It is 540 feet long, each arch 50 feet wide and 80 feet high —that is, from the bed of the river. It took two years to construct it, and during its erection two men lost their lives— one by falling from the parapet into the river bed.

Adjacent to the viaduct is the entrance to Lainshaw Castle, which is at present occupied by Sheriff Anderson. It "consists of a large square tower, with a lesser one of a different style and a number of buildings of more recent date connecting them together, and a large and elegant modern addition." The whole overlooks the Annick, and fronts a handsome park containing trees of great size and beauty. The scene throughout the estate is picturesque, and sufficient to thrill the soul of the most indifferent admirer of Nature's beauties. Ancient Lainshaw belonged to the Montgomeries; but that family becoming extinct the estate passed into the hands of William Cuninghame of Bridgehouse, who acquired it by purchase in 1779. The only thing that makes Lainshaw Castle historically interesting is the murder of Hugh, fourth Earl of Eglinton, which was perpetrated on the 19th of April, 1586. It seems that a feud existed between the Cuninghames of Robertland and the Montgomeries of Eglinton. The vassals of the latter, headed by the Earl, invaded the territory of the first-named and burned their castle. In revenge for this blazing deed the Earl was waylaid by the Cuninghames and shot dead. The whole incident is narrated in "Robertson's Ayrshire Families" in the following graphic manner :—" The good Earl, apprehending no danger from any quarter, set out from his own house of Eglinton towards Stirling, where the court then remained, in a quiet and peaceable manner, having none in his retinue but his own domestics, and called at the Langshaw [close to the village of Stewarton], where he staid so long as to dine. How the wicked crew, his murderers, got notice of his being there I cannot say. It is reported, but I cannot aver for a truth, that the Lady Langshaw, Margaret Cuninghame, who was a daughter of the house of Aiket (others say it was a servant, who was a Cuninghame), went up to the battlement of the house and hung over a white table napkin as a signal to the Cuninghames, most of whom lived within sight of the house of Langshaw, which was a sign agreed should be given when the Earl of Eglinton was there. Upon that the Cuninghames assembled to the number of thirty-four persons or thereby in a warlike manner, as if they had been to attack or to defend themselves from an enemy; and concealed themselves in a low ground near the bridge of Annick, where they knew the Earl had to pass, secure as he apprehended from any danger—when, alas! all of a sudden the whole bloody gang set upon the Earl and his small company, some of whom they hewed to pieces, and John Cuninghame of Clonbeith came up with a pistol and shot the Earl dead on the spot. The horror of the fact struck everybody with amazement and consternation, and all the country ran to arms, either on the one side of the quarrel or the other, so that for some time there was a scene of bloodshed and murder in the west that

had never been known before." Tradition has it that the
Earl after being shot rode a considerable distance and fell
dead off his horse at the ford of the river. The path along
which he rode was known as the "Weeping Path," and the
scene of his death is said to be Bridgend. The road at
Lainshaw Castle gate crosses a bridge, and dives under a
canopy of foliage which excludes the sunshine and darkens
the path. The scene was so lovely that I leaned on the
parapet and looked around enraptured.

By the side of the Annick, and under the shade of the
viaduct, stands Lainshaw Mill. On the top of its chimney
there is a dwarfish rowan tree growing, which is some fifty
years old. It is a curiosity in its way and attracts universal
attention. After a chat with the miller about his mill and
the affairs of the neighbourhood, staff in hand, I sped on to
Kilmaurs.

CHAPTER XII.

From Stewarton to Kilmaurs—The appearance of the Village—The Council House and Juggs—Kilmaurs of the olden time—Its Government and Churches—The Monk's Well—My Lord's Place—Jock's Thorn—Kilmaurs Castle—The Glencairn Family—An Incident.

Near Lainshaw Mill the road to Kilmaurs strikes off to the left. After skirting the new railway for about a mile it is finely shaded on each side with trees as it nears Lochridge, a small, well-wooded estate. The mansion is a quaint building of the olden time, embellished with armorial devices and retaining the latticed windows and porched doorway so peculiar to gentlemen's residences at the beginning of the last century. From Lochridge the road passes over the brow of a height from which the pedestrian has an excellent view of Lainshaw Castle and its policies, the Frith of Clyde, and the vast track of country lying between him and the margin of its shore. The view of the coast continues for a considerable distance and is not lost sight of until the road swoops down to the ancient village of Kilmaurs. When viewing the beautiful scenery as I strayed along this very pleasing road how I wished that some of my readers, whom fate or circumstances have banished from the scenes of their youth, and whose lot is cast in some far distant land, or who in the pursuit of wealth or in the practice of their trades are pent up in some smoke-begrimed city, had been with me; to them it would have been an ever-to-be-remembered ramble.

Upon entering Kilmaurs I found it to consist, for the most part of one long straggling street lined with irregularly built tenements, which are most primitive in construction and appearance. In the centre of the street stands the Council House, a church-like erection with a steeple and clock.* By

---

* On the 28th of August, 1874, the steeple was struck by lightning during the prevalence of a storm. Twelve feet of it was thrown down, but beyond the smashing of the steps in front of the Court House and several panes of glass in its rear no accident occurred.

the side of the steps leading to the hall door the "Juggs" still dangle at the end of an iron chain. They are in a good state of preservation, and attract more attention than any other relic of antiquity about the place, being often handled and curiously examined by strangers, many of whom seem at a loss to understand what the rusty iron collar could have been used for. The last time they were brought into official requisition was in the case of a woman found guilty of theft. After undergoing her sentence she was laid hold of by a mob and drummed out of the parish. This disgraceful affair occurred in 1812.

Kilmaurs, like many Scottish towns, derives its name from the patron saint of the church. The town was erected into a free barony, with power to elect bailies, create burgesses, to hold markets, fairs, and so forth, by King James the Fifth in 1527. From this charter Cuthbert, Earl of Glencairn, as superior, received power to parcel out land in burghal tenements. In November in the above year the Earl and his son granted a charter, and divided equally 240 acres of land amongst forty persons, to be held by them, their heirs, and successors for ever, upon the payment of 80 merks yearly. These individuals were called "tenementers," and had the exclusive privilege "of buying or selling, of brewing or malt-making, and all other arts or trades, as that of shoemakers, skinners, carpenters, woolsters, &c." The design of this charter, which is still in existence, seems to have been to lay the foundation of a manufacturing and commercial population, but the scheme was never successful. The "tenementers," instead of turning their attention to the arts, devoted their whole energy to agriculture, and Kilmaurs in the course of time became famous for growing the best *kail plants* in Ayrshire. The only trades that ever obtained a kind of permanency in the place were the manufacture of steel clockwork and cutlery. These were carried on to some extent. The knives manufactured by the cutlers were noted for their sharpness of edge, and this circumstance gave rise to the old saying, "as sharp as a Kilmaurs whittle," which is often applied to persons of acute understanding or quickness of action. Upon one occasion a Kilmaurs clergyman rose to address an audience after a young divine who had concluded a discourse in flowing English. The gentleman, who was somewhat jealous of the rhetoric of his young friend, is reported to have said—" My friends, we have had a great deal of fine English ware amang us the day, but aiblins my Kilmaurs whittle will cut as sharply as ony English blade!" The cutlers and steel-workers, tradition states, went to Sheffield and laid the basis of the hardware trade of that town. Be that as it may, the manufacture of hardware has long since departed from Kilmaurs, and nothing but weaving, shoemaking, and other crafts incidental to all rural districts were carried on until a few years back, when bonnet-making was introduced. This industry has given an impetus to the trade of the place, and affords employment to many of the inhabitants. The factories of Mr. Woodrow and Messrs. Laughland & Robertson, are in a prosperous condition, and I trust will form the neucleus of many more establishments of a like nature.

The town at this date contains a population of 1145. It is governed by two bailies, the election of whom is vested in the burgesses or "tenementers." That body also elects the town treasurer, fiscal, and clerk. The police force consists of one solitary individual, whose situation seems a sinecure, the inhabitants being for the most part sober and industrious. In the matter of church accommodation it is fairly supplied, being possessed of three places of worship which belong to as many different denominations. First, there is the Parish or Established Church, then the United Presbyterian and Free Churches. The U.P. is the finest building in the place, and presents a handsome appearance. It is built on the site of a former place of worship of the congregation, and was opened on Sabbath, the 26th March, 1865, the inaugural sermon being preached by the Rev. Professor Eadie of Glasgow. This church was constituted in 1738, and was then the only Antiburgher place of worship in Ayrshire. The rev. and popular David Smeeton was the first minister, and the old meeting-house was often crowded on Sabbath-days by people who had ridden many miles to listen to this earnest and eloquent servant of God. Professor Paxton followed Mr. Smeeton. He was a man of considerable literary talent, and under his care the church prospered. When he removed to Edinburgh he was succeeded by the Rev. Mr. Robertson, who laboured for thirty-six years with a popularity that never varied. After Mr. Robertson came Mr.

Christie. He was followed by the Rev. Mr. Taylor, who removed to Bootle, and from thence to New York, where he has had conferred upon him the degree of D.D. The present pastor is the Rev. Andrew Gray. He entered the charge in 1857, and is highly spoken of by the people of Kilmaurs. The Free Church is a plain, unassuming edifice, bearing the date 1854. There is little of interest connected with it. The Rev. Mr. Maxwell is pastor, and is well known as an earnest and devout minister.

From the Cross I entered Fenwick road. At its corner, next the Council House, stands an old-fashioned building that was at one time the residence of the Rev. Mr. Smeeton, the Antiburgher minister. Since his day it has been stripped of its dignity, and is now converted into a spirit shop. A few yards past it I turned down a rural lane, and soon arrived at a rude bridge spanning the Carmel, the streamlet on whose bank Kilmaurs is situated. Crossing, I was delighted to discover a neat bowling-green, upon which Mr. M'Naught, the parish schoolmaster, and other gentlemen were playing off for a silver medal. Near to the bridge, and at the foot of Place Brae, under a canopy of thorn bushes, is situated a very interesting spring named the Monk's Well, from which the lieges of Kilmaurs draw their supply of water. This well has two remarkable peculiarities—it never freezes, and although hundreds of pailfuls of its liquid are carried off daily, it ever remains brimful and pours its superfluous water into the river at its brink. How it obtained its name is a matter of conjecture, but possibly it did so from the fact that the monks in connection with the village church drank of its store when they lacked better cheer. There is a tradition in connection with it worth relating. It is as follows:—Once upon a time the lord of the manor—possibly one of the Glencairn family—forbade the inhabitants of the village to draw water. His mandate was law, and when the villagers ceased to come with their pitchers, the well, to the astonishment of all, dried up. At this his lordship waxed wroth, and applied to a dignitary of the church for a solution of the mystery. "Go," said the ecclesiastic, "restore the well to the people, let them come with their pitchers, and it will flow as of yore." This was done, and the well poured forth its waters, and I suppose has never ceased to do so since the wonderful event.

From a lengthy piece of verse on the Monk's Well by William C. Lamberton, a Kilmaurs poet of some local fame, I make the following extract for the twofold purpose of presenting the reader with a specimen of his poetry and conveying a right idea of the spot which the verses so happily describe.

> " The Carmel sweetly murmurs by,
>   The wild flowers scent the breeze,
> The little birds sweet music make
>   Among the leafy trees.
> The footpath by the streamlet's brink
>   By many feet is worn,
> Down to the little stone-built well
>   Beneath the spreading thorn.
>
> " And here at twilight's quiet hour
>   The village maidens come
> With sportive jest and glee to bear
>   Its priceless treasure home ;
> Both day and night—by young and old
>   Its presence is desired,
> At feast and fast, when sick or well,
>   Its water is required.
>
> " And one of fever dying in
>   A far off land did cry—
> 'Oh for a drink from the monk's well
>   Once more before I die.'
> Ne'er summer's drouth nor winter's frost
>   Does hurt this blessed spring,
> And in its praise our local bards
>   Their sweetest notes do sing."

Bidding adieu to the Monk's Well, I swung myself over a dilapidated paling and began the ascent of Place Brae. Upon its brow stands My Lord's Place, an old-fashioned and partly ruinous building. With the exception of the mansion-house, which is in an excellent state of preservation, blocks of masonry adjacent to it are much decayed, and at first sight seem the remains of a large building that Time has shattered and almost levelled with the ground. But this is not the case. The seeming ruins are nothing more than the remnant of the walls of an elegant structure which was in course of erection during the lifetime of the Lord Chancellor of Scotland, William, ninth Earl of Glencairn. At the death of his lordship the work was abandoned, and no other member of the family proceeding with it the pile was allowed to become a wreck. Several members of the Glencairn family lived in the old mansion-house, and the last individual of distinction who occupied it was a relative of the Eglinton family. It is at present occupied by an obliging old lady, who kindly showed me over the house. From the brow of *The Place* brae the view is delightfully picturesque. At the foot is the neat bowling-green and the little river winding along. On the rising ground opposite stands the village; in the hollow the church, with a well-wooded background; and beyond a widely diversified landscape, through which runs the railway —a thread of that wondrous iron network that has brought many secluded towns and hamlets into direct communication with the large centres of industry. Taking a last look at the old mansion-house and its surroundings, I musingly strayed in the direction of *Jack's Thorn*, a neat farm-steading that tops the neighbouring hill to the east. In its immediate vicinity there are many venerable trees. In some places they form clumps, but elsewhere stand in regular rows, forming as it were a carriage drive. These trees, from their seeming age and diversified appearance, doubtless formed part of the "faire park" spoken of by Pont. From *Jack's Thorn* I passed down an avenue and entered a field. A pleasant walk over the gowan-spangled grass brought me to the top of a sward-covered circular mound, which tradition affirms to be the site of Kilmaurs Castle, but there is not a vestige of the building remaining. The plough has long since passed over the spot, and cattle lowing stray where the ancient castle stood in all the pomp of family distinction. Pont surveyed the district 266 years ago, and wrote as follows concerning the stronghold :—" The castell is ane ancient, strong building, belonging to the Earl of Glencairne, environed with a faire parke, called Carmell wod, from the vatter of Carmell that runs by it." This, reader, is all that is recorded concerning the castle of Kilmaurs. Its pomp and form are matters of conjecture, and were it not for the fact that several old people in the village remember of sporting among some ruined remnants of masonry which occupied the spot the situation would be unknown.

Kilmaurs Castle was the baronial residence of the Cuninghames of Kilmaurs, Earls of Glencairn. The surname, it will be observed, is territorial, and was originally assumed from the bailery of that name, and alludes, according to Van Bassen, to the following circumstance:—"One son of Friskin assisted Malcolm (afterwards Malcolm Canmore), after the murder of his father, King Duncan, in making his escape from the tyranny of Macbeth; and being hotly pursued, took refuge in a barn, where Friskin concealed him by forking straw over him, by command in the words of the motto, 'Over, fork over.' The pursuit being over, the prince made his escape to England, accompanied by his faithful preserver. The prince was no sooner in possession of his kingdom than he rewarded his preserver with the Thanedom of Cuninghame, from which he and his posterity took their name, and grained the shake-fork as the armorial figure, with said motto, to perpetuate the memory of his happy escape." Doctors differ on many subjects, and so do historians. Sir G. M'Kenzie affirms that the shake-fork and motto were assumed by the noble house of Glencairn owing to their having the office of master of horse in the king's stables. I have no doubt that the arms of the family, an argent, a shake-fork, and sable, with the motto, "over, fork over," have reference to some circumstance connected with the family history, but leave the reader to draw his own conclusion. The first of the family upon record is one Warnebaldus de Cunninghame, who flourished in the reign of Edgar and Alexander I. (The latter reigned from 1107 to 1124.) This Warnebaldus is assumed to have been in possession of the lands of Kilmaurs, and possibly the castle may have been built by him, but this is merely conjecture. After Warnebaldus there follows a long list of

"Knights that wight and worthie were,"

but I will not weary the reader by a recital of their numerous virtues, warlike exploits, and doughty deeds, but simply state that the last of the male line of the main stem of the great Cunninghame family was John, fifteenth Earl of Glencairn, who died unmarried in 1796. He succeeded his brother James, the early and indulgent patron of Robert Burns, the ploughman poet. What Scotchman who has read the "Lament" for this Earl of Glencairn can ever forget the soul-stirring effusion ?—especially the last two stanzas, for in them the bard pours forth his grief in the bitterness of his soul.

> "Oh ! why has worth so short a date ?
>   While villains ripen gray with time ;
> Must thou—the noble, generous, great,
>   Fall in bold manhood's hardy prime ;
> Why did I live to see that day ?
>   A day to me so full of woe !
> Oh ! had I met the mortal shaft
>   Which laid my benefactor low !
>
> "The bridegroom may forget the bride,
>   Was made his wedded wife yestreen ;
> The monarch may forget the crown
>   That on his head an hour has been ;
> The mother may forget the child
>   That smiles sae sweetly on her knee ;
> But I'll remember thee, Glencairn,
>   And a' that thou hast done for me !"

Leaving the site of Kilmaurs Castle I struck through a field, and after a brisk walk arrived at a low hedge, which I cleared with a bound, and landed in a secluded road minus my hat, which flew off during my brief suspension between heaven and earth. There was no help for it ; back I had to go to recover my new "felt," which I did at the risk of tearing my unmentionables into ribbons. Moving in the direction of the village, I arrived in Kilmaurs road, turning the corner just in time to see a young gentleman imprint a kiss on the rosy lips of a rather good-looking young lady whose waist the left arm of the happy fellow encircled. She did not seem averse to the salutation ; but oh ! when she discovered that they had been caught in the act,

> "Her face it reddened like the rose, then pale as ony lily"

she hurriedly drew down her veil to hide her confusion. Smilingly I passed, for I thought of my own daffing days, and how the young lady might have chided her lover with the following stanza of an old song :—

> "Behave yoursel' before folk,
> Behave yoursel' before folk,
> Oh ! dinna be sae rude to me
> As kiss me sae before folk.
> It wadna gie me muckle pain,
> Gin we were seen an' heard by nane,
> To take a kiss or grant you ane,
> But guidsake no before folk."

CHAPTER XIII.

Kilmaurs continued—The old Church—Its appearance and history—An Anecdote of the Rev. Hugh Thomson—The Glencairn Isle and Monument—The appearance of the Vault when opened—A Ghastly Keepsake—The Rev. George Paxton—"Wee Miller"—"The Double Suicide"—The Old Manse—Covenanting Relics—A Stroll along Crosshouse Road—The Estate of Plann—Busbie Castle—The Tumulii at Greenhill Farm—Home again.

At the foot of the village of Kilmaurs, in the centre of a small graveyard, stands its old Parish Church—a Gothic structure of considerable antiquity. Finding the gate of the little burying place open I entered and stood for a few moments leaning on my staff surveying the grass-covered mounds where

> " Servants, masters, small and great,
> Partake the same repose ;
> And where in peace the ashes mix
> Of those who once were foes."

Stoical indeed must the man be who unmoved can stray through an old churchyard without musing upon the apparent end of life, or cherishing a passing thought upon the layers of fellow-mortals who moulder beneath his feet.

> " Like leaves on trees the race of man is found,
> Now green in youth, now withering to the ground ;
> Another race the following spring supplies ;
> They fall successive and successive rise."

The church upon near inspection appears to be a quaint old building which has received several additions. According to the author of *Caledonia* it was dedicated to a Scottish saint named Maure, who is said to have died in 899, and who was commemorated on the 2nd of November. "So early as 1170," says Paterson, " Robertus filii Wernebaldi granted the church of Kilmaurs, in the township of Cunninghame, with half a caracute of land, to the monks of Kelso. This charter was confirmed by Richard Morville, Great Constable of Scotland,

and Lord of Cuninghame, the superior; also by Engleram, Bishop of Glasgow, who died in 1174. . . . The monks enjoyed the rectorial revenues, and a vicarage was established to serve the cure. In Bagimont's Roll, as it stood in the reign of James V., the vicarage of Kilmaurs, in the deanry of Cunninghame, was taxed at £2 13s. 4d., being a tenth of the estimated value. The whole passed into lay hands after the Reformation." The interior of the church is in keeping with its exterior, being plain and of a peculiar shape. It contains nothing of interest. In the wall there is a stone slab to the memory of Hugh Thomson of Hill, minister of the gospel at Kilmaurs, his wife, and twelve children. Mr. Thomson died in 1731. "He was a person of great muscular strength," says the writer of the Kilmaurs article in the *Statistical Account*. "We have heard that, being in Kilmarnock on a market day, he approached a stand on which a blacksmith had exposed to sale horse-shoes and other hardware articles of his own manufacture. Mr. Thomson, wishing to purchase some of the horse-shoes, asked the price of them, and on being told, said by way of joke—'So much for these. I could twist them with my fingers.' 'Twist them, then,' said the smith, 'and you shall have the price of your own making.' Mr. Thomson took one of them up and twisted it almost with as much ease as Samson broke the green withes with which he was bound. The blacksmith stood aghast; and thinking his customer *no cannie*, he gave him the shoes on very reasonable terms, and was right glad to see his back turned." Separated from the church by a narrow passage stands the Glencairn Isle—a dungeon-like building with an iron gate, and a small barred window, through which the light of day streams and dimly illumines the interior. Under the window there is a brass plate bearing the following inscription:—

"This ancient burying place of the Glencairn family, which had fallen into ruins, has been restored by Dame Charlotte Montgomery Cuninghame, in memory of her beloved husband, Sir Thomas Montgomery Cunninghame, 8th Baronet of Corsehill, and descendant of Andrew, 2nd Son of the 4th Earl of Glencairn. He passed to his rest 30th August, 1870."

Against the eastern wall stands a handsome mural monument, erected by James, the seventh Earl of Glencairn, in the year 1600. This beautiful specimen of ancient architecture

contains within a recess formed by receding columns—which
are surmounted by an entablature and some beautiful scroll
work—full-sized half-length figures of the Earl and Countess
clad in armour. They stand in the attitude of prayer, with
folded hands and open books before them. Beneath on a
lower level are the figures of two boys and six girls which
represent their family. They also have folded hands and
books before them, and a devotional appearance. Behind the
figures of the adults there is a tablet containing a semi-faded
inscription, now quite unreadable. Upon one of the columns
" NOTHING SHURER THAN DEATH, BE THEREFOR SOBOR AND
WATCH IN PRAYER" is still legible. It was long believed that
this monument commemorated William, 9th Earl of Glencairn,
who died Lord Chancellor of Scotland; but this was fallacious,
because it was erected forty-four years before his death. Some
years ago when the aisle was undergoing repair, the vault was
opened, and the bones and dust of generations of the Glencairn family were seen lying confusedly upon the damp floor
amongst rotten coffins which had fallen to pieces and scattered
their contents. Amongst the skulls there was one of a red-
dish hue supposed to be that of the Chancellor. A tradition
states that his lady, Margaret Montgomery, was so strongly
attached to him that she had his corpse decapitated and the
head embalmed. The ghastly trophy was kept in her bed-
room, and when she died it was—in accordance with a wish
she expressed—placed in her coffin and buried with her.
Both aisle and monument are much decayed. At no distant
date the dust of the once lords of the manor will mingle with
that of their meanest hind in the lap of mother earth. Nature
heeds not the " storied urn" or the obsequies of the wealthy.
She makes no distinction between the loutish clown in his
nameless grass-covered grave and the earl in his vault. They
sleep equally sound, and possibly when the dead wakes at

> " The trumpet's ring,
> The thrust of a poor man's arm will go
> Thro' the heart of the proudest king."

With such thoughts as these crowding on my mind I left the
aisle and began to stray through the ancient burying ground.
One portion lately added has quite a modern appearance, lairs
being laid off and new tombstones erected. But as I love to

stray "in the winding ways of hoar antiquity," I turned my attention to the grassy hillocks, beneath which

"The rude forefathers of the hamlet sleep,"

and discovered that the oldest stone is to the memory of a William Coningham, and dated 1634; also, many others curiously carved, which form antiquarian objects of interest. Among the mementoes of departed worth met with while wandering through the tangled grass, space only permits me to mention two, and a nameless grave in the south corner. The first of these is a monumental tablet commemorative of the wife and family of the Rev. George Paxton. This is the inscription :—" To the memory of Mrs. Eliz. Armstrong, who died 25th August, 1799, in the 37th year of her age. This stone is erected by her affectionate husband, the Rev. George Paxton. Also, to the memory of their beloved children, Martha Paxton, who died 16th Dec., 1792, aged 4 months; and William Paxton, who died 8th Oct., 1799, aged 3 years.

'Insatiate archer! could not one suffice?
Thy shaft flew thrice, and thrice my peace was slain.'"

George Paxton was minister of the Secession Church of Kilmaurs from 1789 to 1807. He then removed to Edinburgh, and rose to be Professor of Divinity to the General Associate Synod. He was the author of the "Villagers and other poems," and was known as a scholar and masterly prose writer.

The next is to the memory of the Rev. Alexander Miller. He was the author of the Kilmaurs article in the old *Statistical Account*, and was the "Wee Miller" to whom Burns refers in his "Holy Fair."

"*Wee Miller* neist the guard relieves,
And orthodoxy raibles,
Though in his heart he weel believes,
And thinks it auld wife's fables.
But faith! the birkie wants a manse,
So caunily he hums them,
Although his carnal wit and sense,
Like bafflins ways o'ercomes him
At times that day."

The inscription is as follows:—" Erected by Jas. Boswell Miller in affectionate remembrance of his father, the Rev.

Alex. Miller, minister of this parish, who died 25th December, 1804, deeply regretted by all who could appreciate his worth as an intelligent divine, dutiful son, watchful father, and a faithful friend."

I will now refer to the obscure grave in the south corner. There the bodies of Mr. and Mrs. Barker repose in the unbroken slumber of death. They committed suicide by drowning themselves in the Irvine, near Wet Bridge, on the 24th October, 1844. The circumstance at the time was spoken of as "the double suicide," and being so romantic and unprecedented it caused a great sensation throughout the country. When found the bodies were tied together with handkerchiefs, and in such a manner that it was evident each had assisted the other in effecting their object, and that they had lain down in the water, for it was only some three feet deep. The remains of the faithful pair were conveyed to Kilmaurs, and placed in the Parish Church to await identification. The circumstance noised abroad, and thousands flocked to view the corpses, but no one identified them. From the apparel in which the bodies were attired it was evident that the deceased had moved in superior society. This set the inventive imagination of many at work, and all kinds of stories and suppositions were circulated, but the facts of the case when known amounted to this:—The ill-fated pair came to Kilmarnock about a week before the sad event and put up at the Commercial Hotel. One evening they called for their bill, and when the gentleman paid it he remarked in an off-hand manner that they were going for a walk. They left but never returned, and the next heard of them was that they had committed suicide. It was supposed they came from England, and that unfortunate business speculations and a dread of poverty had caused the committal of the rash act. They now rest from their troubles unknown, and I may say almost forgotten. Near to the churchyard, and in a garden at the back of it, stand some slight remains of an old monastic building which was supposed to be in conjunction with the church at one period. Sir Hugh de Morvile is said to have resided in it while engaged building a portion of Kilwinning Abbey in the twelfth century, and it is affirmed that it was occupied so late as 1630. It is now in a ruinous condition, and occupied by swine, who seem to have a greater taste for clean straw and good swill than antiquities.

Leaving the churchyard and all its melancholy associations, I walked towards the village, and having crossed a little bridge spanning the Carmel, stopped before an old building on the left, which is said to have been a manse at one period. It is antique in appearance, and presently occupied by families in poor circumstances. Above one of its windows in rude characters is

"WALK IN THE LIGHT."

Tradition states that the man who built this house did so with stones which he purloined during the night from a neighbouring quarry, and that being discovered he consented to the above inscription being graven above his window rather than be prosecuted for the theft.

From the old manse to the Council House the main artery of the village is most primitive in appearance, the houses being for the most part thatched, low-roofed tenements, but notwithstanding this they have a cosy, bien look about them, which is greatly enhanced by the kail-yards and flower-plots at their back doors.

Although Kilmaurs does not contain a stone to the memory of one man who laid down his life for the Covenant, yet it is possessed of relics of that period. These consist of a drum and flag which are said to have passed through the battles of Drumclog and Bothwell, and to have been carried by a detachment of the villagers who marched to the roll of the first and fought round the second on the memorable fields.

The Drum is in the possession of Mr. David Smith, and is in every way similar to the one in the possession of the Howies of Lochgoin, an account of which the reader will find in page 129.

The Flag is in the possession of Mr. Robert Harper. Unfortunately it is in tatters, and in an attempt to preserve it, it has been in a great measure destroyed. The following inscription is still legible :—" Drumclog, 1679 ; Bothwell, 1679. Kilmaurs for the Presbyterian interest of Christ, Reformation in Church and State, agreeable to the Word of God and our Sworn Covenants."

Upon reaching the Cross I stepped into an inn to partake of refreshments before starting on my homeward journey.

Having done so, and indulged in a chat with the cheerful landlord, I took my leave, and staff in hand turned into the road leading to Crosshouse. Passing the station of the new line of railway which has brought Kilmaurs into something like direct communication with the outer world, and which doubtless will yet be the means of introducing a larger measure of trade and commercial enterprise into its sluggish system, I pushed onward and soon left the old village behind. Straying along the hedge-bordered highway, amusing myself from time to time by knocking the tops off thistles with swinging blows of my stick, I stopped occasionally to survey the landscape and the fields of yellow grain all ripe for the sickle that waved in the cool afternoon breeze. The sickle? well that is hardly correct in this era of wonder-working machinery, for the reaping machine is now universally used, and in fact I heard its click, clicking sound, and saw it at work in several fields where rakers and binders were busy "stooking" the golden-eared treasure as it fell before the advancing juggernaut. I did not meet with anything calling for special notice in this road until I arrived at the handsome bridge which spans the old line of railway. I lingered on it for some time and watched the trains glide along like things of life, and their engines vomiting forth clouds of smoke and steam which floated away in flakey, fleecy clouds and melted into nothingness. From the west parapet I looked down upon Crosshouse station and over a wide expanse of country through which the railway runs into dim perspective.

To the south of the railway is the estate of Plann, and on some rising ground near the bridge the extensive fire-clay works of John M'Knight & Son. The estate is the property of the senior partner, who has been very successful in his mining operations. Some years ago, while sinking a pit in the vicinity of the mansion-house, a seam of ironstone of a very high quality was discovered somewhat accidentally, and contrary to the expectation of the most eminent geologists. When the discovery was made known many who are deeply interested and engaged in geological studies came and carried away specimens of the ore, with a sceptical feeling that would scarce admit the fact that ironstone is in the locality. Besides ironstone the estate is rich in coal and fire-clay. The coal is of a first-class kind, while the fire-clay contains properties

M

which enable it to withstand intense heat, and it is pronounced to compare favourably with the most celebrated clays of a fire-resisting nature by the eminent R. Carter Moffat and the well-known Robert A. Tatlock, F.R.C.E., F.C.S.

From the bridge a short walk brought me to Knockentiber, a row of old houses at present occupied by miners. Near to it stands the ruin of Busbie Castle, once the residence of a family named Mowat, who alienated their lands somewhere about 1630. Being somewhat curious, I went to inspect the pile, and found it situated in a garden a short distance from Crosshouse road. It seems to have been a fortified feudal mansion of three storeys. Round the architraves there is a sculptured cable which winds fantastically round the walls. The wreck is in a most ricketty and seemingly unsafe condition—so much so, indeed, that I would not be surprised to hear of it being blown down during a storm. Little is known regarding it. It is supposed to have been built by a David Mowat, who received a grant of the lands from Robert III. somewhere about 1390. His descendants seemingly never attained distinction. If we are to believe the indefatigable Wodrow, the last of the Mowats who dwelt in the castle was not an over scrupulous observer of the Sabbath, for he profaned the holy day by having great gatherings at his house, and by playing at football and other games. "Mr. Welsh took the liberty to write several prudent and civil letters to the gentleman, desiring him to suppress the profanation of the Lord's day at his house. The gentleman not loving to be received a Puritan, slighted all, and would not amend. In a little time after, Mr. Welsh, riding that way, came to his gate, and called for the gentleman, who, coming out, invited Mr. Welsh in, which he declined, and told him he was come to him with a heavy message from God, which was, that because he had slighted the advice given him from the Lord, and would not restrain the profanation of the Sabbath in his lands and beside his house, therefore, the Lord would cast him out of his house and lands and none of his posterity should ever enjoy them. This was visibly fulfilled; and though the gentleman was in very good circumstances at the time, yet from that day forth all things went cross, and he fell into one difficulty after another until he was compelled to sell his estate; and when he was giving the purchaser possession of it, he said with tears before his wife and children, 'Now, Mr. Welsh is a true prophet.'" This is Wodrow's account of the vacuation of the castle and lands, and no doubt he penned it in good faith and believed every word of it. Paterson says, that "in 1661, Hugh, Earl of Eglinton, was served heir to his predecessor in the lands of Busbie, Knockentiber, and Robertown. It had been in their possession, however, some years previously. Among the Eglinton papers there is a receipt for the rents of Robertown and Busbie for crop 1638, amounting to one thousand four scoir sevintein pundis, threttein shillings, four pennies. The Mowats of Busbie," he adds, "are now wholly extinct, and the name in Ayrshire is rare." From inspecting the castle I returned to Knockentiber, and took the nearest road home, which is an old and very hilly one. Descending a pretty steep brae I arrived at the Carmel, crossed a neat bridge, and sped onward. On my left, near the bank of the stream, I observed, on some rising ground, a circular mound which wakened my curiosity to such an extent that I determined to visit it, and for that purpose introduced myself to the tenant of the farm of Greenhill. The mound is situated at the back of the farm-house, on the top of a steep bank, but there is nothing about it externally to excite interest. At first I conjectured the eminence to be a justice mound, but upon enquiry this proved fallacious, for there is good authority for supposing that it is an ancient barrow or tumulus, beneath which the dead of some forgotten conflict lie buried. Some years ago several stone coffins were discovered in a field on the farm of Waterpark in the parish of Kilmaurs. The newspaper account of the discovery, from which I quote, goes on to say:—"These graves have been found within the circuit of one of three large barrows or tumulii, situated on either bank of the Carmel water; the tumulus to which they pertain being, as already stated, upon Waterpark Farm, and the others being situated upon Greenhill farm—the most remarkable of the three, indeed, being close to Greenhill farmhouse. The surface being now pared from the Waterpark Cairn, it presents the usual aggregation of stones piled over the forgotten dead of ancient times." After chatting some time with the occupants of the farm, I resumed my homeward journey, and sped on my way, up hill and down dale, until I came within sight of the town, and as

I stood on the high ground looking down into the valley where it nestles, the following lines of M'Queen of Barkip came to mind:—

> "There stands the town—populous and dense,
> The monstrous, moving, and promiscuous mass
> Of all that's evil and of all that's good.
> There vice and virtue, ignorance and pride,
> Learning, humility, justice, and gross fraud,
> Stern avarice and sympathy benign
> Dwell with each other 'neath one common roof;
> And there, too, wealth and deepest misery
> Rush side by side, like two twin sister streams.
> Meet, mix, and mingle, and yet, strange to tell,
> Break not each other's surface, but remain
> Like oil and water pour'd in the same glass,
> Distinctly separate as they ne'er had met."

Passing Bonnyton Square, I soon gained Portland Street, and mingled with the jostling throng.

CHAPTER XIV.

From Kilmarnock to Grougar—The Ruins of Tammie Raeburn's Cottage—His self-imposed vow, personal appearance, courtship, witticisms, etc.—Grougar Row—Loudoun Kirk—The Queir—Lady Flora Hastings—Her melancholy death—The character of her Poems—Janet Little, the poetical correspondent of Robert Burns—George Palmer—An obscure Covenanter—A relic of Loudoun Kirk.

ONE Saturday morning while aimlessly straying through the town I resolved to retire from its noise and bustle for a space and seek the quietude of the country. For this purpose I crossed Green Bridge, and after a short walk arrived at Holehouse road. Turning into it, I entered the first road on the right and held onward. This road—as the reader in all probability is aware—runs between Kilmarnock and Loudoun Kirk, and is one of the good old undulating sort that winds over heights and hollows in such a manner that the pedestrian meets with a good deal of ups and downs while traversing it. Any little toil, however, that I encountered during my walk was amply repaid by the extensive and beautiful views obtained of the valley of the Irvine, and of the ever-memorable district,

"Where Loudoun Hill rears high its conic form,
And bares its rocky bosom to the storm."

From Bonnyhill, where the view is exceptionally fine, a lengthy walk brought me to the Irvine, at a point where it sweeps round a curve and tears along its channel through some beautiful scenery from which it emerges triumphantly, and passes placidly on its way to the sea. From the margin of the river the road diverges and becomes somewhat steep for a short distance. Along it, on the brow of a hill, a little off the highway, stands the beautiful villa of Mr. John Murray, factor for Grougar, and in the hollow behind, concealed from view, the ruin of the humble cottage of Tammie Raeburn, the Ayrshire Hermit. Being anxious to visit what was at one time the residence of a peculiarly interesting personage, I climbed over a field gate and alighted in a kind of roadway which runs along the side of a hedge and terminates in a small holm. Rounding a turn of the path the roofless, ruinous domicile suddenly came into view—a circumstance that caused me to pause and ruminate upon the changed scene before me. Where now, I asked myself, are the swains and braw lasses who made this hollow ring with their laughter and daffing glee forty years ago? Some are removed far from the place of their nativity, others slumber in the lethe of death, and the few living are wrinkled with care and fast hastening to "the bourne from whence no traveller returns." I found two gables of the cottage entire, but the back and front walls much broken down, and the interior strewed with the *debris*, out of which grew tall nettles and rank weeds. The tresseled ivy twined fantastically about one of the gables, and clutched the tottering stones with its tendrils, as if anxious to hold the fabric together. The eccentric Thomas Raeburn, whose memory gives to the ruin a kind of interest, died on the 23rd of June, 1843, in the 74th year of his age, after spending the greater part of his life in the fulfilment of a foolish self-imposed vow which he rigorously kept until the day of his death. He now sleeps in Stewarton Kirkyard, but his name and personal appearance will long be spoken of, and numerous anecdotes of him will form the subject of many a story at firesides in town and country. Raeburn inherited the house and a few acres of land, which constituted his farm, from his father. Curiously enough the small property was surrounded by that of other people, and there was no direct road into it save one through a field belonging to a neighbour. This the neighbour closed, and forbade Raeburn to use it; but Raeburn, imagining that "use and wont" constituted a right to continue what had been a privilege, went to law, lost the case, and was mulcted in heavy expenses. The result of the trial so preyed upon his mind that he became morose and gloomy, for he believed that justice had not been meted out, and that the judge had dealt harshly with him. In this frame of mind he took a solemn vow upon himself that he would never shave his beard, cut his hair, or renew his clothing until he received his rights. In course of time he became an odd-looking personage. His hair grew long and matted, and his beard, which was unkempt, hung in long tangled masses down his breast. His clothes, too, in course of time lost their identity, and became so patched and darned that it was ultimately a matter of difficulty to discover an original piece of any garment. Naturally enough such a peculiar individual attracted many visitors from all parts of the country, but more so from Kilmarnock—a favourite rural walk with young people of both sexes being from the town to Tammie's residence and back. He was of a parsimonious, money-loving disposition, lived sparingly, and drank nothing but water when bacchanalian cheer was not supplied to him gratis or procured without making a call on his purse. Tammie was never married, although in early life he had a desire of being so to the daughter of a neighbouring farmer who had attracted his attention at church. Peeps at her charms during the hours of divine service did not satisfy the would-be suitor long, for he resolved to call at the farm and offer the maiden his hand and heart. With this object in view he dressed himself in his Sunday clothes one fine day and set out to her residence, fully sensible of the delicate nature of his mission. With a palpitating heart he knocked at the door. It was opened by his affianced, who enquiringly looked, as if anxious to ascertain his business. Tammie stared at her, but not a word could he utter. Ultimately, by a prodigious effort, he managed to stammer out—" Could ye tell me the road to Finnick ?" The nymph gave the required information, and so ended the only courtship that he was ever known to engage in. After this event an old woman kept house for him, and managed his dairy, for he kept several cows and was famed for making cheese of an excellent quality. Tammie welcomed visitors of all grades to his residence, and was ever ready to crack a joke, and that as often as possible at their expense; but these were mostly tame and childish, savouring more of catches than witticisms. For instance, upon being asked if his clock was with the town, he replied in a self-satisfied manner—" No, it's twa mile an' a half aff it." If a visitor asked to light his pipe, he was generally told by the "hermit" that "There's no as muckle fire in the house as wad licht a pipe, but ye may licht yer tobacco." Upon being asked if he was ever drunk, he replied—"There's naebody wi' a throat big enough to swallow the like o' me." Tammie had a strange influence over the feathered tribe. Often for the gratification of visitors he would go into his garden and cry " Bobbie,

bobbie;" then place a small piece of bread between his lips and stand still until a robin would alight upon his beard, take the morsel from his mouth, and fly off to a neighbouring bough with the prize. To accommodate visitors he dealt in lemonade and ginger-beer, and occasionally in a more stimulating beverage. This infringement of the excise law, however, did not go unpunished, for upon one occasion he was convicted and fined in twenty-five pounds. Raeburn has passed away. The wealth he so avariciously scraped together was divided amongst his relations, the trees of his orchard have been cut down, and his bit farm is now included in the estate of Grougar. His parsimony would not allow him to enjoy life, and he, I have no doubt, assumed eccentricities with a desire to appear odd, and ultimately because it brought in the bawbees.

Leaving the shattered hermitage I crossed a stubble field and strolled up the river bank. Passing Milton Mill I regained the highway, and after a brisk walk arrived at Grougar Row—a collection of miners' dwellings remarkable for nothing save the number of rosy-cheeked children sporting in front of them as happy and as frolicsome as fairies. It is somewhat curious that wherever working-people are located bairns are plentiful. Were they a source of wealth, as they are said to be in some parts of the globe, how well off many a poor man would be. Beyond the Row, stately trees line the road for some considerable distance, and render the walk a pleasant one. I enjoyed it immensely, and arrived at Loudoun Kirkyard well satisfied with the scene through which I passed. The gate was locked, and by the long rank grass that grew about the entrance it was evident that it had not been opened for some time. In a dilemma I eyed the wall, but abandoned the idea of climbing by turning into a side road where I observed a cottage. Passing it I stopped before the entrance to a neat garden where roses and flowers of various hues luxuriantly bloomed, and beautified the spot. Venturing within the flowery threshold, I was met by a motherly middle-aged woman, who kindly directed me through the garden to a little wicket which opened into the churchyard. This lady afterwards proved to be the occupant of the cottage, and the daughter of the late James Nisbet, who was sexton of Loudoun churchyard for a long series of years, and on that account is invaluable to the visitor, as she is well versed in the antiquities of the burial place and the lore of the district. The ancient place of sepulture is surrounded by a wall and a row of sombre trees, through which the passing wind soughs as if mournfully sighing for the oblivious dead mouldering beneath their shade. Its interior is unadorned with shrubbery, and the headstones and monuments are few and scattered, but in the absence of pompous decoration, Nature has spread a grassy coverlet over the spot, and on the occasion of my visit it was decked with gowans, buttercups, and a variety of wild flowers, which she scatters so profusely over hill and dale. In the centre stands a meagre remnant of Loudoun Kirk, consisting of one gable and a portion called the "queir," which has been used as the Loudoun family sepulchre from a very early date. The kirk was erected in 1451 by a donation to the monks of Kilwinning by the lady of Sir John Campbell. The queir has a very ancient appearance, and is embellished with the Loudoun family arms and other curious devices. In the back wall there is a small grated window which I looked through until my eyes became accustomed to the internal gloom and revealed to me the outlines of several coffins on the floor, whose mountings glistened in the faint light and whose appearance caused a strange shudder to thrill my frame. These encasements were all renewed some years ago, the old ones having become so decayed that they had fallen to pieces. Within the queir rests the mortal remains of the gifted but unfortunate Lady Flora Hastings. When one of the ladies of the bedchamber to H.R.H. the Duchess of Kent, a most cruel and unmerited slander was raised against her, which so preyed upon her mind and wounded her feelings that she died of a broken heart in Buckingham Palace in July, 1839. Nearly the whole nation at the time deeply sympathised with her, and greatly deplored her untimely end. By her request her remains were conveyed to Loudoun and deposited alongside those of generations of her ancestors. The body was followed to its last resting place by her mother (the Dowager Marchioness), her sisters and brothers, and other relations of her family, and also by many parishioners who felt a deep commiseration for her. The mother survived her favourite daughter for little over a year, and it is believed that the melancholy circumstances which accelerated her daughter's death hastened her own. Lady Flora was an accomplished poetess, and shortly after her decease her poems, which are distinguished by much purity of thought, sweetness and grace, were collected and published. An able reviewer has said that "such a deep love for the beautiful, the exalted, and the holy reigns throughout them all, that it is impossible to repel the conviction that her actions accorded with her words, and that her words gave but the utterance to the calm and sinless feelings of her heart."

> "O, ill befa' the raven wing
> That brake her harp o' gouden string!
> The dove-like harp whose siller lays
> Pour'd music sweet on Loudoun braes."

From the queir I turned my attention to the little burying-place and the unassuming memorials it contains. Near to its door the oldest stone in the yard is to be met with. It is embellished with masonic emblems, and is to the memory of "Matho Fultun, maister mason—ane richt honest man who died in the year of God 1632." There are some verses in its centre which are most difficult to make out, but the gist of them is that Matho went to his grave as to his bed, with the intention of rising at the resurrection. The stone is very curious, and well worth the attention of those who are expert at deciphering semi-obliterated inscriptions. A few yards from this, and near to the ivy-mantled gable of the auld Kirk, a plain slab marks the spot where lie the remains of Janet Little, the celebrated poetical correspondent of Robert Burns. It bears the following inscription:—"In memory of John Richmond, who died August 10, 1819, aged 78 years; and Janet Little, his spouse, who died March 15, 1818, aged 54 years, and five of their children." Janet Little, authoress of a poetical work which never gained any great or lasting popularity, spent her early years about Ecclefechan, and came to serve in the capacity of a domestic servant in the family of Mrs Henrie, a daughter of Mrs Dunlop of Dunlop, the distinguished friend of the poet Burns, who rented Loudon Castle during the years 1788—89. While in their service, she met with a volume of the bard's poems, and seemingly was so enraptured with its contents that she conceived a partiality for the author and wrote him a poetical address, which she forwarded along with a letter of explanation. A few verses from it may not be out of place :—

> " Fair fa' the honest rustic swain,
> The pride o' a' our Scottish plain ;
> Thou gi'es us joy to hear thy strain,
>   And notes sae sweet ;
> Old Ramsay's shade reviv'd again
>   In thee we greet.
>
> " Lov'd Thalia, that delightfu' muse,
> Seem'd long shut up in a recluse ;
> To all she did her aid refuse
>   Since Allan's day ;
> 'Till Burns arose, then did she chuse
>   To grace thy lay.
>
> " To hear thy sang all ranks desire,
> Sae weel you strike the dormant lyre
> Apollo with poetic fire
>   Thy breast does warm ;
> An' critics silently admire
>   Thy art to charm.
>
> " Cæsar and Luath weel can speak—
> 'Tis pity e'er their gabs should steek,
> But into human nature keek,
>   And knots unravel ;
> To hear their lectures once a week
>   Nine miles I travel."

Near to Janet's grave, there is a handsome monument erected by the parishioners of Loudoun as a tribute to the memory of their late pastor, the Rev. James Allan, who died 1st June, 1864; and at a short distance from it a stone, unassuming in appearance, to the memory of Margaret Reid (spouse to John Campbell, smith, Alton), who died December, 27th, 1821, aged 65 years. It bears the following reminder to the passer by :—

> " Time was I was as thou art now,
> Looking o'er the dead as thou dost me ;
> Ere long thou'lt lie as low as I,
> And others stand and look o'er thee."

Upon reading these rude lines I leaned on my staff and mused, " for other feet will tread the street a hundred years to come," and we will rest from our labours forgotten. In life death is feared, and its approach dreaded, because of its mystery; but could we penetrate the gloom of the grave, perchance we would hail the dread spectre with as much joy as the tempest-tossed mariner does the sight of his native shore.

In the vicinity of the last named stone, there is a very handsome one of recent erection bearing the following inscription :—" Erected by Helen Fulton, in memory of her husband, George Palmer, who died 26th May, 1874, aged 77 years. He was teacher of the Free School, Kilmarnock, for 31 years. His duties, discharged with conscientious diligence, gained the entire approbation of its directors. He was a man of rare abilities, breathed the very spirit of the Gospel, lived its life, and his end was peace." The name of George Palmer will be familiar to many elderly natives of Kilmarnock, and on this account the sleeper 'neath the green turf deserves more than a passing notice. Born of parents who belonged to that class designated " the industrious poor," he was early apprenticed to the loom, and continued at it until well up in manhood. Being possessed of a fine intellect, he thirsted after knowledge and gradually acquired an education that fitted him for a better position. During the Radical years he zealously entered into politics, and being gifted with a calm, discriminating mind, and power of language, he soon became a leading spirit amongst those who were infected with similar opinions. To be a Radical, especially an intelligent one, was to be a marked man, and the subject of this notice began to be looked upon as a dangerous individual by the authorities, and, with many others, was apprehended on the night of the 14th of April, 1820, when a regiment of Yeomanry Cavalry invaded Kilmarnock. When made prisoner, Bailie Porteous, who accompanied the captors, searched his house, and when rummaging through his desk, remarked, " George, you are a beautiful writer." Perhaps this incident had something to do with his future prosperity, for it was this veritable Bailie who introduced him to the Free School. After suffering three months' imprisonment in Ayr Jail, he was discharged *without a trial*, and returned home to abandon politics for matters of a more profitable nature. Shortly afterwards he received the appointment to the Free School, and after labouring in it for thirty years was granted by the directors a retiring salary, which he enjoyed for nearly twenty years. Mr Palmer was the author of several school manuals, and contributed to the local papers. For a long period he was an elder in King Street Church. When he retired from public life he settled in Galston, and became a member, and ultimately an elder, in the church of the Rev. Mr Matthewson. He fought the good fight, and closed a life of usefulness at a ripe old age. Besides the stones noticed here at random, there are several others both ancient and modern that will prove very interesting to the visitor. One near the little gate that I noticed when leaving the churchyard I cannot omit. It bears the device of a cross and crown, and the following inscription :—" Here lies Thomas Flemming of Loudoun Hill, who, for his appearance in arms in his own defence, and in the defence of the Gospel, according to the obligations of our National Covenants and agreeable to the Word of God, was shot in an encounter at Drumclog, 1st June, 1679, by bloody Graham of Claverhouse." Nothing seems to be known of Thomas Flemming further than what the inscription tells. His name does not occur in Wodrow or any other work I have met with.

When leaving the secluded burying place, Mrs Semple, the occupant of the cottage already mentioned, showed me a relic of Loudoun Kirk in the shape of a moderately-sized bell, which, tradition states, was sent from Holland as a present to the parishioners by James second Earl of Loudoun, eldest son of the Lord Chancellor. It was anciently the custom to toll this bell in front of funeral processions on their way to the churchyard; but it has been discontinued, and the relic is now a curiosity. The words "Loudoun Kirk" is cast upon it in raised letters.

CHAPTER XV.

The Policies of Loudoun Castle—The external and internal appearance of the Building—The Family Portraits—The Library—The old Yew Tree—The Loudoun Family, and salient points in the History of some of its Members—The old Castle of Loudoun—Its destruction by the Kennedys, &c.

From Loudoun Kirk I passed along a very romantic road, and after a sharp but pleasant walk arrived at the entrance gate of Loudoun Castle. The policies are thickly wooded, exquisitely picturesque, and possessed of a wild romantic beauty that charms the eye and thrills with ecstasy the lover of romantic scenery. Throughout the estate there are very many aged trees of symmetrical loveliness, whose gnarled arms in the vernal season of the year are almost hid from view by wealth of foliage. These monarchs of the lawn and dark wood are mementos of that enterprising and zealous nobleman, John, fourth Earl of Loudoun, who is said to have greatly improved the estate and imparted to it its sylvan beauty by planting upwards of one million trees which he collected from all parts of the globe. The drive to the castle is lined on each side by a neat grass border and by stately trees, which shadow the path with their leafy boughs. Admiringly viewing it, I stood in the roadway irresolutely scratching my head, for I felt somewhat perplexed upon this occasion as to the ways and means of gaining admittance to the castle and grounds. Summoning up courage, and putting on an air of importance, I passed through the gate without being stopped or questioned by the people in the lodge, and on and on until I came within sight of the imposing and magnificent mansion of the Loudoun family. Through the trees on my left I observed the neat villa of Mr. Robert Mackie, the manager of the estate, and from that quarter feared an abrupt termination to my explorations, but in this I was agreeably disappointed.

Arriving at the castle, I was struck by its massive appearance, and was delighted to find upon examination that it combines the gracefulness of modern architecture with the massive strength of early times. One turreted, battlemented, square tower was erected in the twelfth century, and another which overlooks the entire building in the fifteenth. To these antiquated structures Sir John Campbell who was created Lord Chancellor in 1642, made an extensive addition, and in 1811 the whole was augmented by a large and stately portion, which gives to the pile quite a palatial appearance. The interior is fitted up with great magnificence and sumptuously furnished, the walls of the principal apartments being literally covered with finely executed portraits of the Loudoun and Rowallan families. Some of these paintings are very old and recall to one's mind many stirring events in the good old days when plain speaking and hard blows were in fashion, and when the four feet of cold steel which dangled by every gallant's side was used to enforce arguments and settle differences. Among the family likenesses a portrait of Charles I. is very interesting at this date on account of its disfigurement. When the castle was besieged by Cromwell's soldiers it hung in the gallery, and after the capitulation of Lady Loudoun—who defended the place right gallantly—formed an object for the soldiers, who ransacked the rooms whereon to vent their contempt for his Majesty by making thrusts at his picture with their swords—a pastime, no doubt, which was well seasoned with jokes and laughter. The library is very extensive and contains nearly 10,000 volumes, besides ancient manuscripts, some of which are very curious. Close to the castle wall grows a patriarchal yew tree of unknown antiquity. Under its deep shade, in the time of William the Lion, one of the family charters was signed, and when the union between Scotland and England was entered into, Lord Hugh Campbell of Loudoun subscribed the articles beneath its umbrageous boughs. During the reign of Charles II., when James, second Earl of Loudoun, was banished to Holland, he held secret communication with his lady, and addressed his letters " to the gude wife at the Auldton, at the old yew tree, Loudoun, Scotland." The aged veteran at this day looks healthy and strong, and appears to be as capable of withstanding the blasts of another century as any tree on the estate.

No family in Ayrshire can boast of a more lengthened possession of their property or a more honourable pedigree than that of Loudoun. About the year 1189 the barony was granted to James, son of Lambrinus, by Richard de Morville, overlord of the district of Cuninghame and minister of William the Lion. At his death he left an only daughter, who married Sir Reginald de Craufurd, hereditary Sheriff of Ayrshire, and by him had four sons, from one of whom are descended the Craufurds of Craufurdland. Their great-grand-daughter (Margaret, only child of Hugh de Craufurd) married Sir Malcolm Wallace of Ellerslie, and was mother of Sir William Wallace, the famous hero. In the fifth generation the ancestral line of the Craufurds of Loudoun terminated in the only daughter of a Sir Reginald, who fell in battle in 1303 while fighting for Scottish independence. This lady married Sir Duncan Campbell of Lochow, and from this union sprang the first Campbells of Loudoun. In the twelfth generation the Lochow Campbells were merged into those of Lawers by the marriage of Margaret, Baroness of Loudoun, with Sir John Campbell in 1620. In the fifth generation the Lawers Campbells terminated in Flora Mure, Countess of Loudoun, who married in 1804 Francis Rawdon Hastings, Earl of Moira. In 1816 he was created a British Peer by the title of Marquis of Hastings, Viscount of Loudoun, etc. He was Governor of India and Commander-in-Chief of Malta. He died in 1836, and was succeeded in the Loudoun estate by his descendants, in whose possession it now is.

Perhaps it may not be out of place here to notice the salient points in the history of some members of the Loudoun family. Sir John Campbell of Lawers, who was created Earl of Loudoun, Tarrinzean, and Mauchline in 1633, and afterwards Lord Chancellor of Scotland, was a staunch Covenanter, and acted a conspicuous part in the stirring events of his time. He distinguished himself in 1637 by his active resistance to the ill-judged and unconstitutional attempt of Charles I. to force Episcopacy upon Scotland. He was one of the commissioners from the Scots army who settled the pacification of Berwick with Charles I. in 1639, and was subsequently committed to the Tower on a charge of high treason. After remaining there for some time, he was, through the influence of the Marquis of Hamilton, liberated. He commanded the Scots army at the Battle of Newburn, and was afterwards appointed First Commissioner of the Treasury, with a yearly pension of £1000. After taking an active share in the Civil War at the Restoration he was deprived of the office of Chancellor, and fined 12,000 pounds Scots. He died in 1652, and is interred in the queir of Loudoun Kirk. The third Earl of Loudoun was a Privy Councillor in 1697, and was appointed in 1704 one of the Commissioners of the Treasury, and made a Knight of the Thistle. In the following year he was appointed joint Secretary of State for Scotland, and named one of the commissioners for the Union. In 1708 he was appointed keeper of the great seal in Scotland, with a pension of £2000 a year. In 1715 he was made Lord Lieutenant of Argyleshire, and served as a volunteer under the Duke of Argyle at Sheriffmuir. He was also one of the sixteen Scots representative peers from 1707 to 1731. His countess was a remarkable woman, having greatly improved the grounds around her residence at Sorn Castle, where she died in her hundredth year. Their only son John—the fourth Earl of Loudoun—was a distinguished military officer, and sat as a representative peer for forty-eight years. He was a staunch royalist, and in 1745 raised a regiment of highlanders for the service of government, and on the breaking out of the rebellion of that year joined Sir John Cope, under whom he acted as adjutant-general. After taking part in the highland campaign, he was appointed captain-general and governor-in-chief of the province of Virginia, and was constituted commander-in-chief of all the British forces in America. Although thus busily engaged abroad, he was the first agricultural improver of the district of Loudoun. In 1740 he commenced operations by making roads through the parish and causing a bridge to be built over the Irvine. He was also a vigorous planter and encloser, and was the first to introduce foreign trees into the West of Scotland; in fact, he may be said to have bequeathed to Loudoun braes that sylvan beauty for which they are so justly celebrated. During his time ten entire swivel brass cannon marked with the Campbell arms were discovered near to the castle, buried some two feet below the surface of the ground, but how they came to be there was never ascertained. This enterprising nobleman died in 1782, aged seventy-seven years.

After lingering about Loudoun Castle for some time I entered the principal avenue and leisurely strolled in the direction of Newmilns. Now the path would pass through a strip of wood and be darkened by the foliage of stately trees, then it would emerge into the open glade and wind along a verdant bank, or down a dell and over a burnie, bickering amongst the brackens. At a shady nook by the side of a little streamlet, a good half-mile distant from the castle, I diverged from the path, passed over the brow of a well-wooded bank, and arrived at the brink of a broad gully which partly encircled a rugged and almost unascendable mound. Descending the chasm, I with difficulty reached the bottom and passed through a luxuriant crop of nettles and up the opposite bank, a feat accomplished by laying hold of whatever would assist my ascent. Gaining the summit, several half-buried blocks of masonry and portions of foundations made known that I stood on the site of the old castle of Loudoun—a building which was anterior to any portion of the present magnificent structure. Regarding its history there is nothing authentic known, but it is preserved in the traditional mind that it was burned by the clan Kennedy during a fray. This is very probable, and is partly borne out by the fact that a family on the estate, who have occupied their farm for centuries, claim descent from a noble liegeman, who at the risk of life and limb dashed into the burning pile in spite of chief and clansmen and dragged forth the charter chest of the Loudoun family and bore it off in triumph. This family tradition is somewhat strengthened by history, for a deadly feud existed between the Campbells of Loudoun and the Kennedies of Carrick about the year 1527. During a foray which the former made into the territory of the latter, the Earl of Cassillis was slain, but to avenge his death the Kennedies entered the district of the Campbells on several occasions and laid it waste by fire and sword; therefore it is possible that during one of these raids the old castle was attacked and left a smoking ruin. A ballad, from which I make the following extract, was at one time very popular in the district, but as it ascribes the burning of the castle to "Adam o' Gordon and his men," it is probably an adaptation, for it is well known that the wandering minstrels of old, by changing the names of persons and places, adapted their lays to suit similar incidents in different localities :—

>Out then spake the Lady Margaret,
>   As she stood upon the stair—
>The fire was at her goud garters,
>   The low was at her hair—
>
>" I would give the black," she says,
>   " And so would I the brown,
>For a drink o' yon water
>   That runs by Galston toun."
>
>Out then spake fair Annie,
>   She was baith gimp and sma',
>" O row me in a pair o' sheets,
>   And tow me doun the wa'."
>
>" O hold thy tongue, thou fair Annie,
>   And let thy talkin' be,
>For thou must stay in this fair castle,
>   And bear thy death with me."
>
>" I would rather be burnt to ashes sma',
>   And be cast on yon sea foam,
>Before I'd give up this fair castle,
>   And my lord so far from home.
>
>" My good lord has an army strong,
>   He's now gone o'er the sea,
>He bade me keep this gay castle
>   As long as it would keep me.
>
>" I've four-and-twenty braw milk kye
>   Gangs on yon lily lee,
>I'd give them a' for a blast of wind
>   To blaw the reek from me."
>
>O pittie on yon fair castle,
>   That's built o' stone and lime,
>But far mair pittie for Lady Loudoun,
>   And all her children nine.

The scenery in the vicinity of the mound is wild and romantic. After gazing upon it for some time I reluctantly left the spot, and returned to the avenue with my mind made up to go as far as Newmilns, for, as the reader is probably aware, the principal drive through the policies of Loudoun Castle merges into a road which terminates in the ancient village.

CHAPTER XVI.

Loudoun Braes—Newmilns, its appearance, history, and trade—The Radical proclivities of the inhabitants—The old Tower and incidents associated with it—The Parish Church—Norman Macleod—The Churchyard—Interesting Tombstones commemorative of Nisbet of Hardhill and other Covenanting natives of the Parish who suffered during the Persecution—The Workmen's Institute—"The Lass o' Patie's Mill."

BEYOND the site of the old castle the path gradually loses its sylvan beauty and merges into a rough, undulating road which winds over braes that called forth the admiration and awakened the muse of the sweet singer, Tannahill. Since his day they have lost none of their attractions, but appear as verdant and picturesque as they did when he strayed over their heathy summits admiring "Loudoun's bonnie woods," and possibly planning the song which has given them a world-wide celebration. Straying onward, viewing the classical scenery and the finely-wooded slopes of Lanfine, which rise abruptly from the vale lying between it and the Loudoun estate, a walk of some two miles brought me to a turn where the hedge-bordered road ran through a glade and shortly afterwards abruptly terminated at a spot called Bore Brae. From the summit of the brae the spectator looks down upon Newmilns, which lies at his feet in a narrow vale through which the river Irvine winds serpent-like as it passes by the quaint village and through scenery whose magnificence calls forth the admiration of every visitant.

> "There as I pass'd with careless steps and slow,
> The mingling notes came soften'd from below;
> The swain responsive as the milk-maid sung,
> The sober herd that lowed to meet their young,
> The noisy geese that gabbled o'er the pool,
> The playful children just let loose from school,
> The watch-dog's voice that bayed the whispering wind,
> And the loud laugh that spoke the vacant mind,"

"in sweet confusion" smote my ear as I looked down upon the picturesquely-situated hamlet. No stately building save the Parish Church, which is topped with a beautiful spire, greets the eye, the village being composed nearly wholly of humble, unostentatious buildings, primitive alike in construction and appearance, and totally destitute of architectural beauty. But humble as it is, it has a history which dates back to a very remote period, it having been a place of some little importance when Kilmarnock was an obscure village, and when other towns which surpass it in elegance and importance were almost unknown. A royal charter under the superiority of the Earls of Loudoun was conferred upon it in the reign of James IV., but how it began to be is a matter of uncertainty. Possibly it grew up in the vicinity of grain mills erected on the bank of the river, for its water at this date drives the wheels of not a few as it courses to the sea.* The inhabitants have always been noted for their Radical proclivities, and not a few of them have suffered for their enthusiasm in the cause of reform. Several suffered death and many underwent imprisonment for standing up in defence of the Solemn League and Covenant during the troublous times of the persecution; and during the Radical period they were so much dreaded by the Government that a detachment of soldiers was placed in the village to keep them in order, it being considered one of the greatest hotbeds of Radicalism in the country. Newmilns of to-day contains a population of 3028. The inhabitants are mostly engaged in muslin-weaving, and the music of the shuttle has a merry echo in its streets, but it is a wretchedly remunerative employment, the industrious workman being able to earn little over a bare subsistence.

Strolling down Bore Brae, I entered the main street of the village, and found it to be broad and respectable, although somewhat rustic in appearance. Partly concealed behind some houses on its north side, I discovered the oldest building in the place, which consists of a massive square tower of some historic interest, being at one time a residence of the Loudoun family† and at another the headquarters of Captain

---

* Sir Hugh Campbell of Loudoun had a charter of the lands of Newmilns, with the mill and granary, dated 4th October, 1534.—*Paterson's Ayrshire Families.*

† The Master of Loudoun died in March, 1612. His latter will was made at "the Newmylnes, the sevint day of Merche." His lady also died the same month and year. Her latter will was made also at "Newmylnes, the penult day of Merche." They seem thus to have resided at the tower of Newmilns.—*Ibid.*

Inglis, a notorious scourge of the Covenanters, who, as related in a former chapter, surprised the men who had met in Little Blackwood for devotional purposes.

The writer of the Loudoun article in the *Statistical Account* in mentioning this tower says—" In one of the expeditions of Inglis's troops in the search of conventicals, eight men who were discovered praying in the Blackwood, near Kilmarnock, were taken prisoners. One of them, it is said, was immediately executed, and the soldiers in mockery kicked his head for a football along the Newmilns public green. Inglis was about to shoot the others when it was suggested to him that it would be prudent to get a written order from Edinburgh for their execution. The seven men in the meantime were confined in the old tower. But while the troop was absent on one of its bloody raids, with the exception of a small guard, a man named Browning, from Lanfine, with others who had been with him at Aird's Moss, got large sledge hammers from the old smithy (still in existence), with which they broke open the prison doors and permitted the Covenanters to escape. John Law (brother-in-law to Captain Nisbet) was shot in this exploit, and is buried close to the wall of the tower. The dragoons soon went in pursuit of the prisoners, but they had reached the heather, and where no cavalry could pursue them. The soldiers, however, having ascertained that John Smith of Croonan had given the runaways food went to Smith's house, and meeting him at his own door shot him dead! Within a short period his grave was to be seen in the garden of the old farmhouse."

Tradition states that only *one* soldier played football with the martyr's head, and that shortly afterwards he fell from the top of the tower into the court below and broke his neck —a fit consummation certainly to a heartless villain's life. Set into the gable of an old thatched house near the tower there is a tablet to the memory of the man who was shot when assisting to set the prisoners at liberty. It bears the following inscription:—" Renewed in 1822. Here lies John Law, who was shot at Newmilns, at the relieving of eight of Christ's prisoners who were taken at a meeting for prayer at Little Blackwood, in the parish of Kilmarnock, in April, 1685, by Captain Inglis and his party, for their adherence to the Word of God and Scotland's covenanted work of Reformation.

> "Cause I Christ's prisoners relieved
> I of my life was soon bereaved,
> By cruel enemies with rage,
> In that encounter did engage;
> The martyr's honour and his crown
> Bestowed on me! O high renown!
> That I should not only believe,
> But for Christ's cause my life should give."

The old tower at this epoch of civil and religious liberty is untenanted, but its rooms are occasionally made to ring by the Newmilns Brass Band, who use it to practise in. It has also been used as the village jail, and at one time pigeons were kept in it, which circumstance gave to it the name of "the dookit," a term by which it is locally spoken of.

From the tower I passed over to the Parish Church, a handsome building with a beautiful spire. It stands in an old burying-ground, and occupies the site of a former and much smaller place of worship, which a wag states was thrown through the windows of the new erection. I gained admittance to the burying-ground by a side door, and to the church by the kindness of an elderly woman who was engaged dusting out the sanctuary. Internally it is commodious and neatly fitted-up, and contains a beautiful white marble monumental tablet which bears the following inscription:—"In memory of Norman Macleod, D.D., one of Her Majesty's Chaplains for Scotland, and Dean of the Knights of the Order of the Thistle. Ordained to the charge of the Parish of Loudoun, 15th March, 1838; translated to Dalkeith, 15th December, 1843; and to Barony Parish, Glasgow, 17th July, 1851. Moderator of General Assembly in 1869. Died 16th June, 1872. 'Blessed are the dead which die in the Lord. They rest from their labours, and their works do follow them.'" Norman Macleod was too popular as a preacher, an author, and an editor to render any remarks of mine necessary, but I cannot refrain from stating that he was the most liberal-minded clergyman I ever knew; *good words* flowed from his lips, and what left his pen will form a valuable addition to the literature of our country.

The churchyard, although small and unkept, contains several interesting tombstones which commemorate martyrs to the cause of liberty. The first I met with bore the following inscription:—"To the memory of John Nisbet of Hardhill, who suffered martyrdom at the Grassmarket, Edinburgh, 4th December, 1685. Animated by a spirit to which genuine religion alone could give birth, the pure flame of civil and religious liberty alone could keep alive. He manfully struggled for a series of years to stem the tide of national degeneracy, and liberate his country from the tyrannical aggressions of the perjured house of Stewart. His conduct in arms at Pentland, Drumclog, and Bothwell Bridge, in opposition to prelatic encroachments and in defence of Scotland's Covenanted Reformation, is recorded in the annals of those oppressive times. His remains lie at Edinburgh, but the inhabitants of his native parish, and friends to the cause for which he fought and died, have caused this stone to be erected."

John Nisbet of Hardhill—an account of whose capture is given in a former chapter—was born in Newmilns about the year 1627. When Claverhouse was advancing the Covenanting army at Drumclog, a message was despatched to Hardhill to apprise him of the fact and induce him to join the little band. Although he had suffered much from prelatic persecution he hesitated not a moment, but mounted a horse and rode with all possible speed to the scene of action, merely stopping on his way through Darvel to induce John Morton, the village blacksmith, to accompany him and assist with his brawny arm to discomfit the foe. Both arrived on the field in time to be of immense service to the Covenanters, for they fell into their ranks in time to take part in the successful charge which decided the fate of the battle. In the thick of the fight, the smith encountered a dragoon who was entangled in the trappings of his wounded horse, and was about to dispatch him, but being moved by the man's piteous appeal for mercy, he disarmed him and led him from the field a prisoner. Many of the Covenanters, however, were not so humane, for they demanded that the dragoon should be put to death, on the ground that he was an enemy to their cause. This the smith strongly objected to, and declared that whoever touched a hair of his head he would cut down, for having given the man quarter, he would defend his life at the risk of his own. None feeling inclined to cross swords with the resolute champion, he was allowed to have his own way, but was expelled the fold, and ever after looked on with suspicion. To the left of the stone to the memory of John Nisbet, there is another which states that it was " Erected September 1829 by the Parishioners of Loudoun in testimony of their deep admiration of the noble struggle in defence of the civil and religious liberties of their country against the despotic and persecuting measures of the house of Stuart, maintained by the undernamed martyrs belonging to this parish, who suffered and died for their devotedness to the Covenanted work of Reformation :—

MATTHEW PATON, shoemaker in Newmilns, who was taken at Pentland, and executed at Glasgow, Decr. 19th, 1666.

DAVID FINDLAY, who was shot at Newmilns, by order of Dalziel, 1666.

JAMES WOOD, taken at the battle of Bothwell Bridge, and executed at Magus-muir, Nov. 25th, 1679.

JOHN NISBET, in Glen, executed at Kilmarnock, April 14th, 1683 ; and

JAMES NISBET, in Highside, executed at Glasgow, June 11th, 1684.

'These are they who came out of great tribulation. Rev. vii. 11.'"

Matthew Paton was tried along with three others who had been taken prisoner with him, and in spite of every plea set up in their behalf all four were put to death. Wodrow says " they were executed that day. The men were most cheerful, and had much of a sense of the Divine love upon them, and a great deal of peace in their suffering."

David Findlay belonged to Newmilns. Happening to be in Lanark when the Covenanting army passed through, he very foolishly spoke of the circumstance upon his return to his native village. The fact coming to the ears of Dalziel, he had Findlay brought before him, and because he was unable to answer certain questions as to who he saw, to the surprise of every one the tyrant ordered him to be shot. The wretched man pleaded hard with the lieutenant for one night to prepare for eternity, but that was denied him, for when Dalziel heard of the request he told the officer that he would teach him to obey without scruple, and " so," says Wodrow, "the man was shot dead, stripped naked, and left upon the spot."

James Wood when taken prisoner carried no arms, but because he would not call the rising at Bothwell rebellion, and Bishop Sharp's death murder, he was sentenced to be hanged.

John Nisbet was executed in the Cross of Kilmarnock. The circumstances of his death have been narrated in a former chapter.

James Nisbet was noted for his piety and for his enmity to the apostacy of his time. When attending the funeral of John Richmond of Knowe, who was executed in Glasgow for his adherence to the Covenanted work of Reformation, he was taken prisoner, but although no definite charge could be brought against him yet the subtile questions of his persecutors so entangled him that his answers became unsatisfactory, and he was found guilty of rebellion and sentenced to death. In the "Cloud of Witnesses" the following note is appended to his testimony:—"This martyr was so inhumanly treated and constantly watched that it was with much difficulty he got anything written, and that only a line now and then." He was executed at Howgatehead, a place in the vicinity of Glasgow at the period, but long since included within its limits. I remember when a mere youth of tracing the old Howgate, and with some degree of certainty indicating the situation of the gallows, and of spelling out the almost defaced words on a slab behind which this and other two martyrs lay buried. In fact, at this date, after having my own experience of toils and cares, anxieties and troubles, joys, sorrows, and reverses, I can distinctly remember the inscription, for then as now a martyr's grave, an auld kirkyard, or an ivy-mantled ruin, suited my poetic temperament, and possessed a charm for me that few others experienced. In 1862 the old slab, which was indented into a wall in Castle Street, a little beyond the corner of Garngad Hill, was removed and substituted by a beautiful tablet of polished granite, which was subscribed for by the citizens of Glasgow. It bears the following inscription, which is somewhat similar to that on the original stone:—"The dead yet speaketh. Behind this stone lyes James Nisbet, who suffered martyrdom at this place, June 5th, 1684. Also James Lawson and

Alexander Wood, who suffered martyrdom, October 24, 1684, for their adherence to the Word of God and Scotland's Covenanted work of Reformation." At its base is a drinking fountain, above which is inscribed the words, "Drink and think."

Among the many stones which the churchyard of Newmilns contains there are only two beside those already noticed which may be said to be of interest to the visitor. The one marks the spot where the dust of John Gebbie reposes, and the other where that of John Morton mingles with kindred earth. Gebbie fought at Drumclog, and was carried off the field mortally wounded, and like the mighty Nelson died with the shouts of victory ringing in his ears. Morton was tenant of Broomhill, a farm in the parish of Loudoun, and was shot by Claverhouse at the same engagement.

From the churchyard I regained the main street of the village and stopped before the Working Men's Institute, a very handsome two-storeyed building which was presented some years ago to the inhabitants by Miss Brown of Lanfine, a lady who takes a deep interest in the welfare of the working classes in the neighbourhood of her estate.

After straying through the village, and spending an hour in the house of an esteemed friend whose hospitality will not readily be forgotten, I turned my face towards Kilmarnock. Near to the western extremity of the village I passed a curious old bridge which crosses the Irvine and gives access to the terminus of the Galston branch of the South-Western Railway, and a little beyond it stopped and looked over to the scene of Ramsay's popular song, "The Lass o' Patie's Mill." A mill of modern appearance occupies the site of the erection which graced the bank of the Irvine in Ramsay's day, but the field wherein the rustic beauty was making hay when she attracted the attention of the Earl of Loudoun is still pointed out, and although one hundred and fifty years have passed since the event the stranger still stops by the brink of the stream and enquires for the song-hallowed scene. The story of the song is well known. The poet and the Earl of Loudoun were riding along the highway when it occurred to the latter that the comely appearance of the "lass" would form a fit subject for Allan's muse. At the suggestion the bard lagged behind, composed the ditty, and produced it the same afternoon at dinner.

CHAPTER XVII.

The Village of Darvel, its appearance and trade—Loudoun Hill and its Historic Associations—Wallace's Attack on the English Convoy—A Scottish Victory—Drumclog—The Laird of Torfoot's account of the Battle—His fight with Captain Arrol and his encounter with Claverhouse—The appearance of the field after the engagement—The Covenanters and their achievements.

ABOUT two miles east of Newmilns stands Darvel, a small village with 1729 of a population. It contains nothing historical or important, and consists of a long street lined with unassuming tenements, which are mostly occupied by muslin weavers, that industry being the staple of the place. The principal building is the Workmen's Institute, which was erected by Miss Brown of Lanfine as a memorial of her sister. It contains the village library and a hall capable of holding 500 individuals, which is divided by a moveable partition and converted into a recreation and reading room. The whole is open to the villagers at little more than a nominal fee of membership. From the village street there is a striking view of Loudoun Hill, which is only some two and a half miles distant. Its locality possesses many historical associations, and on this account deserves something more than a passing notice, for it must for ever constitute an engrossing object of interest not only to the tourist, but to every individual who is interested in the struggles of Wallace and Bruce, and of a bold peasantry who fought for Christ and the covenanted work of reformation. The hill stands some two hundred and fifty feet above the surrounding country. The side towards Darvel is clothed with wood, and that to the east is composed of bare trap-rock, which is studded here and there with a solitary tree. From its summit there is an excellent view of the surrounding country. Away to the westward is the picturesque valley of the Irvine—a vista little short of twenty miles in length —studded with dense woodlands and luxuriant holms, fertile fields and neat farm-houses; while on both sides the ground rises gracefully and to the southward attains a considerable elevation. In almost every other direction the eye rests on a vast expanse of moorland, which cannot fail to strike the dwellers in large cities as something novel. But there is an interest connected with Loudoun Hill that is far more fascinating than its rugged beauty or the prospect obtainable from its summit. Near to its eastern base a spot is yet pointed out where the hero Wallace with a small party of trusty patriots lay all night in ambush waiting the advance of a troop of English soldiers who were conveying provisions from Carlisle to the garrison at Ayr. In the grey dawn of the morning the unsuspecting convoy advanced, and when entangled in a narrow pass Wallace and his men rushed upon them like a whirlwind and smote them hip and thigh. The odds were fearful, but Scottish valour turned the tide in favour of the assailants, and the English fled and left behind them their rich stores. Near the hill also the noble Bruce with six hundred followers met in battle array the Earl of Pembroke and an army of six thousand. The battle, which was fought in May, 1307, we may depend, was both fierce and bloody, but the English were defeated, and Pembroke and his overwhelming host fled before the handful of brave men, which shows that "the race is not always to the swift, nor the battle to the strong." This was one of the most glorious victories that ever graced the laurels of Scotland, but in later times, and nearer our own day, the persecuted supporters of the Covenant—in the cause of God and their country—defeated Claverhouse on the field of Drumclog, which lies about a mile eastward of the eminence. The most graphic account of the fray, and the most interesting picture of the eventful scenes of that ever memorable Sabbath morning, is narrated by the Laird of Torfoot in an article which he penned when he returned from exile and from it I condense. "It was," says the Laird, "a fair Sabbath morning, 1st June, A.D. 1679, that an assembly of Covenanters sat down on the heathy mountains of Drumclog. We had assembled not to fight but to worship the God of our fathers. We were far from the tumult of cities—the long dark heath waved around us, and we disturbed no living creature save the peesweep and the heather cock. As usual, we had come armed—it was for self-defence, for desperate and furious bands made bloody raids through the country, and pretending to put down treason they raged war against religion and morals. They spread ruin and havoc over the face of bleeding Scotland. The clergyman had commenced the service, and was waxing eloquent on the wrongs of Scotland and the Church when the watchman posted on Loudoun Hill fired his carabine and ran towards the congregation. This announced the approach of the enemy, and the minister hastily concluded his discourse and said:—'I have done. You have got the theory—now for the practice. You know your duty. Self-defence is always lawful. But the enemy approaches.'" The officers now collected their men, and placed themselves each at the head of those of his own district. Sir Robert Hamilton placed the foot in the centre. A company of horse, well armed and mounted, was placed along with another small squadron on the left. All being in readiness, the women and children, and the old men, with their bonnets in their hands, and their long grey locks streaming in the wind, retired to a convenient distance, fervently singing a psalm to the tune of "The Martyrs." The Covenanters were all in good spirits, and gave a hearty cheer as Hamilton hastened from rank to rank inspiring courage into the undisciplined peasants. Gradually Claverhouse and his troops advanced amid a sound of trumpets and drums. Halting, he viewed the position of the Covenanters, and after a consultation with his officers sent a flag of truce with the message that they were to lay down their arms and deliver up their ringleaders. The request was contemptuously refused by the little army. They were full of religious zeal and true to each other, and while waiting the result of the flag of truce they engaged in the singing of a psalm. When Claverhouse heard that they scouted his request he passionately cried, "Their blood be upon their heads; be no quarter the order of the day." This announcement was received with yells from his troop, who at the word of command advanced. The Covenanters were not slow to meet them, but when Claverhouse's party stopped to fire the Covenanters dropped to the earth and allowed the volley to pass over. Quickly springing to their feet they returned fire and made every bullet tell. The fire now became incessant, and for some time resembled one blazing

sheet of flame along the lines of the Covenanters. A moss
hag dividing the belligerents, Claverhouse tried to cross
it with the intention of breaking the centre of the small
army. Observing this, Hamilton cried, "Spearmen to the
front! kneel. to receive the enemy's cavalry. God and our
country is the word." The spearmen knelt, and those on foot
poured volley after volley into the ranks of Claverhouse.
After several unsuccessful attempts to cross the moss, Claverhouse was about to flee, when the Covenanters rushed
forward, and a dreadful hand-to-hand conflict ensued. At
this juncture the Laird says, "My gallant men fired with
great steadiness. We could see many tumble from their
saddles. Not content with repelling the foemen, we found
our opportunity to cross and attack them sword in hand.
The captain, whose name I afterwards ascertained to be
Arrol, threw himself in my path. In the first shock I discharged my pistols. His sudden start in his saddle told me
that one of them had taken effect. With one of the tremen-
dous oaths of Charles II. he closed with me. He fired his
steel pistol. I was in front of him; my sword glanced on
the weapon, and gave a direction to the bullet which saved
my life. By this time my men had driven the enemy before
them, and had left the ground clear for the single combat.
As he made a lunge at my breast I turned his sword aside
by one of those sweeping blows which are rather the dictate
of a kind of instinct of self-defence than a movement of art.
As our strokes redoubled my antagonist's dark features put
on a look of deep and settled ferocity. No man who has not
encountered the steel of his enemy in the field of battle can
conceive the looks and manner of the warrior in the moments
of his intense feelings. May I never witness them again!
We fought in silence. My stroke fell on his left shoulder, it
cut the belt of his carabine, which fell to the ground. His
blow cut me to the rib, glancing along the bone, and rid me
also of the weight of my carabine. He had now advanced
too near me to be struck with the sword. I grasped him by
the collar, pushed him backward, and with an entangled blow
of my Ferrara I struck him across the throat. It cut only
the strap of his head-piece, and it fell off. With a sudden
spring he seized me by the sword-belt. Our horses reared,
and we both came to the ground. We rolled on the heath

in deadly conflict. It was in this situation of matters that my brave fellows had returned from the route of the flanking party to look after their commander. One of them was actually rushing on my antagonist when I called to him to retire. We started to our feet; each grasped his sword; we closed in conflict again. After parrying strokes of mine enemy, which indicated a hellish ferocity, I told him my object was to take him prisoner; that sooner than kill him I should order my men to seize him. 'Sooner let my soul be branded on my ribs in hell,' said he, 'than be captured by a Whigamore. No quarter is the word of my colonel and my sword. Have at thee, whig—I dare the whole of you to the combat.'—'Leave the madman to me, leave the field instantly,' said I to my party, whom I could hardly restrain. My sword fell on his right shoulder. His sword dropped from his hand. I lowered my sword and offered him his life. 'No quarter,' said he, with a shriek of despair. He snatched his sword, which I held in my hand, and made a lunge at my breast. I parried his blows until he was nearly exhausted, but gathering up his huge limbs he put forth all his energies in a thrust at my throat. My Andrea Ferrara received it, so as to weaken its deadly force, but it made a deep cut. Though I was faint with loss of blood, I left him no time for another blow. My sword glanced on his shoulder, cut through his buff coat, skin, and flesh, swept through his jaw, and laid open his throat from ear to ear. The fire of ferociousness was quenched in a moment. He reeled, and falling with a terrible crash poured out his soul in a torrent of blood on the heath. I sunk down insensible for a moment. My faithful men, who had never lost sight of me, raised me up. In the fierce combat the soldier suffers most from thirst. I stooped down to fill my helmet with the water which oozed through the morass. It was deeply tinged with human blood, which flowed in the conflict above me. I started back with horror, and Gawn Witherspoon bringing up my steed, we set forward in the tumult of the battle." While the hand-to-hand fight in which the Laird was engaged was going on, the battle raged fiercely on each side of him, and ultimately Claverhouse and his men were driven into the moss. The firing had by this time ceased, and the fighting was hand to hand and man to man, any of the Covenanters who were on horseback dismounted to engage in the fray, for they well knew that their steeds would sink in the bog if they attempted to follow the enemy. Coming in close proximity with Claverhouse, the Laird describes his appearance in anything but flattering terms. "Three times," he says, "Claverhouse rolled headlong on the heath as he hastened from rank to rank, and as often he remounted. In one of his rapid courses past us my sword could only shear off his white plume and a fragment of his buff coat. But in a moment he was at the other side of his square. Our officers eagerly sought a meeting with him. 'He has the proof of lead,' cried some of our men; 'take the cold steel or a piece of silver.'—'No,' cried Burley, 'it is his rapid movement on that fine charger that bids defiance to anything like an aim in the tumult of the bloody fray. I could sooner shoot ten heather-cocks on the wing than one flying Clavers.' At that moment Burley, whose eye watched his antagonist, pushed into the hollow square. But Burley was too impatient. His blow was levelled at him before he came within its reach. His heavy sword descended on the head of Clavers' horse and felled it to the ground. Burley's men rushed pell-mell on the fallen Clavers, but his faithful dragoons threw themselves upon them, and by their overpowering force drove Burley back. Clavers was in an instant on a fresh steed. His bugleman recalled the party who were driving back the flanking party of Burley. He collected his whole troops to make his last and desperate attack." Under the charge which followed the Covenanters were giving way, but Hamilton placed himself in the front of the battle with the white flag of the Covenant in his hand and cheered them on. Here the Laird crossed swords with Claverhouse. He relates the incident as follows:—"He struck a desperate blow at me as he raised himself in the saddle with all his force. My steel cap resisted it. The second stroke 1 received on my Ferrara, and his steel was shivered to pieces. We rushed headlong on each other. His pistol missed fire; it had been soaked in blood. Mine took effect, but the wound was not deadly. Our horses reared. We rolled on the ground. In vain we sought to grasp each other. In the *melee* men and horse tumbled on us. We were for a few moments buried under our men, whose eagerness to save their respective officers brought them in multitudes down upon us. By the aid of my faithful man, Gawn, I had extricated myself from my fallen horse, and we were rushing on the bloody Clavers, when we were again literally buried under a mass of men, for Hamilton had by this time brought up his whole line, and had planted his standard where I and Clavers were rolling on the heath. Our men gave three cheers and drove in the troops of Clavers. Here I was borne along with the moving mass of men and almost suffocated, being faint with the loss of blood. I knew nothing more till I opened my eyes on my faithful attendant. He had dragged me from the very grasp of the enemy and borne me into the rear, and was bathing my temples with water." At this juncture of the battle the Royal troops got into confusion, and being hard pressed by the Covenanters were driven back; but every inch of ground was sternly disputed, and nought was heard save the clashing of weapons, the neighing of horses, the shrieks of the wounded, and the groans of the dying. But allow the Laird to describe the closing scene of the battle:—" At this instant his (Claverhouse's) trumpet sounded the loud notes of retreat, and we saw on a knoll Clavers borne away by his men. He threw himself on a horse, and without sword, without helmet, fled in the first ranks of the now retreating host. His troops galloped up the hill in the utmost confusion. My little line closed with that of Burley, and took a number of prisoners. Our main body pursued the enemy two miles, and strewed the ground with men and horses. I could see the bare-headed Clavers in front of his men kicking and struggling up the steep sides of the Calder Hill. He halted only a moment on the top to look behind him, then plunged his rowels into his horse and darted forward; nor did he recover from this panic till he arrived in the city of Glasgow. . . . I visited the field of battle next day, but I shall never forget the sight. Men and horses lay in their gory beds. I turned away from the horrible sight. I passed by the spot where God saved my life in single combat, and where the unhappy Arrol fell. I observed that in the subsequent fray the body had been trampled on by a horse, and his bowels were poured out." I need not relate how the Covenanters after this successful engagement were flushed with victory, or how they marched to Bothwell, and sustained a disastrous defeat. Suffice it to say that they played a noble part on the stage of Scottish history. They did much to burst the bands of tyrannic oppression, and set a groaning nation at liberty. They may have been somewhat fanatical, but they did good service, and we are now reaping the rich harvest of political and religious liberty that they in the past sowed.

> " Praise to the good, the pure, the great,
>   Who made us what we are—
> Who lit the flame that yet shall glow
>   With radiance brighter far.
>
> " Glory to them in coming time,
>   And through eternity;
> They burst the captive's galling chain,
>   And bade the world go free."

> " Yes! though the sceptic's tongue deride
> Those martyrs who for conscience died;
> Though modish history blight their fame,
> And sneering courtiers hoot the name
> Of men who dared alone be free
> Amidst a nation's slavery;
> Yet long for them the poet's lyre
> Shall wake its notes of heavenly fire:
> Their names shall nerve the patriot's hand,
> Upraised to save a sinking land,
> And piety shall learn to burn
> With holier transports o'er their urn."

CHAPTER XVIII.

From Newmilns to Galston—The Institute—Barr Castle—The Boss Tree—Cessnock Castle—The appearance of the buildings—The Campbells of Cessnock—Sir Hew, and the charges brought against him—The alienation of the Castle and Lands—The Main Street of Galston—The Parish Church and Graveyard—Stones commemorative of local Covenanters—John Wright, the Galston Poet—Titchfield Street—A Mining Settlement—From Galston to Hurlford—The Village: its buildings and inhabitants—Crookedholm—Back to Kilmarnock—Conclusion.

THE road from Newmilns to Galston, which is nearly two miles in length, is remarkable for sylvan beauty and picturesque scenery, being draped with hanging boughs, and fringed on the one hand with the thickly-wooded policies of Loudoun Castle, and on the other by stripes of plantation through which the waters of the Irvine gurgling sing a continual farewell to "Loudoun's bonnie woods an' braes" as they roll on to mingle with the mighty deep. I enjoyed the walk immensely, and stopped now and again to feast my vision on the prospect or to catch glimpses of the castle, for its stately form is now and then seen through openings between the branches of the magnificent old trees. Towards the end of the road I observed the town of Galston lying in a hollow on the left bank of the Irvine, and as my way home passed through it I pushed onward at a brisk pace, so that I might rest and partake of refreshment in the house of ex-Bailie Murdoch, who retails not only the staff of life but also the "broo o' the barley." Arriving at a stately bridge which spans the river I crossed and entered the town of Galston, which contains 4727 of a population, and has a general trade of muslin-weaving and woollen manufacture. Of late years it has undergone a transition which has not been for the better—an influx of miners who are employed in pits in the vicinity having taken place, it has become both populous and rough, for a shifting, unsettled class of any kind rarely adds to the moral status of a community. Passing the Mechanics'

Institute—a handsome building lately presented to the inhabitants by the philanthropic Miss Brown of Lanfine—I gained the main artery of the town, and after partaking of my promised rest and refreshment started to explore the antiquities. The principal is Barr Castle, an old square tower, which stands in a hollow in the vicinity of the railway station. It is seemingly a remnant of a more extensive building, but it is without a history, little being known regarding it beyond what tradition has handed down. It is at present a seed store, but in early times it was doubtless the residence of some baron of no mean order. By its side grows an old plane-tree, which a juvenile tradition affirms once served as a means of escape to the valiant Wallace, who when pursued by enemies leaped from a top window of the edifice into its branches and descended to the ground. According to *M'Crie's Life of Knox*, Barr Castle must have been occupied about the year 1556 by a John Lockhart, who was a warm supporter of the Reformed doctrines and a zealous assistant at the spoliation of various churches, for that writer states that Knox preached in the building and addressed the people of Kyle from one of its windows. It was also a favourite haunt of John Wright, a gifted but unfortunate local poet, who repeatedly refers to it and very happily as follows in one of his shorter pieces:—

"Barr Castle! tenantless and wild!
  Dome of delight! dear haunt of mine!
The shock of ages thou hast foiled,
  Since fell the last of Lockhart's line;
Thou'rt left a hermit to grow gray
O'er swallow, crane, and bird of prey.

"Proud edifice! no annals tell
  What thou hast brooked, what thou hast been,
Who reared thee in this lovely dell,
  What mighty baron—lord, I ween,
Of hardy Kyle; no bordering tower
Possessed more independent power.

"O for a pinion from the wing
  Of pelf to lift me from the mire,
And crown a wish, formed in life's spring,
  When life was all desire!
These walls should ring with minstrel's lay,
These turrets fall not to decay."

"The Barr" at this day and since the earliest recollection of the oldest inhabitant is the resort and play-place of the youths of the town, and many a keenly-contested game of handball is played against the tower. During my visit a group were engaged at the pastime, and their noisy, good-humoured ejaculations recalled to my mind the following verse of Wright's "Retrospect":—

> "To Lockhart's tower now flocked we forth—the prey
> To wreck of ages, and the pride of song;
> Where many a gambol circled round the gray,
> Dark, feudal vestige, and its dells among;
> But o'er all sports athletic, nimble, strong,
> Was handball pastime; young, mid-aged, and old,
> As equals mingled, after practice long;
> And scarce a neighbouring village was so bold
> As struggle with our own the sovereignty to hold."

Near to "the Barr" there is a dilapidated wall surrounding an old garden which is said to be that which belonged to the castle. It is still under cultivation, and has every appearance of the antiquity ascribed to it. In a field adjacent to the vestige of feudal times stands the remains of a majestic elm of gigantic proportions which was known by the name of "the boss tree," from the circumstance of a cavity in its trunk. The botanical curiosity was blown down some twenty years ago, and all now remaining of it is a rotten hollow stump in which four men might conveniently stand erect; but notwithstanding its condition, and that it is decayed to a mere shell, it still retains one healthful guarled bough which somewhat astonishingly manages to draw sustenance from its apparently sapless parent. Tradition has it that the Wallace Wight hid from his foes in the branches of this tree; but whether it was or was not the case is of little consequence, the shattered remnant being a sufficient curiosity. M'Kay in his *Ingleside Lilts* makes the tradition the subject of a poem which he entitles "The Warrior's Tree." It concludes as follows:—

> "Then boldly he sprang from the green leafy shade,
> His eye sternly rolling in wrath;
> The glen's lonely echoes resounded his tread,
> As on to the combat majestic he sped,
> Regardless of ruin or death.

> "The vision has passed; but the Warrior's Tree,
> Though fading 'neath Time's chilling blight,
> Still waves its broad branches alone on the lea,
> Where the peasant oft pauses, delighted to see
> The haunt of brave Wallace the Wight."

From the boss tree I leisurely strolled towards the railway station, crossed a bridge which spans the line, and after a walk of little over a mile along a beautiful road, from which the pedestrian has a delightful view of the woods of Loudoun, the braes of Laufine, and a vast track of level country, stopped before an old-fashioned gateway with a turnstile. Finding it to be the entrance to the policies of Cessnock Castle, I entered, passed up the avenue, and in a short time arrived in a courtyard lined on three sides with old buildings of various heights and designs. On the right, near to the top of what appeared to be the principal one, an old clock whose hands had ceased to indicate the passing hour displayed its weather-beaten face and looked down upon the apparently deserted residence as if conscious that its services were no longer necessary, for there was no appearance of life, all being still and in a semi-ruinous condition. Leaning on my staff I viewed the old place, and while thus engrossed fell into a reverie, out of which I was roused by a low growl in close proximity with my heels, which had the effect of nearly frightening the life out of me and causing me to spring a couple of feet into the air. Turning I beheld a large dog tugging at the end of a chain, and doing its best to scare me from the scene. With thoughts of the seat of my best trousers being torn out, I was making a hasty retreat when a door in the left wing of the building opened and a young man made his appearance, to whom I related the object of my visit. After changing the tune of the noisy brute into an apologetic howl he kindly conducted me over the buildings and showed me everything that he considered interesting connected with them, but I did not observe anything very remarkable, and after passing through one empty room after another I was glad when I regained the outer world. I do love old buildings, but Cessnock is not sufficiently wrecked for me; it is by far too clean and destitute of cobwebs, but nevertheless it is a fine place and will amply repay a visit. It stands on the top of a steep bank overlooking Burnawn, a romantic streamlet whose banks are bright with bloom and melody, and whose channel is famous for the number of pebbles and jaspers that have periodically been found in it. Originally the building consisted of a solitary square tower of great strength, but additions were from time to time made to it until it became very extensive; and though now deserted and in a measure abandoned to decay, it retains not a little of its old grandeur and presents a very interesting appearance. Ivy in many places has begun to creep up the walls and peer into some of the windows, as if anxious to see what progress decay is making within. The Campbells of Cessnock were descended from a second son of George Campbell of Loudoun, who married Lady Janet Montgomerie, seventh daughter of Hugh, first Earl of Eglinton, in November, 1513. The connection with the Loudoun family was made closer by the pious but unfortunate Sir Hew Campbell of Cessnock, who about 1630 married Lady Elizabeth, second daughter and co-heiress of George, Master of Loudoun. Amongst the many associations of Cessnock Castle the history of Sir Hew is the most mournful, that nobleman being persecuted to the death by a secret enemy who is supposed to have been John Drummond, Viscount of Melfort. Sir Hew belonged to the Presbyterian party, and took part in the political troubles which ended in the death of Charles I. Upon the ascension of Charles II. he became a favourite at court, and was knighted by that monarch about 1649, and was by Parliament appointed Lord Justice-Clerk. At the Restoration he retired from public life, but here his troubles commenced. Without any apparent cause he was exempted from the act of indemnity passed in 1662, and, after suffering various terms of imprisonment and paying heavy fines, was in 1683, along with his son George, thrown into prison upon a trumped-up charge of being connected with the Covenanters in the district, and accessory to the rising at Bothwell. At the trial they would have been found guilty had not a conscience-stricken witness broken down. This event caused their acquittal, but they were detained in prison, and in the year following were brought to trial for being connected with the Ryehouse Plot. This they partly admitted, and threw themselves upon the mercy of the Court, but were found guilty and sentenced to be removed to the Bass until the King's pleasure should be known. Their estates were forfeited and annexed to the Crown, but afterwards were conferred upon the supposed secret instigator of the charges. Under this harsh treatment the health of Sir Hew broke down, and after a lengthened imprisonment on this account he was released, but died shortly afterwards at Edinburgh, on the 20th September, 1686, aged 71 years. When the troublous times of the Revolution were over a bill was laid before Parliament to rescind all fines and forfeitures that had occurred after the year 1665. The bill after much opposition was passed, and the castle and lands of Cessnock were restored to the family. Sir George Campbell of Cessnock, the sharer of much of the persecution directed against his father, came into possession in March, 1691, but having no male issue the property devolved upon Sir Alexander Hume, Earl of Marchmont, who married his daughter Margaret. In turn he was succeeded by his son Hugh, who alienated the estate and confined his landed property to Berkshire. Since that time Cessnock has been in the possession of several individuals. It was for some considerable time occupied by a John Wallace, a relative of the Wallaces of Cairnhill; but in 1786 the trustees of Miss Scott, late Duchess of Portland, acquired it, and it is now in the possession of his Grace the Duke. Bounding down the steep bank on which the castle stands, I strayed along a footpath that skirts the Burnawn, which at this point jinks round a curve and runs zig-zag through a beautiful glen.

After a pleasant walk I arrived in the highway and shortly afterwards in the main street of Galston, a closely-built, populous thoroughfare, and entered the Crown Inn to fortify my inner man before starting for home. I found Mr and Mrs Ferguson very courteous, a circumstance that did much to make my refreshment doubly refreshing, and causing me to think lightly of the five lang Scotch miles that lay between me and Kilmarnock.

At the head of the main street on an eminence stands the Parish Church, a commodious building topped with a beautiful spire in which there are clock dials. It stands in the centre of a very ancient graveyard, and was erected in 1808 upon the site of an old place of worship which previous to the Reformation belonged to the Friars of Faile, a fraternity who, as the reader will doubtless remember,

"Loved gude kail on Fridays when they fasted."

In the graveyard I met with several very chaste monuments and tombstones which mark the burying-places of some very old Galston families, and also with two humble slabs commemorative of Galston Covenanters. One of these bears the following inscription:—" In memory of John Richmond, younger of Know, who was executed at the Cross of Glasgow, March 19th, 1684, and interred in the High Churchyard there; and James Smith, East Threepwood, who was shot near Bank on Burnawn, 1684, by Captain Inglis and his dragoons, and buried there. Also, James Young and George Campbell, who were banished in 1679, and the Rev. Alex. Blair, who suffered imprisonment, 1673."

John Richmond was captured in Glasgow by Major Balfour. Wodrow tells how he was taken to the guard-house, and bound neck and heel, and left for hours on the damp floor bruised and bleeding from wounds received in a struggle with his captor. The reader will remember that it was at his funeral James Nisbet, in Highside, was taken and shortly afterwards executed at Howgatehead, Glasgow, as related in the last chapter. Nothing is known of James Smith beyond what is graven on the stone. James Young and George Campbell were taken at Bothwell, conveyed to Edinburgh, and imprisoned in Greyfriars' Churchyard, and afterwards along with two hundred and fifty others banished to the plantations, but the ship was wrecked when off the Moul Head of Deerness, and they both perished. The Rev. Alex. Blair was minister of Galston, and a man of more than ordinary talent. In 1662 he suffered imprisonment for refusing to submit to prelacy, and was stripped of his clerical rights. In 1669 he was charged with the crime of *preaching and baptizing*, and was dismissed with a caution, and was afterwards imprisoned for refusing to give thanks to God for the restoration of Charles II. on a day appointed by the Government, but the confinement so injured his health that he died "in much joy," says Wodrow, "and full assurance of faith."

Near to the door of the church and close to the side walk there is another stone which marks the spot where rests one of "bloody Graham's" victims. On the top there is a wretched bas-relief representation of one man shooting another. Between the figures there is a sand-glass two-thirds of their size, and the gun is as thick as the leg of the holder and longer than himself; the whole is very ridiculous, and ill accords with the inscription, which is as follows:—" Here lies Andrew Richmond, who was killed by bloody Graham of Claverhouse, 1679, for his adherence to the word of God and Scotland's Covenanted work of Reformation.

" When bloody tyrants here did rage
Over the Lord's own heritage,
To persecute His noble cause,
By mischief framed into laws;
'Cause I the Gospel did defend,
By martyrdom my life did end."

Nothing is known regarding Andrew Richmond beyond what the stone states.

Amongst the many memorials of departed worth in this churchyard the absence of a tribute to the memory of John Wright, the local poet already referred to, is conspicuous. The people of Galston may consider the nativity of this ill-starred votary of the muse no great honour, but nevertheless it is undeniable that his poetry is highly creditable to the unlettered muse of Scotland, and would not disgrace a town of greater pretensions. But who is John Wright? some of my readers may ask. Well, John Wright was a native of Galston, a harness weaver, and the author of a volume of poems entitled *The Retrospect, or Youthful Scenes*, and many other poems and songs. In early life he was sober, well-conducted, and industrious, and continued to be so until Fame found him out, but after that he allowed himself gradually to be drawn into the vortex of intemperance. When at the loom he wrote *The Retrospect*, a long poem of undoubted merit, but as neither it nor any of his shorter pieces met with the approbation of his friends he determined to visit Edinburgh and get some literary man's opinion regarding the whole. Collecting his manuscripts, he set out with them and one halfpenny in his pocket and walked to the capital, living by the way upon turnips or whatever he could procure. While strolling friendlessly, and I may say objectlessly, through the city—for he possessed no recommendation—he met with a Galston lad who was studying at the college, and by him was taken by the hand and introduced to John Wilson, professor of moral philosophy. The professor took John's poems, read them, and wrote a notice of the author, which he published in an Edinburgh magazine. In that notice he says—"Mr Wright is a self-taught poet, and has encountered difficulties in his progress more depressing to genius than any I have seen recorded of either Burns or Hogg." The cry arose, who is this new poet? and every one was desirous of obtaining a copy of his work, which was speedily published. The first edition appeared in 1833, and two others during the course of his life. A copy of one before me contains a list of subscribers, and I observe the names of twenty-two clergymen and several of the most eminent literary men then living. Fame was within his grasp, and he might have done well, but drink ruined him, and during the latter years of his life he wandered from town to town living as he best could, and that generally upon the charity or hospitality of friends who had known him in other circumstances. J. K. Hunter, in his *Life Studies*, speaks of meeting with him in Paisley Road, Glasgow. He must then have fallen very low, and I would fain hope that the picture Hunter draws of him is overdone. He says—"A different sort of study made its appearance—a sair-worn something that had once borne resemblance to a man, now rowed up in a bundle of auld claes that might have adorned a scarecrow in a potato field without exciting the envy of a dealer in cast-off raiment; an auld Kilmarnock bonnet pulled down to the eyes; the head leaning forward, the shoulders rounded and high as the crown of the head; an earthy coat that might once have been black—the very dirt on it glazed—buttoned to the throat; the skeleton of two pairs of trousers, torn to strips; and a pair of bauchles on the stockingless feet. . . . . . I could not have fancied that form the abode of poetry; it would have been the last element of thought I should have guessed to have ever lodged in that clay tenement." After borrowing pins from women on the way with which to pin the rags of the poet together, Hunter gave him a few coppers (all the money he had with him, he states), bade him good-bye, and saw him no more.

John Wright died "unwept, unhonoured, and unsung,"

aged thirty-nine—one account states in the Glasgow Police-office and another in the Royal Infirmary. A few Galston natives residing in Glasgow followed his remains to their last resting place, and defrayed the expenses of the funeral amongst them. In a nameless grave he found a lethe for all his self-inflicted woes, but for all that a simple slab might be raised in the churchyard of his native village to commemorate this gifted but unfortunate son of song.

Closing the churchyard gate I entered the Cross, glanced at the clock on the church steeple, and was surprised to find that the day was far spent, and that the gloamin' would be set by the time Kilmarnock would be reached. Buttoning my coat, I grasped my staff firmly, took a last look around, turned my face in the direction of home, and walked at a brisk pace down Titchfield Street. The buildings in this line of street are unostentatiously plain, and through several of the windows I observed looms and grey-headed "wabsters" industriously plying the shuttle. At one door I paused a moment and listened to the clickity-clack and the birr of a pirn wheel, for they are sounds that I seldom hear, but when heard they awaken fond memories and recall to my mind the happy, joyous days "when I was a callant and gaed to the schule." At the foot of Titchfield Street are situated a collection of miners' houses called the Boyd, the Gauchlan, and the Goatfoot Rows, which have sprung up mushroom-like within the last few years. They have a cleanly and comfortable look, and their occupants a bien and respectable appearance. Here Titchfield Street merges into the Kilmarnock road. Following its course I passed on my right another mining settlement named the Tarry and New Goatfoot Rows. The first is so named from the circumstance of the roofs of the houses being covered with tarred canvas. It was in the New Goatfoot Row that my old friend James Garret lived. Although a miner he was well read and highly respected, and is now sadly missed by his family and fellow-workmen, for they often profited by his long experience and wise counsel in trade matters. He was generally averse to strikes, but if a dispute had no other alternative old James never lifted a pick until it was settled. But he has gone—gone to the narrow house, and my small circle of friends and well-wishers counts one less.

Beyond New Goatfoot Row the road for a long distance is broad and level, and traverses a delightful district which presents many fine alternations of hill and dale, wood, fell, and russet lawn. I enjoyed the scene immensely as I walked at a brisk pace on my homeward journey, but did not meet with anything worthy of remark until I came to Hoodstone Bridge. This bridge spans the Cessnock—a streamlet which Burns has rendered classic by his muse, and which at this point forms an eccentric curve before it empties itself into the Irvine. The stream also divides the parishes of Galston and Riccarton, and bounds the estate of Holmes, a residence of the Fairlies. The mansion-house can be seen in the distance through the trees, but is a modern erection possessed of no feature of interest. After lingering a short time watching the rippling Cessnock, I followed the line of road, which after some two miles of a continuous level becomes somewhat steep and irregular. Passing through Hillhead Toll I gradually attained the summit of the brae, and paused at a small bridge that spans a single line of rail that communicates between the main railway and some coal pits belonging to the Messrs Gilmour. Here I had a splendid view of the surrounding country. The prospect from the bridge is as extensive as it is beautiful, and the eye rests with delight upon a fertile and highly picturesque track of country. Farther on I passed a roadside public-house, into which a number of miners were entering seemingly with the intention of "wetting their whistles" and washing the dust of the week out of their throats. I was certain it was pay-day with them, for the buxom landlady smirked and smiled upon the motley group, and welcomed them ben with great frankness. A little beyond this "public" the road takes a turn, and when rounding it the somewhat scattered but populous village of Hurlford bursts into view.

Passing rows of miners' dwellings of the usual class, and remarkable only for the number of children gambolling about them, I arrived in the village of Hurlford. Old Hurlford, which consists of a few thatched houses of mean appearance, stands on an old and now disused road in a hollow to the north of the modern village. These houses—some half-dozen in number—were all that constituted the hamlet seventy years ago; but had it not been discovered that the district of Hurlford was rich in mineral the Hurlford of then would have been the Hurlford of to-day, and the ground whereon the new portion of the village stands would have been furrowed by the plough and yielded crops to the husbandman. Hurlford of to-day, however, is a place of considerable importance and bustle. It contains a population of 2718, or, including Crookedholm, 3488, and is possessed of two handsome churches, a commodious academy, and a beautiful jail, which I trust the inhabitants patronise as little as possible, and also a prosperous Co-operative Society. It depends chiefly on the Portland Iron Works, the extensive fire-clay goods factory of J. & R. Howie, and the numerous collieries in its vicinity.

Crossing a splendid bridge which spans the Irvine, I passed on the north side of the road the Free Church, a very neat edifice with a spire, and a little farther on, on the same side, stands Hurlford Parish Church, a recently-erected building, and one of the finest places of worship in Ayrshire. Opposite it, to the south, is the Portland Iron Works, the glare of whose furnaces on a dark night illumines the whole district.

Passing through Crookedholm, a straggling row of irregularly-built dwellings that line the road at a spot where the Irvine, far below the level of the highway, sweeps round a curve as it ripples onward, I soon arrived at Woodend, the beautiful residence of Allan Gilmour, Esq. The house is built of red sandstone, and occupies a position that commands a capital view of the surrounding country. The road beyond it is nearly a dead level, and continues so until Kilmarnock is reached.

After a pleasant but lengthy walk I passed through a tollbar and entered London Road, an aristocratic suburb already noticed, and soon reached Green Bridge. Traversing Duke Street, I arrived once more in the Cross as the gloamin' was setting in, and wearily sought the seclusion of my home, where my return was hailed by the gleeful shouts of my little ones, who one and all were so glad to see my face that they accorded me a hearty welcome—yes, such a welcome as little truthful, loving souls only can give. One laid hold of my staff, the other of my hat, while a third set my arm-chair in a cozy corner and fetched my slippers. I drew up to the ingle cheek, and felt grateful that I was once more at "my ain fireside."

READER,

  I've wandered by yon country side,
   And viewed the lowly graves
  Where Scotland's martyr'd heroes sleep,
   O'er whom the green grass waves.
  I've gathered tales o' auld langsyne,
   And climbed the braes sae steep;
  I've stood upon the castle wa'
   And viewed the ruined keep;

but now we must part. You have obtained the benefit of my jottings, and I trust they have entertained you, and not only awakened fond memories of youthful haunts and associations, but added something to your stock of knowledge. If this be the case, then my object in giving them a permanent form has been attained, and we take leave of each other mutually satisfied.

www.ingramcontent.com/pod-product-compliance
Lightning Source LLC
Chambersburg PA
CBHW022010220426
43663CB00007B/1031